Pro .NET Directory Services Programming

Erick Sgarbi
Ajit Mungale
Mikael Freidlitz
Noel Simpson
Jamie Vachon

Pro .NET Directory Services Programming

ISBN (pbk): 1-59059-269-7

Printed and bound in the United States of America 12345678910

Trademarked names may appear in this book. Rather than use a trademark symbol with every occurrence of a trademarked name, we use the names only in an editorial fashion and to the benefit of the trademark owner, with no intention of infringement of the trademark.

Technical Reviewers: Rick Delorme, Mark Horner, Shefali Kulkarni, David Schultz, Julian Skinner

Editorial Board: Dan Appleman, Craig Berry, Gary Cornell, Tony Davis, Steven Rycroft, Julian Skinner, Martin Streicher, Jim Sumser, Karen Watterson, Gavin Wray, John Zukowski

Assistant Publisher: Grace Wong

Project Manager: Kylie Johnston

Copy Editor: Rebecca Rider

Production Manager: Kari Brooks

Production Editor: Kelly Winquist

Proofreader: Linda Seifert

Compositor: Katy Freer

Indexer: Bill Johncocks

Cover Designer: Kurt Krames

Manufacturing Manager: Tom Debolski

Distributed to the book trade in the United States by Springer-Verlag New York, Inc., 175 Fifth Avenue, New York, NY, 10010 and outside the United States by Springer-Verlag GmbH & Co. KG, Tiergartenstr. 17, 69112 Heidelberg, Germany.

In the United States: phone 1-800-SPRINGER, email orders@springer-ny.com, or visit http://www.springer-ny.com. Outside the United States: fax +49 6221 345229, email orders@springer.de, or visit http://www.springer.de.

For information on translations, please contact Apress directly at 2560 Ninth Street, Suite 219, Berkeley, CA 94710. Phone 510-549-5930, fax 510-549-5939, email info@apress.com, or visit http://www.apress.com.

The information in this book is distributed on an "as is" basis, without warranty. Although every precaution has been taken in the preparation of this work, neither the author(s) nor Apress shall have any liability to any person or entity with respect to any loss or damage caused or alleged to be caused directly or indirectly by the information contained in this work.

The source code for this book is available to readers at http://www.apress.com in the Downloads section. You will need to answer questions pertaining to this book in order to successfully download the code.

I would like to thank the whole Apress team for working together and constructively on this book—excellent work! Lastly, I wanted to thank Mum and Dad, Tia Ottilia and Seu Altair, Chris and Ale, and Pat and Mileth for their continuous support and friendship.
–Erick Sgarbi

All my love and thanks to Sucheta—my inspiration. Special thanks to Apress and Rebecca Rider for the efforts they had taken with this book.
–Ajit Mungale

I would like to thank my wife and daughter for their patience and understanding of my constant refrain of "just-one-more-hour."
–Mikael Freidlitz

This is dedicated to my father Brian, my mother Rosemary, and the guys at iGEN Knowledge Solutions Inc. Each of them, in one way or another, has helped me get to where I am today.
–Noel Simpson

I want to thank all the people who have supported me during my move to Australia and during the writing of my part of this book. This is for you Mom, Dad, Ron, and Kat.
–Jamie Vachon

Contents at a Glance

Contents

Chapter 4
ADSI in .NET   113

Chapter 5
Directory Service Security   133

Chapter 8
Exchange Administration   251

Index   275

About the Authors

Erick Sgarbi is a system specialist/consultant and programmer with experience in designing and developing large systems and solutions by various type of framework. He is now focusing more on .NET Technologies and designing applications for Mobile and Smart devices for distributed and web enabled solutions. Erick can be reached at erick@ihug.com.au.

Ajit Mungale is a senior software engineer and has experience in Microsoft and Java technologies. His expertise includes Microsoft .NET, IBM MQSeries, and WebSphere. Ajit is currently writing an IBM Redbook on Microsoft .NET and WebSphere coexistence in Research Triangle Park, North Carolina.

Mikael Freidlitz is a consultant and lead architect at Consignit. He lives and works in the beautiful seaside city of Gothenburg, Sweden. Besides partaking in amazing software projects and spreading the gospel of a proper architecture, Mikael has been seen downtown on a mountain bike, trying to find the courage to get that front wheel off the curb. Contact Mikael at mikael@mikael-freidlitz.com.

Noel Simpson is a database administrator and programmer in the city of Calgary in Alberta, Canada. In addition to his DBA and programming tasks, he is putting his directory service knowledge into practice as he embarks on a project to integrate a large organization's many disparate systems with a popular directory service as the focal point. Visit Noel on the web at www.noelsimpson.com.

Jamie Vachon is a Microsoft MVP for Active Directory working as a senior IT architect in Sydney, Australia for Expert IS. He specializes in Microsoft solutions, focusing on .NET. Prior to moving to Australia, he lived and worked in the United States for various companies in Boston, and Washington, D.C.

Introduction

Directory Services encapsulates and exposes objects within a network, offering a unified way of accessing different types of data. Of particular interest on the Windows platform is the Active Directory, which supplies powerful and flexible methods for managing users, servers, and resources in a single information store that is globally accessible throughout an enterprise.

Knowing how and when to use a directory service effectively will enable you to develop applications that store infrastructure information safely, as well as perform management or administrative tasks.

In this book, we will show you the .NET Framework's support for programming Directory Services, and the Active Directory in particular. You will learn how to create applications to view, search, or manage directory entries such as users, as well as physical resources such as printers.

What Does This Book Cover?

The book is divided into two main sections. The first part, "Programming Directory Services in .NET," includes Chapters 1 to 5 and covers all the techniques and the theory that you need to know to access Directory Services from .NET code. Then, in the second part, "Directory Services in Action" (Chapters 6 to 8), we look in more detail at some specific scenarios for applications that need to use Directory Services.

To give you an overview of what you'll learn from this book, let's look in more detail at what each chapter covers:

> **Chapter 1, "Directory Services in a Nutshell,"** presents an overview of Directory Services, and looks at their structure and typical uses. We provide a quick tour of the Active Directory Service Interfaces (ADSI), which is a set of COM interfaces that represent objects in a directory service and provide a way to program against Directory Services that is independent of the directory service provider. After that, we show you how ADSI and the .NET Framework's support for Directory Services fit together.

> **Chapter 2, "Directory Services and .NET,"** kicks off our discussion of programming Directory Services in .NET. The key namespace for working with Directory Services in .NET is System.DirectoryServices, which provides wrapper classes for underlying ADSI functionality. In this chapter, we explore the DirectoryServices.Directory Entry class, which encapsulates an object in the directory, and provides many methods and properties for working with directory objects. We also create a Windows Forms Directory Browser application to apply our knowledge of System.DirectoryServices.

> **Chapter 3, "Searching Directory Services,"** is about searching Directory Services, most notably Active Directory. The main class for this functionality is the System.DirectoryServices.DirectorySearcher class; in this chapter, we explore its methods and properties and see examples of Windows and web-based Active Directory search functionality.

> **Chapter 4, "ADSI in .NET,"** revisits ADSI and shows you how to work with some of the key interfaces from .NET. You see how methods of the ADSI interfaces and their System.DirectoryServices counterparts correspond and learn how to perform tasks such as controlling Windows Services with ADSI.

> **Chapter 5, "Directory Service Security,"** is about Directory Service security. In this chapter, we discuss some basic security concepts that you need to be familiar with to use Directory Services, and then we look at managing permissions on directory entries using Access Control Entries (ACEs), which specify access rights, and Access Control Lists (ACLs), which is a container for ACEs. We then explore the ADSI security interfaces and create a managed wrapper for these interfaces that you can use in your applications.

The last three chapters show Directory Services (and the Active Directory) in action.

> In **Chapter 6, "User Management,"** you'll see how we manage Active Directory users and groups by building a sample application that allows you to create and delete users and groups, and assign users to and remove them from groups.

> **Chapter 7, "Server and Resource Management,"** looks at aspects of server management such as creating computer accounts, discovering domain controllers and group policy objects, publishing Service Connection Points, and creating custom resource classes and attributes.

> In **Chapter 8, "Exchange Administration,"** we cover Exchange administration with System.DirectoryServices, and we show you how to search for Exchange-enabled Active Directory objects and how to create and manage Mailboxes. Finally, we look at Exchange administration with other libraries such as CDO and CDOEXM to present a more complete picture of Exchange development.

Who Is This Book For?

This book is for .NET programmers who want to make better use of Directory Services resources, or for Active Directory administrators who are interested in developing more sophisticated and customized administrative tools.

We do not assume that you have prior knowledge of Directory Services programming.

All the code examples in this book are in C#, and we assume that you do have a working knowledge of this language.

What You Need to Use This Book

In order to run the samples in this book, you must have a machine that has the .NET Framework installed.

You also need access to a directory service. In this book, we concentrate on Active Directory, which means that you will need access to an Active Directory installation of either of these operating systems:

- ❏ Windows 2000 Server
- ❏ Windows Server 2003

Conventions

We've used a number of different styles of text and layout in this book to help differentiate between different kinds of information. Here are examples of the styles we used and an explanation of what they mean.

We have represented code in several ways. If we are referring to a single code word in the text–for example, when we are discussing a `for (...)` loop–it's in `this font`. If we are discussing code that you can type as a program and run, then we list it on its own line, separate from the rest of the text:

```
DirectoryEntry de = new DirectoryEntry();
```

Sometimes we just refer to one line, but often, we discuss an entire block of code, like this:

```
DirectoryEntries children;
DirectoryEntry de = new DirectoryEntry();
try
{
    Console.WriteLine(de.Name);
}
```

Advice, hints, background, and other important information are represented like this.

We have also used several types of styles and fonts to highlight other types of information.

Important words and words that are defined are in italic type font in the paragraph text; or, when they are defined as part of a list of other terms that are being defined, they may take the following format:

Important word: Followed by definition.

Words that appear on the screen, or in menus like Open or Close, are in a similar font to the one you would see on a Windows desktop.

Part I

Programming Directory Services in .NET

Directory Services in a Nutshell

Businesses often require a single global information repository with enterprise scope to hold information such as user passwords, group policy, computer locations, or even a phone book. With the added impracticality of storing this type of data separately on each site, businesses also need to access this information from different locations, either across remote networks or from different platforms. Thus they need a place for a single general container that has adequate protocols and policies to handle such services, and this is the role of the directory service.

It is becoming increasingly common to integrate large and complex applications with Directory Services, and the need to manage information centrally becomes particularly evident in the context of developing distributed applications that require sophisticated authentication functionality.

In this chapter, we'll focus on the following:

❑   Understanding what Directory Services are

❑   Managing and using Directory Services

❑   Exploring common directory service providers

❑   Getting to know Active Directory

❑   Understanding the Lightweight Directory Access Protocol (LDAP)

❑   The basics on Naming Services, Directory Services, and .NET

❑   Using the Active Directory Service Interfaces (ADSI)

❑   Introducing the `System.DirectoryServices` namespace

What Is a Directory?

Primarily, a *directory* is a container for data structures that model something in a network. A directory itself is a catalog of information about these objects, organized in such a way to make this information readily available.

> *Elements in a network, such as users, groups, or a piece of hardware such as a printer, can be conceptually characterized by objects in a directory.*
>
> *In this chapter, and throughout the book, when we refer to a directory, we will be referring to this formally defined schema, and not a physical directory in the file system.*

These directory objects can represent living entities, such as users or groups, or highly organized models, such as companies and enterprises as well as hardware. The term *object* is used, in the context of a directory, for the data that is stored about such an entity. An object that can include other objects is referred to as a *container*. The relationship between a container and the objects within it is described using the usual terminology for hierarchical relationships: the objects within a container are known as the *child objects*, and the container is called the *parent object*.

Even though information can be easily stored in directories, they are most frequently used for reading rather than for updating. Much like the way you use a phone book or a dictionary, you use directories frequently to look up of some specific information, and because they are used in this manner, they are optimized for finding the relevant information quickly and easily. For example, in a phone book, some data may change from time to time as individuals, families, and businesses change phone numbers, but the majority stays essentially unchanged. Data is usually added, rather than changed.

Since directories are mostly read-only, being able to perform context-based searches upon them is very important. We look at searching directories in Chapter 3.

What Are Directory Services?

In brief, a *directory service* is a specialized database that maintains typed and organized information about the objects stored in a directory (defined earlier). It also carries a schema that defines these objects and their attributes, thereby encapsulating network elements as logical objects.

In practice, a directory service is a type of resource available in a network that distributes directory information to clients. For example, suppose you have just developed an application that uses a SQL server on a Windows domain, but keeps the authentication data such as username and passwords in the database. After a few months, you are asked to include data from a different department that is currently being housed in an Oracle server, and this is when the nightmare begins. All authentication data from SQL Server must be exported to Oracle; in other words, when running the application, you are forced to authenticate the same user twice because the Oracle server is out of the SQL Server or network context. To compound the nightmare, the company decides to use Novell NetWare instead of Windows Server, and so the users must have three different credentials—one for each of the operating systems, Oracle, and SQL Server databases—as well as their own credentials for accessing e-mails that can be serviced by Microsoft Exchange Server or Groupware.

The example we just related is not very far from the "spaghetti" infrastructure that occurs in businesses regularly. The easy way out for this example is to store all the credential data (username, passwords, etc.) in a directory that can be queried by any application dependency. This way, if the application wants to know who you are, it simply asks the directory. If the database server wants to know who you are, it asks the directory. And, if the e-mail server wants to know who you are, it asks the directory.

> *A directory service has a further role—to expose the directory programmatically to other contexts—and it is this task that we will focus on for the remainder of this book.*

Thus Directory Services provide an expandable, logical representation for all components of a network, including the physical, logical, and policy building blocks. An important part of this support is through a hierarchical namespace that provides a set of conventions that define relationships between the various objects and attributes. For example, to relate an object of type User to other User objects, you can set up a group containing the related users.

Since you have such typed objects like users, groups, printers, or computers stored in the directory, if your company were to purchase a new model of printer, then it may need some extra properties in the directory. You can achieve this by modifying the existing schema (which describes the object) in order to accommodate new properties of objects that are already present in the directory. The same network representation depicted in a hierarchical and scalable model of directories can expand the schema by adding extended information and structure. Furthermore, you can also define new objects so that you may create objects in the directory schema to represent a completely new type of peripheral on your network.

A Directory Service's logical representation of entities within a domain can provide secure integration between foreign networks sharing information. This enables users to be authenticated in foreign networks and can be achieved by linking networks via trusted-relation protocols rather than hardwiring networks within the same Internet Protocol (IP) range. This obviously offers scalable advantages; we will have a look at these soon.

Directory Services vs. Relational Databases

The role of a directory service is often confused with that of a Relational Database Management System (RDBMS); a general misconception is that directories can replace an RDBMS. Although an RDBMS and a directory share some similarities (such as data storage), they are optimized for different functions.

Directories are mostly used for storing static information, such as names, addresses, and passwords. For this reason, directory services and their resources are optimized for reading rather than writing, whereas the typical RDBMS is optimized for both reading and writing.

An RDBMS can also consolidate operations into a single, logical piece of work using transactions, and it can allow an action to be rolled back after it has been performed. This means that, when something goes wrong in the middle of a process, the entire process can be rolled back, and the data can be restored to its original state. For example, when you are transferring funds from one account to another, you must debit the source account and credit the target account, and if something goes wrong when you are crediting the target account, you need to make sure that the source account is not debited. With transactions, this is possible in a RDBMS. Directory services do not embed any type of transactions because this is not required when data is being read, only when it is being updated.

You can easily add more directories from different domains to expand a directory service. Just add trusted networks to the Global Catalog (we will look at this shortly), which can be seen as the directory namespace. This is not a very complex task for directories because of their well-formed security protocols that establish this type of negotiation across different domains. However, it is a different story with an RDBMS because it does not have such protocols available, and maintaining collaboration between different RDBMSs is a far from trivial activity that requires much thought and planning, particularly from a security point of view.

Both a directory and an RDBMS can be replicated or placed in a load-balanced environment, meaning that the same data can reside in different physical locations, and if data fails on one server, another will take over.

A final important similarity between an RDBMS and Directory Services is that they both interact via a common language or interface. For example, standard relational databases make use of Open Database Connectivity (ODBC) or the Structured Query Language (SQL) to retrieve tables or rows, and Directory Services can also distribute objects across networks using the Lightweight Directory Access Protocol (LDAP). We will look at LDAP later in the chapter.

Thus RDBMSs and Directory Services should be seen as two different resources that may work in collaboration with each other. An RDBMS should be used for daily updates of work such as online processing, and typically Directory Services should be used to read more static information like user profiles.

What Can Directory Services Do for Me?

Before we get deeper into Directory Services, let's have a look at some of the benefits Directory Services can offer to programmers and administrators in the typical scenarios of authenticating users and providing programmatic access to system resources.

Even the simplest of applications can have a complex infrastructure due to the requirements of today's business needs. For example, in a web application, you may be required to authenticate customers and make sure that they are who they claim to be, or you may need to provide an administrative interface for the application that allows users to be added and permissions to be granted, or even allows some configuration in Internet Information Server (IIS) to be tweaked.

To meet these needs, Directory Services offers the following:

❑ Distributed authentication

❑ Management and administration benefits

❑ Scalability enhancements

Distributed Authentication

Consider a company that requires you to write a client application that performs data entry into a database using current programmatic technologies such as ADO.NET. Once designed, such applications are normally very straightforward to write and implement, mostly because of the simple requirements of data entry, validation, and database updates. Suppose further that one of the requirements is to authenticate users that are entering data into the application, meaning the application must make sure those users entering data are really who they claim to be. To add further complexity, the application needs to be deployed to several sites.

No matter what technology is used to distribute the application (.NET Remoting, ASP.NET, or even Web Services), it must provide a way of exchanging data. Now, our application must be able to authenticate users within a common network context. At first glance, you probably understand the need for the data store to contain sufficient data for authentication, such as usernames and passwords, so why not use a database such as SQL Server or Oracle instead of a directory service container? As mentioned previously, relational databases are not integrated with basic standards for interdomain communication. Moreover, they do not encompass suitable protocols such as LDAP for communicating with other providers over network contexts.

Take, for example, a person who wants to get an Internet account from a local Internet service provider (ISP). Once the account is set up, the user can log on to the network via a Point-to-Point protocol (PPP), which is the main authentication method employed by the ISP after the user dials into the account. Further, the new user must provide the username and password. Once logged into the ISP's network, the user may want to check for e-mail; consequently he opens a mail client program to retrieve e-mail. To retrieve this e-mail, the client must access the Post Office Protocol (POP) server, which again asks for a username and password. Often enough, the username is the e-mail address, which is the same username the user employed to log on to the PPP account.

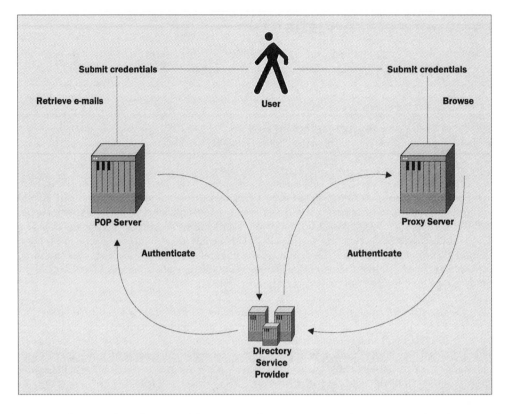

As seen in the preceding diagram, if the user needs to access any other service within the network, he must show the appropriate credentials (username and password) upon request. As a result, the services provided by the ISP give access to users who are bound by authenticated sessions that take place in various parts of the system. This process is often known as single logon.

The inclusion of Directory Services in cases like this shows the distributed authentication process, which is critical for typical distributed applications. In this way, you can effectively implement the single logon by getting different applications to authenticate credentials against the same directory without asking the user to supply credentials separately for each application.

Management and Administration

Larger networks often pose complex problems for administrators, and especially for users. The problem begins when you are looking for a specific object, such as a printer, computer, or user within a network. It can be tiresome to deal with so many, and usually unrelated, network objects, but most of all, you may know exactly what you are looking for but not where to look for it.

Fortunately the structured hierarchical model of a directory service allows it to provide a searchable resource approach that categorizes all objects within the information model; thus users can browse for printers, computers, or other users.

Administrators also can benefit from this functionality when they create new users, change user and group information, change network settings (adding printers), and perform many other routine tasks.

For example, using Directory Services, an administrator can use a script to perform the following tasks:

❏ Create an account.

❏ Include the account as part of a group.

❏ Apply security policies.

❏ Create a corresponding e-mail account.

❏ Generate and set a password.

❏ Create a home directory.

❏ Send a notification of successful account creation.

From the administrator's point of view, using Directory Services is also very effective when she is looking into more complex tasks such as setting up trusts with other domains or changing settings for security. Moreover, because of interfaces available from different Directory Services providers, remote administration can be easily incorporated into a web-based application such as ASP.NET. You'll see examples of performing administrative tasks programmatically in the second part of the book, "Directory Services in Action."

Scalability

One very important aspect of directories is their ability to grow without losing performance. Furthermore, directories can communicate with other directories; for example, if one company merges with another company, then their directories can interoperate without needing any extra hardware.

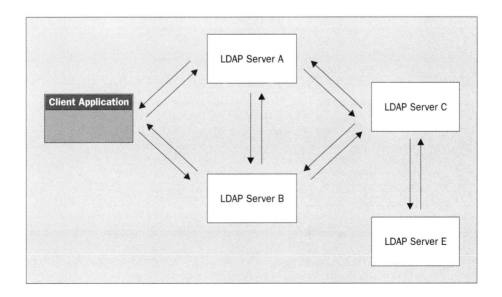

The preceding diagram shows how you can get different directories to trust each other, which, consequently, adds a great deal of scalability to your system. For instance, you may have Server A, which you use primarily to look up information about customers. After some time, your company may expand, adding more directories (in this case, Server B), or it may even merge with other companies that already have existing directories (such as C) and existing trusted access to other company's directories (represented here as Server E).

The Lightweight Directory Access Protocol (LDAP)

Different data containers expose different ways to access data, and directory services have their own protocol for accessing the data they hold–LDAP. Simply speaking, LDAP is to Directory Services what SQL is to an RDBMS, and it plays a very important role in helping client applications communicate with and query directories.

LDAP is a subset of the Directory Access Protocol (DAP), and it was designed at the University of Michigan to support Transmission Control Protocol/Internet Protocol (TCP/IP) and follow the X.500 standards.

The X.500 specification was primarily designed to work with the Open System Interconnection (OSI) model before the existence of the Internet, and it does not support TCP/IP. Basically, TCP/IP combines three layers (the Application, Session, and Presentation layers) of the OSI seven-layer model into a single layer called the Application layer, where protocols such as the Hypertext Transfer Protocol (HTTP) are defined. It is not possible to deliver HTTP in the OSI model because the TCP/IP's Application layer is segmented into three different layers by the OSI model, and because DAP is not designed to exist within the TCP/IP Application layer. LDAP was introduced to compensate for DAP's limitations and therefore it can work under TCP/IP standards.

The X.500 standard specifies the interaction between the directory client and the directory server (the directory server provider) and it uses DAP. X.500 providers to organize directory entries in a hierarchal namespace that is capable of supporting a great quantity of information. They also define very useful and powerful search resources for information retrieval. On the other hand, DAP needs the whole OSI protocol stack to function, and so it demands a lot more resources from the environment. Consequently, an interface to an X.500 directory server using a less resource-intensive, more lightweight protocol was desired.

LDAP is based on four models that map the X.500 standards into its architecture:

Information: Describes how data is stored in the LDAP directory structure.

Functional: Denotes the operation that can be performed on the information structure.

Security: Mainly describes how can the information structure can be protected from unauthorized access.

Naming: Specifies how objects located in the information structure are identified.

These four models make up the LDAP architecture and provide integration with various operating systems and platforms, as long as they support TCP/IP communication.

Most of today's browsers, such as Netscape or Internet Explorer (IE), and even integrated operating system applications, such as Microsoft Outlook Address Book, can easily connect to a directory provider using LDAP. For example, just enter the following LDAP address into your web browser:

ldap://ldap.itd.umich.edu/o=University of Michigan,c=US

Windows will ask if you want to open Microsoft Address Book; if you click Yes, you should see the following Properties dialog:

This demonstrates how LDAP works over TCP/IP; it retrieved the directory object that was referenced as ldap://ldap.itd.umich.edu/o=University of Michigan,c=US from a directory. This process was not possible under the X.500 model because there was no support for TCP/IP protocols, such as HTTP. LDAP can transport information based on the TCP/IP Applications layer without consuming resources from other OSI layers (as DAP required).

Why LDAP?

When developing an application, you often have to define some type of data storage, either local or centralized. For example, when you are designing a small contact list application, you may use local storage such as an Extensible Markup Language (XML) file, a serialized data structure, a comma-delimited file, or anything else that can sit on the local drive within the application. This way you are basically defining an application-specific type of directory. Suppose, however, that you need to distribute a contact list structure with several names and addresses to several applications, including those that haven't been written yet! In such situations, you must consider an application-independent type of directory communication, and the best option is to adopt an industry-standard protocol. Here, LDAP will be useful no matter what directory service provider you use.

LDAP is defined in the Request for Comments (RFC) document RFC 1777, and has been adopted by several vendors as the communication model for their Directory Services products. The RFC documents from the *Internet Engineering Task Force (IETF)* are nothing more than RFCs on standards and specifications about the Internet and related technologies. The earliest RFCs were written over 30 years ago. We are going to cover several very important topics that originated from RFCs, because today's vendor standards for Directory Services have their very beginnings in RFCs. You can find out more about the IETF and RFCs at `http://www.ietf.org/rfc`.

Some other RFCs are well worth having a look at because they don't just denote the current LDAP specification; they also document the progress from X.500 to today's LDAP:

❑   RFC 1778, "The String Representation of Standard Attribute Syntaxes"

❑   RFC 1779, "A String Representation of Distinguished Names"

❑   RFC 1959, "An LDAP URL Format"

❑   RFC 1960, "String Representation of LDAP Search Filters"

These standards are the key for several commercial, free, and open-source Directory Services implementations, ensuring that different directory services can be accessed in the same way using LDAP.

How Does LDAP Work?

LDAP encapsulates all operations in an envelope called an `LDAPMessage`, which defines the operation to carry out. This `LDAPMessage` is submitted to the server, and an integer called a `messageID` is allocated for both the client and server in order to distinguish to which operation the `LDAPMessage` is referring. One other construct is also sent back from the server—an `LDAPResult` envelope, which carries the response from the initial request.

In this example, we begin with a `bindRequest` operation—a request for connection. The `bindRequest` operation is encapsulated within the `LDAPMessage` and is sent to the server over TCP/IP (including the `messageID` unique to the operation). Once the server receives the `bindRequest`, it sends a reply back to the client as an `LDAPResult` including the same `messageID` field, mapping the response to the initial request so that the client can identify to which operation the server is responding.

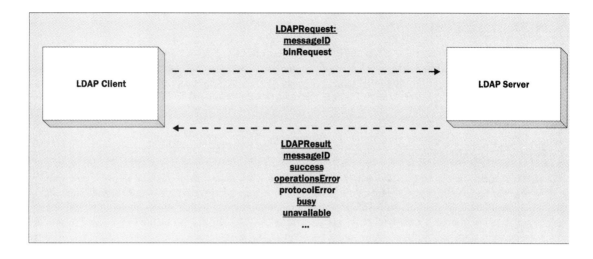

> The bindRequest also carries an authenticationType value, which demands that the server perform a specific type of authentication. Authentication will be covered in Chapter 5.

After the `bindRequest` gets a success response, the client can proceed with other operations, such as an `addRequest` that sends another `LDAPMessage` envelope. The `addRequest` defines an operation to add an entry to the directory catalog. The server will then return another `LDAPResult` encapsulating the result of the operation. Finally, the client can submit an `unbindRequest` within the `LDAPMessage` in order to terminate the protocol session.

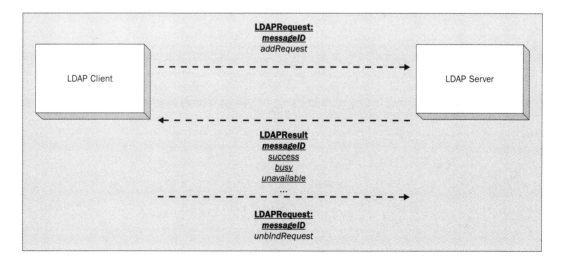

The `unbindRequest` has no return value. The client assumes that the server will receive the `LDAPMessage` with the `unbindRequest` and therefore it no longer needs to wait for any response from the server. Later in this chapter we will cover the main functions in LDAP.

Naming Services

Imagine how productive you'd be today if you were obliged to use IP addresses instead of domain names when working with the Internet. The association of a sensible name with an object is fundamentally important to identifying that object. In a directory service, the association between names and directory objects such as users, groups, or computers in the directory is handled by Naming Services, an extension of Directory Services. Naming services also allocate objects with their attribute names in the directory.

Distinguished Names

Naming services must be able to identify these objects with a naming standard in order to expose them to connecting clients. They do this by identifying each object with a *Distinguished Name (DN)*. If you wish to expose an object inside a container and you already have a reference to the container object, you can use a Relative Distinguished Name (RDN). Think of your file system and how it is organized into system folders and subfolders containing files–DNs act like a path in the file system, with the end point of the path identifying the object.

> *The DN of an object in a directory uniquely identifies it, and because it holds ample information, a client can retrieve the object by referencing its DN. It is also possible to refer to a directory object by its global unique identifier (GUID), a 128-bit number generated when the object is created in the directory.*

In order to standardize the naming for these objects, you must follow the LDAP standard set down in RFC 1617,"Naming and Structuring Guidelines for X.500 Directory Pilots," which you can find at `www.ietf.org/rfc/rfc1617.txt`. The DN consists of a comma-delimited list of name/value pairs that represent the location of the object in the directory hierarchy. For example, in the example we saw earlier, o=University of Michigan, c=US represents an organization called the University of Michigan in the country the US. A DN can include a number of elements to represent this hierarchy, as described in the following table.

Notation	String Type Representation
O	OrganizationName
OU	OrganizationalUnitName
CN	CommonName
L	LocalityName
C	CountryName
ST	StateOrProvinceName
STREET	StreetAddress
DC	domainComponent
UID	userid

Before we go any further let's look into some further Naming Services definitions.

Schema

A *schema* is the blueprint for the structure of a directory because it defines what types of objects and properties are contained within the directory. For example, the schema of a directory can depict an object called `office`, denoting a location that carries properties such as `streetAddress`, `faxNumber`, `phoneNumber`, and `businessHours`. From this schema you can create many office objects representing different locations.

Trees

The objects located within the directory are called *entries* and are organized in a tree structure called a *Directory Information Tree (DIT)*; the objects held in these trees are known as *leaf* objects. In the same way as a folder in a file system can contain subfolders and files, you can view a tree structure as a container of directory objects that can contain other objects.

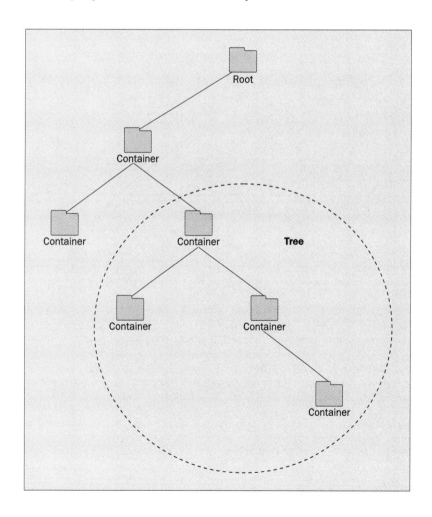

Forests

A collection of trees that share the same schema configuration is known as a *domain tree*, and connecting several domain trees into a single collection of trees produces a *forest*. All trees in a forest have a common schema but can actually define different domains. Consider the following diagram:

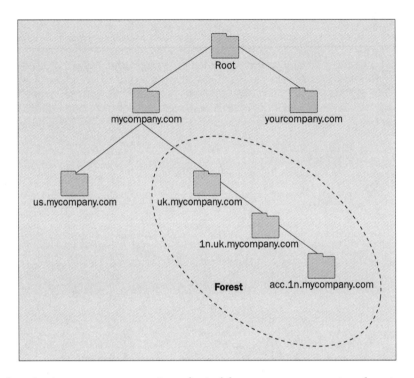

The tree domain uk.mycompany.com is a subset of the mycompany.com tree domain; consequently all the following domain trees under uk.mycompany.com are subsets of it as well.

Forests automatically create a transitive trust relationship, which is basically a two-way trust relationship between domains. This means that directory servers can add trust relationships to other directory servers so that mycompany.com will trust yourcompany.com.

The downside of these types of structures is that you cannot join an already existing domain into a tree, nor can you even join an existing tree into a forest. If you want to tackle this problem, you must build your domain or tree from scratch in an existing tree or forest.

Global Catalog

Global Catalog (GC) is the namespace that can view and manipulate the information within directories from all domains that make a forest. Essentially, a GC contains every single domain in the forest. It keeps a copy of all tree structures and properties that are relevant for creating and changing trusts between domains. In order to bind to a GC using LDAP, you just need to point to the namespace LDAP; this will bind to the enterprise-level root containing all domains in the forest.

Binding to Objects in the Directory

To actually get at an object in a directory, you need to specify binding information. Consider the following diagram showing a user object Gary in a directory and the hierarchy of containers:

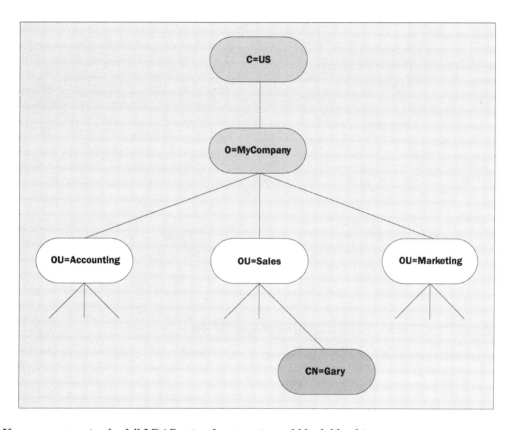

If you were to write the full LDAP string for Gary it would look like this:

```
LDAP://CN=Gary, OU=Sales, O=MyCompany, C=US
```

Notice how the hierarchy of the directory is indicated as you read the string from right to left. Each one of these LDAP strings points to a distinct object in the directory. Just like the primary key of a database table, the distinguished name is unique within the directory because it cannot be repeated.

Each object also has a collection of properties. This collection is an extensible structure that can take different types of data.

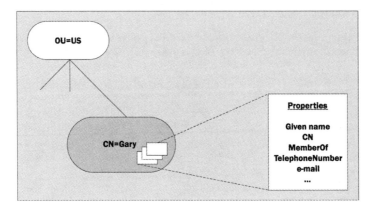

This diagram shows the object CN=Gary and depicts some of its properties. These properties can store values that are relevant for the object, such as the e-mail address and telephone number.

> **Properties can be added by extending the directory schema. However, once a schema is extended, there is no way back! Thus modifying a directory schema must be carefully planned.**

We'll look at schema extensions in the next chapter.

Mandatory and Optional Properties

A mandatory property is a basic object requirement for updating or adding information to the structure, and it is crucial to maintaining the identity of the object within the directory. Mandatory properties have to be specified when an object is created in the directory, or else the creation will fail, since there will be no way to distinguish this object from any others.

In the schema, we can also include optional properties to hold custom or enterprise-specific information such as department codes or work hours.

Directory Providers

We have already talked about Directory Services and how the introduction of LDAP has enabled clients to connect to a directory provider over TCP/IP instead of merely via OSI protocols. As mentioned before, a directory service is basically a directory that allows clients to access it from a different context using the API supplied by that service. Directory service providers come in different packages and are very much related to the environment that will be used by the organization itself. Another point to consider is how user-friendly the directory provider is—before choosing a directory provider, you should always assess the tools for management, migration, and administration provided with the package. Here we are going to look into some of these directories.

Netscape DS

Netscape Directory Server (Netscape DS) is an LDAP-based server that maintains application settings such as user profiles and privileges, as well as network settings, in a centralized environment. It simplifies user administration by eradicating data redundancy with automation management, and it provides total compatibility with LDAP.

Novell's Directory

Novell set a strategy a long time ago to introduce Directory Services as a fundamental resource in Enterprise networks. The first release was called Novell Directory Services (NDS), which was introduced in the NetWare 4 operating system. The most recent release of Novell's directory is called eDirectory, and it is part of the latest generation of Directory Services server provided by Novell. It too supports LDAP.

OpenLDAP

OpenLDAP is a free, open-source implementation of an LDAP-compliant directory service. The source code can be downloaded from http://www.openldap.org/software/download/, while precompiled binaries for Windows NT/2000/XP are available from http://www.fivesight.com/downloads/openldap.asp.

Microsoft Active Directory

Active Directory was introduced and shipped with Windows 2000 Server (initially it was deployed in the beta version known as NT5) in order to replace the NT4 domain structure. It is important to note that Active Directory is not just a Directory, but it is also a very important resource in a network. It holds objects that represent network entities such as computers, printers, scanners, and the users that are part of the domain–Active Directory is the mechanism that defines a computer as a **domain controller** (DC). A *domain* is the security boundary of a Windows network. When you set up Active Directory on a machine running Windows 2000 Server or Windows Server 2003, it becomes a domain controller. A single domain can have multiple domain controllers, each of which can store all of the objects within that domain. However, unlike NT domains, there is no master server, and all domain controllers are treated equally.

What Is ADSI?

People often confuse the Microsoft Active Directory provider with the Active Directory Service Interfaces (ADSI), mainly because of the similarity in their names, but they are completely different things. In fact ADSI existed long before Active Directory.

ADSI is essentially a definition of a directory service model together with a set of COM interfaces that represent this model. ADSI was designed to let developers use the same set of libraries to connect to several different types of directory service providers and to perform tasks within these directories without needing to know an application programming interface (API) for each individual provider. Thus, using ADSI, the code to connect to Active Directory is the same as the code for connecting to NDS.

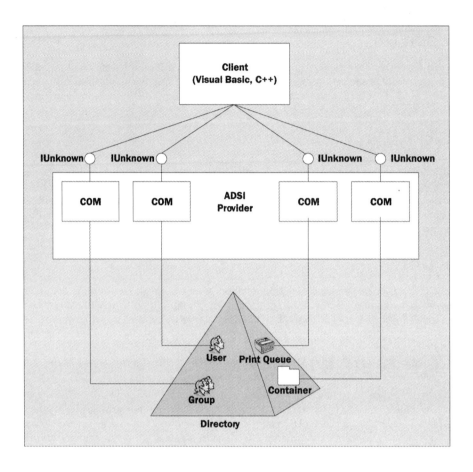

As described in this diagram, the ADSI interfaces represent different objects in a directory.

In many ways, ADSI facilitates the development of Directory Services–driven applications. As you shall see later in the chapter and throughout the book, the .NET Framework has improved on ADSI, effectively providing an even more straightforward implementation of ADSI.

ADSI Providers

ADSI providers are directory services that implement the ADSI interfaces. Writing your own provider is no easy task and beyond the scope of this book; instead we are going to look at some of the most well known ADSI providers available.

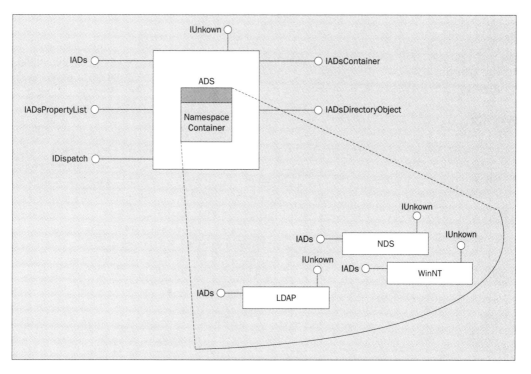

This diagram represents an ADSI COM interface that is able to define various namespaces with a great level of abstraction. We are going to look at these objects shortly.

WinNT

As we've said before, Active Directory was only available from Windows 2000 on; prior to that, the WinNT provider for Windows NT stored the local resources of a computer, including printers, users, and groups. This provider basically gathered the necessary information from local resources and presented it as an ADSI directory composition. This approach is rarely used nowadays in current projects since the schema available with it is much more limited than that of LDAP providers. For example, it has no searching support; however, using WinNT it is a very good way for administrators to manage local network resources in the NT4 environment.

> **Active Directory can also be accessed using the WinNT provider, but as a result, it will be restricted by the WinNT limitations. Needless to say, this backward compatibility was implemented only for migration purposes from NT4 to Windows 2000.**

IIS

Internet Information Server (IIS) is a web application service that is responsible for handling web pages. It also implements ADSI interfaces that are widely used for administrative scripting for creating web directories or File Transfer Protocol (FTP) points.

LDAP

As expected, the LDAP provider can be accessed by ADSI. As mentioned before, ADSI uses an LDAP provider in order to establish communication with other providers. Consequently, ADSI can talk with any provider that is natively LDAP-compliant, such as Exchange Server or even IIS. The LDAP provider is the provider we normally use to access the Active Directory.

ADsPath

Earlier, we looked at the LDAP strings that point to a particular container or leaf and are used to bind to a particular object in a directory. In ADSI, an LDAP string is known as an *ADsPath* because it actually points to an object in the directory but not necessarily from a LDAP provider. The idea of the ADsPath is to be able to use ADSI interfaces to bind to a number of different providers. Here are some of the provider namespaces:

Namespace	ADSI Support For:
WinNT:	WinNT provider
LDAP:	LDAP providers
IIS:	IIS provider
NDS:	Novell Directory Services

The ADsPath is guaranteed to uniquely identify each object in the directory to which it is pointing. Note that the namespace part of the ADsPath is case sensitive. Here are some examples of binding to particular directory objects:

```
WinNT://DomainName//Users/Guest

NDS://DomainName/O=Users/CN=Guest
```

To bind to a particular WWW service running on localhost in IIS, you would use this:

```
IIS://localhost/w3svc/service1
```

Finally, the ADsPath for the LDAP provider is as follows:

```
LDAP://cn=Guest,cn=users,dc=DomainName,dc=com
```

Because of different implementations of LDAP standards, all the following are valid LDAP strings that can be used by ADSI:

```
LDAP://domainname.com/cn=guest,cn=users,dc=domainname,dc=com

LDAP://domainname/cn=guest,cn=users,dc=domainname,dc=com

LDAP://DC=com/DC=domainame/CN=Users/CN=Guest
```

If the object is not supplied, you must at least bind to the root of the directory and iterate across the tree objects—we are going to look at this process shortly.

Exploring ADSI Interfaces

ADSI interfaces can be categorized into different groups, with each group responsible for a particular directory service task. Here is a listing of these groups and a brief explanation of their responsibilities:

Core interfaces: Provide objects for essential management functionality that is performed on the underlying directory. These interfaces are responsible for binding to the directory, loading objects and properties, and performing updates.

Persistent Object interfaces: Define objects that persist in directory interfaces such as computer, users, and groups.

Schema interfaces: Responsible for schema maintenance and are very important for schema extensibility.

Property Cache interfaces: Take care of the local client caching mechanism.

Dynamic object interfaces: Deal with objects that are not specifically of a directory service nature, such as working with file streams, network commands, and even print job queues.

Security interfaces: Deliver the security requirements of a directory-driven application; they mainly allow ADSI to control credentials in a directory.

Non-automation interfaces: Let applications written in C/C++ use ADSI without using COM, by using VTables. This approach can be highly complex but it maintains a low overhead on directory connections.

Extension interfaces: Give vendors the ability to extend ADSI objects to add product-specific functionality. This group contains the single interface that is responsible for the entire ADSI application extension model.

Utility interfaces: Used in common tasks such as deleting an object or setting and retrieving directory paths.

Data type interfaces: Provide the ability to access ADSI data types.

Some of these categories are beyond the scope of this book, but we are going to discuss the others because they are very important to your work with the .NET Framework. The categories we are going to visit are the Core, Schema, and Property Cache interfaces.

Core Interfaces

The Core interfaces in ADSI provide ways to create representations of objects in a directory. Here are the interfaces that are the heart of the Core category:

❑   IADs

❑   IADsContainer

❑   IADsNamespaces

❑   IADsOpenDSObject

The IADs interface allows a representation of an object in a directory to be created. Consequently, any object retrieved from a directory using ADSI must implement this interface. It also gives the application the ability to implement objects to perform basic directory operations such as loading properties, modifying and updating property values, and getting the directory location of the object.

The IADsContainer interface provides methods for dealing with ADSI container objects that represent directory containers such as computers or domains. A typical usage of this interface would be to query a top-level directory object to retrieve its IADsContainer object in order to gather information about its child objects. In this way, you could iterate through a whole tree from top to bottom. The way to determine if an object is a leaf is just to check whether it supports IADsContainer; if it does, it must be a container object, and you can continue drilling down the tree.

The IADsNamespaces interface is responsible for managing namespaces for the different providers. Each directory service provider has a different namespace and this interface is able to allocate different namespaces for different types of providers. The implementing object contains only one property, defaultContainer. This property allows you to specify a default container object, so that clients can bind to that particular namespace, even if no object was chosen.

The IADsOpenDsObject interface connects to the underlying directory object. It maintains a single method called OpenDSObject that supports authentication through user credentials. Basically, in order to bind to a directory object using OpenDSObject, you would need to pass in the path where the object is located in the directory as well as the credentials.

ADSI Schemas

The definition of a particular object in a directory must be in the schema, or else it would be impossible to create such an object. When you ask a directory to create an object, it will look up at the schema and say, "Yes, I can support that object!" or "No, I don't know that particular object!" In order to create, manipulate, and change objects in a directory, ADSI has to be able to represent the directory schema within its interfaces. Let's look at two of the most important ADSI schema interfaces:

❑   IADsClass

❑   IADsProperty

The IADsClass interface defines the main identity of an object schema, determines whether or not an object will be a container, and specifies all the mandatory and optional properties an object can support. This interface defines the high-level structure of a schema object.

The IADsProperty interface defines the names of the properties in the IADs object. It also states what the maximum and minimum values of properties may be, the data type of the value, or if the property will support multiple values. For example, the memberOf property defines which groups an object can belong to, and the email property is simply a single string value representing an e-mail address.

The schema container itself must implement IADs and IADsContainer in order to define object schemas, and in fact, all directory objects implement the IADs interface. In the next chapter, we will revisit directory schemas and show some practical examples.

Property Cache Interfaces

As mentioned previously, data is read from a directory far more often than it is written to one. When reading information about a container object in a directory such as a forest containing several trees with groups, users, network objects and more, you must ensure that you are not continually making round trips to the server. Imagine if you were using an RDBMS to look at a single row in a table but it retrieved an entire table with thousands of rows; to get at that single row would be unfeasible. On the other hand, when reading information from a directory, you may retrieve a list of employees in a company, stored in directory objects that each contain several properties. You know that this listing will not be changed that often, so there is no need to refresh this list on a single-request basis.

ADSI allows the client to cache information about a whole directory on the client. Furthermore, it provides functionality for managing this cache, such as refreshing and retrieving specific parts of the data cached. The Property Cache interfaces define this functionality:

- ❏ IADsPropertyEntry
- ❏ IADsPropertyList
- ❏ IADsPropertyValue
- ❏ IADsPropertyValue2

The IADsPropertyEntry interface defines the value of a single property in an IADs object. It is important to note that this interface reflects a cached entry of an IADsProperty that can define single or multiple values.

Whereas the IADsPropertyEntry represents a single property, the IADsPropertyList defines an object that represents a list of properties. It allows the IADs object to read, modify, and update several properties from an object at once.

Finally, you have the IADsPropertyValue and IADsPropertyValue2 interfaces. These interfaces maintain similar names because they have the same purpose—to define a property value in the IADsPropertyEntry. The difference is that IADsPropertyValue is used to represent predefined ADSI data types such as Long Integer or System Time, and IADsPropertyValue2 is used to represent user-defined object values. This is very useful if you need to represent the value of an object from a different provider than the one in which you are working.

ADSI in Action

Interfaces are very useful for getting different applications that don't know much about each other to communicate. ADSI is used to accomplish such tasks. For example, consider an Office application (such as Word or Excel) that needs to run a macro to retrieve a series of groups and its users from a directory; it will retrieve all users and their attributes (say, addresses and telephone numbers) by implementing ADSI interfaces in order to create representations of directory objects without knowing anything about the underlying Directory Services activity.

In this section, we are going to look at how ADSI works conceptually, without giving reference to any specific language. The following diagram shows an example of how such a process can be possible using ADSI to retrieve data from a directory:

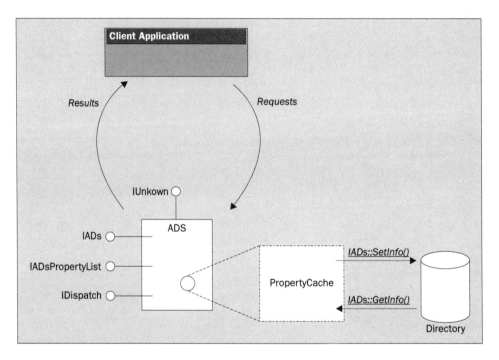

This diagram shows a conceptual picture of how the client application can use ADSI. The client application creates an instance of an IADs object, which can be a user, group, or even an entire tree from a directory.

At first, it requests certain information about an object in the directory by calling the GetInfo() method defined in the IADs object. The GetInfo() method is used to fill the client's property cache defined by the IADsPropertyList of the ADSI object. Once the client has a cache of the requested information, it can read and change the data, including deletions. Since this is a local cache, any changes you make must be committed back to the directory in order to make any change to the data permanent, and this is done with the IADs method SetInfo().

> It is very important that you commit any changes you make to the property cache to the directory; otherwise these changes will not be made to the physical directory.

You can commit changes with the `IADs` method `SetInfo()`. We'll look more at committing changes in the next chapter.

ADSI works as more than a bridge between the client and the directory; it will also be a type of translator between them. Also note that the directory provider will run in a completely different process (probably on a different machine), and ADSI is located in the client in the form of a DLL exposed as a COM component. This makes access from the client more reliable and efficient. ADSI accomplishes a fast communication between server and client by wrapping each directory as a COM object and caching it on the client, giving the impression that communication is being performed on the directory (server side) while the changes are actually being made on a local cached process.

The client COM object stores all directory objects' properties as well as the methods to perform operations on the directory. Thus it basically represents a cached directory structure using instances of ADSI containers and leaf objects.

.NET Directory Services Model

As part of the .NET Framework, the `System.DirectoryServices` namespace is included in the `System.DirectoryServices.dll` assembly. The following diagram shows how this namespace fits in with the other concepts we've encountered in the chapter.

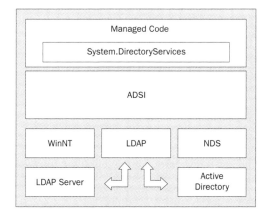

In this diagram you can see that `System.DirectoryServices` is managed code, written on top of ADSI. Thus the key functionality of ADSI is retained, particularly the support for the ADSI and LDAP providers. Another key benefit is that `System.DirectoryServices` hides some of ADSI's complexity, and exposes a simpler programming interface.

Before .NET, ADSI was widely used to create applications that communicated with directories. If you have already used ADSI in the past, either through C++ or VB6, you already know some of the major complexities of ADSI, such as cleaning up objects or error handling. As much as ADSI facilitates access to directories, it can be time-consuming to code ADSI applications from scratch; as a result, when using ADSI, you would usually create wrappers around it–the same approach is taken by the .NET Framework.

There are two very important classes in the System.DirectoryServices namespace:

❑   DirectoryEntry

❑   DirectorySearcher

The DirectoryEntry is a managed representation of an entry in the directory, and it has an underlying native ADSI object defined by the IADs interface. We'll see more about this in Chapter 2.

The DirectorySearcher includes the functionality to search objects in the directory. The most important aspect of this class is that it encapsulates the IDirectorySearch ADSI interface to perform queries on the directory. We'll look at searching with DirectorySearcher in Chapter 3.

Even though the underlying communication structure of System.DirectoryServices uses the existing ADSI functionality, it encapsulates the usage of these objects in a very efficient and simple model by hiding some of ADSI complexities when performing straightforward tasks such as retrieving a user list, or updating information. It also includes a rich set of collection-type classes for searching, enabling developers to create efficient and functional applications in a much shorter time. However, not all of ADSI is exposed through dedicated System.DirectoryServices classes and namespaces, and there are times when you will want to get your hands dirty with ADSI to perform some task on a directory.

We'll see more about the interplay between System.DirectoryServices and ADSI in the remaining chapters.

Summary

In this chapter you looked at directories and Directory Services, and saw an overview of their structure and their importance as resources in an enterprise network.

You have seen some of the advantages and properties of a directory service, including the following:

❑   The ability to store network information such as user, groups, computers, and their descriptive properties

❑   The ability to expose high availability across platforms and networks due to support of appropriate network protocols

❑   Highly optimized reading ability, enabling rich queries to be done against directory objects such as users and groups

❑   Centralized management and control over network resources

❑   Administrative delegation; control over system services, enabling system administrators to delegate users with passwords and levels of security

2

Directory Services and .NET

In this chapter, we are going to explore some of the classes within the System.DirectoryServices namespace of the .NET Framework and discuss what you can do with them. System.DirectoryServices provides resources to create Directory Services–enabled applications. We are going to look at the main component of the namespace, the DirectoryEntry class, and explore its functionality for tasks such as adding, removing, and updating information in a directory service.

We are also going to explore some navigation approaches using the DirectoryEntries class; we'll also show you how to iterate and retrieve the DirectoryEntry object's properties as well as perform changes on it. Later, you will use the DirectoryEntry class to extend existing class definitions in the directory schema by adding custom attributes.

Most of the tasks you perform using System.DirectoryServices classes in this chapter will be implemented in a Windows forms directory browser application that you'll build as you progress through the chapter.

In this chapter, we'll focus on the following:

- ❑ Exploring the System.DirectoryServices namespace
- ❑ Investigating the DirectoryEntry object functionalities
- ❑ Retrieving, modifying, deleting, and updating a DirectoryEntry
- ❑ Getting and setting DirectoryEntry properties
- ❑ Exploring other ADSI providers
- ❑ Understanding DirectoryEntry's caching
- ❑ Investigating and extending the DirectorySchema

The System.DirectoryServices Namespace

In the last chapter, you learned that the .NET Framework provides resources to access Directory Services and that these resources are built on top of Active Directory Service Interfaces (ADSI), which encapsulates existing interfaces for effective communication with ADSI and Lightweight Directory Access Protocol (LDAP) providers. We must point out that these ADSI resources are now available for managed as well as for unmanaged code—you'll see more about using "raw" underlying ADSI in Chapter 4.

Now you'll take a look at the functionality available within this namespace. We're not simply going to provide a list of all the available methods and properties—you can find these easily in the .NET Framework SDK documentation—instead, you will see how the methods and properties relate to real Directory Services tasks.

The DirectoryEntry Class

The purpose of the DirectoryEntry class is to manipulate an entry from a directory. In .NET, an instance of the DirectoryEntry class represents an object in a directory that encapsulates a node or object in the directory hierarchy. The DirectoryEntry class is considered to be the core of the System.DirectoryServices namespace, mostly because it is the class that encapsulates the actual ADSI objects and interfaces that are used to perform the communication between the .NET Framework and a directory.

Working side by side with the DirectoryEntry class, is a collection-type class named DirectoryEntries, which comprises several DirectoryEntry objects grouped together into a single collection. The DirectoryEntries class has a very important place in the namespace because it retains the hierarchy between parent and children objects in a directory, and in this way, it offers a clean representation of the directory structure.

The DirectoryEntry class has a number of methods for manipulating objects in a directory, and it has the amusingly named Properties property, through which you can access the properties of objects in a directory. The name is amusing because it means that when reading about the DirectoryEntry class, you can often find the words "properties" and "property" appearing several times in the same sentence, often with a different meaning! (You just saw this in the previous sentence.)

What Can You Do with a DirectoryEntry?

You can perform many tasks using a DirectoryEntry object because it wraps a real entry in a directory container and these tasks have a special relationship with the directory. Moreover, DirectoryEntry possesses methods and properties that make it possible to accomplish the following actions on directory objects:

- ❑   Modify properties.
- ❑   Rename or move an entry.
- ❑   Enumerate child objects.
- ❑   Create children.

❑   Delete child objects.

❑   Get object identity.

The `DirectoryEntry` class also has the native `Invoke()` method; this is a reflection-based resource that allows developers to call native methods on the underlying ADSI object, thus adding great extensibility to the instantiated `DirectoryEntry` object. Furthermore, it saves the developer from creating her own reflection code from `System.Reflection` when dealing with native ADSI resources.

Search Functionality

The `System.DirectoryServices` namespace also provides a way to query objects and implement search functionality in a directory. We will explore this functionality in greater depth in the next chapter, but we'll have a quick look at the relevant classes first:

> **DirectorySearcher:** Performs queries against Active Directory.
>
> **ResultPropertyCollection:** Contains properties of a `SearchResult` instance.
>
> **SearchResult:** Encapsulates a single node from a search performed by a `DirectorySearcher` object.
>
> **ResultPropertyValueCollection:** Contains values of properties within a `SearchResult` instance.
>
> **SearchResultCollection:** Contains several `SearchResult` instances returned from a query made using a `DirectorySearcher`.
>
> **SortOption:** Specifies how to sort the results of a search.

The `System.DirectoryServices` namespace contains powerful searching support since most of the work that is done with the classes is basically for querying and reading the directory.

Schema Structure

A schema is a definition of classes that are stored in the directory that enforces the rules and constraints that manage the structure of the data being stored. The schema defines the classes (such as user, group, and organizational unit) that can appear in the directory, and the optional and mandatory properties (such as `accountExpires`, `telephoneNumber`, and `department`) for each class. Every object in the directory is an instance of at least one class in the schema, and this class encompasses a set of attributes and syntax that defines the schema itself.

> *Note that property names in a directory follow a camel-casing convention—the first letter of each property name is lowercase, and the first letter of any other words contained in the name is capitalized.*

The `DirectoryEntry` class exposes properties such as `SchemaClassName`, which denotes the name of the schema that defines the object, and `SchemaClassEntry`, which is the actual `DirectoryEntry` instance that represents the object's schema. Later in the chapter, we explore how to take advantages of these properties to extend the resources of Directory Services.

Code Security

The .NET Framework provides a way to add security at the code level; in other words, security within the assemblies you build. For example, if you want to create an assembly that changes the properties of directory objects, you will want to make sure that the only assemblies, either executables or libraries, that have permission to access a certain method, are the assemblies to which you have granted these permissions.

The classes that are used for code access security in the `System.DirectoryServices` are as follows:

> **DirectoryServicesPermission:** Allows you to control code access security permissions for `System.DirectoryServices`.
>
> **DirectoryServicesPermissionAttribute:** Allows you to make declarative `System.DirectoryServices` permission checks.
>
> **DirectoryServicesPermissionEntry:** Defines the smallest unit of a code access security permission set for `System.DirectoryServices`.
>
> **DirectoryServicesPermissionEntryCollection:** Contains a strongly typed collection of `DirectoryServicesPermissionEntry` objects.

These classes follow the same functionality that is applied in the `System.Security` namespace; in fact, these classes are inherited from other classes in the `Security` namespace. Code security is not just available for `System.DirectoryServices` but for many other namespaces in the .NET Framework.

Retrieving an Entry from a Directory Service

In `System.DirectoryServices`, all objects in a directory service are represented as instances of the `DirectoryEntry` class. The `DirectoryEntry` instance connects to other objects located in the directory, returning a reference to it back to the client as a `DirectoryEntry` instance.

Even though .NET has made it very straightforward to manipulate entries from a directory, you must consider a few basic topics that were primarily defined in ADSI in order to effectively understand what you need to perform different actions.

> In order to use the `System.DirectoryServices` namespace, you must add a reference to the `System.DirectoryServices.dll` assembly, either from the **Add Reference** menu option in VS.NET or with the **/r** switch if you are compiling from the command line.

To retrieve an object from a directory, you have three things to consider:

❑   Naming

❑   Binding

❑   Navigation

Naming

Naming identifies different objects in the directory. We are going to use Active Directory for our examples, but objects in other directories may be in a different namespace, which uses different namespaces to access different directories. In Active Directory, we'll be using the distinguished naming convention, which is used to identify the name of the domain that holds the service as well as the referenced object. We already introduced the naming convention in Chapter 1; here we are going to use only the following:

Notation	String Type Representation
OU	organizationalUnitName
CN	commonName
DC	domainComponent

This convention can produce ADsPaths such as `LDAP://DC=ADSERVER,DC=COM`, which represents the root hosted by a directory service. Consider the following ADsPath that represents a user in the Users container:

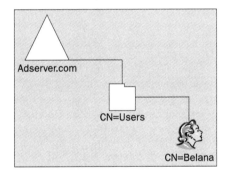

From this diagram, you can assume that the AdsPath of the Belana user is `LDAP://CN=Belana,CN=Users,DC=ADSERVER,DC=com`. This is the path that the `DirectoryEntry` instance will use when it binds to that particular object.

If the current user doesn't have the required permissions to access the directory, then you will have to include user credentials with the binding request. These are used for the authentication process when you are retrieving a `DirectoryEntry` object. The username and password are represented by the `Username` and `Password` properties of the `DirectoryEntry` instance; they describe the user who is requesting information to the directory service.

Binding

The process of retrieving an entry from a directory service must begin with binding. *Binding* involves finding the directory service and providing the appropriate credentials for performing all types of operations on that particular entry determined by the path passed to the `DirectoryEntry` object. There are five constructors that allow you to bind to a directory object when you instantiate a `DirectoryEntry` object:

1. Empty constructor, serverless binding:

```
DirectoryEntry de = new DirectoryEntry();
```

2. Passing the object's ADsPath:

```
    DirectoryEntry de = new
DirectoryEntry("LDAP://CN=Users,DC=ADSERVER,DC=com");
```

3. Passing the path, username, and password:

```
DirectoryEntry de = new DirectoryEntry( "LDAP://CN=Users,DC=ADSERVER,DC=com",
                                        "administrator",
                                        "avatar");
```

4. Passing the path, username, password, and authentication type (represented by the AuthenticationTypeEnum, covered in **Chapter 5**):

```
DirectoryEntry de = new DirectoryEntry( "LDAP://CN=Users,DC=ADSERVER,DC=com",
                                        "administrator",
                                        "avatar",
                                        AuthenticationTypes.Secure);
```

5. Passing a native ADSI object:

```
DirectoryEntry de = new DirectoryEntry(IADSObject);
```

Sometimes you need to keep track of directory objects even after they move location–for example, when you are attempting to migrate objects from one tree to another. In this case, you can use the actual Global Unique Identifier (GUID) of the object that you met in the previous chapter to perform the bind process: LDAP://{GUID=<*guidvalue*>}. The GUID will never change if the object is moved from one parent to another because this GUID is a value generated by the host operating system when the object is initially created in the directory. You can retrieve the GUID of a DirectoryEntry object from its NativeGuid property, which returns a string representation of the number.

Another very important point to consider is when you wish to rebind to a directory. For instance, suppose that you have instantiated a DirectoryEntry and have performed a bind to the path LDAP://DC=MYSERVER,DC=COM, and now you want to bind to CN=Users. You can of course create another DirectoryEntry instance, passing in a different path, but an overhead is associated with creating another object, and this can be expensive if you have to perform many binds to a directory. Instead, you can reuse the existing DirectoryEntry, by setting a new path with the Path property, and then refreshing the cache.

```
    //Bind to default naming context
    DirectoryEntry entry = new DirectoryEntry("LDAP://DC=MYSERVER,DC=COM");
    ...

    //Perform work on entry
    ...
```

```
entry.Path = "LDAP://CN=Users,DC=MYSERVER,DC=COM"; // different path;
//Re-Bind
entry.RefreshCache();
```

Take a look at this code; here we showed you how to bind the `DirectoryEntry` instance to the `defaultNamingContext`. After doing your work on the directory entry, you changed the value of the `Path` property to point to the new directory entry and called the `RefreshCache()` method. `RefreshCache()` refreshes the local cache and also performs a bind to the current path stored in the `Path` property. You will learn how to apply this approach later in the Directory Browser application; also, we will discuss the local cache in more detail later in the chapter.

Serverless Binding

The ADSI Software Development Kit (SDK) documentation advises you never to hardcode a server name; this practice mostly keeps software configuration more flexible, but it also avoids the security issues that may arise from having details of your server embedded in your code. Remember, your code can be easily read when disassembled and exposed in Microsoft Intermediate Language (MSIL) form. From the flexibility point of view, if you deploy a client application to a different directory service context (such as a server with a different name), the application will, of course, break. To avoid the problem of initially specifying a server name, you perform the initial binding on the root of the directory, a process known as **serverless binding**.

You accomplish serverless binding by binding the object to `LDAP://rootDSE`, which is defined in LDAP 3.0. This is not a namespace, but the root of the server that is available to the client. For example, if an application is placed in a directory context (network location) in which the server name is `SERVER.COM`, using `LDAP://rootDSE` will bind the context to `DC=SERVER,DC=COM`. However, if you deploy the same application to a different context in which the server is called `YOURSERVER.COM`, then `LDAP://rootDSE` will return `CN=YOURSERVER,DC=COM`. The main purpose of the `LDAP://rootDSE` approach is to provide necessary information about the server to the client.

When using `DirectoryEntry` instances, you don't need to implement the process of acquiring the root because the logic of doing it is already within the `DirectoryEntry` class. If a path is supplied either through the `Path` property of `DirectoryEntry` or one of the constructor overloads, that path will be used for binding. Otherwise, if no path is specified, then the `DirectoryEntry` will automatically bind to the path retrieved from `LDAP://rootDSE`–this path is known as the `defaultNamingContext`, which is one of the properties of the root entry.

Thus when working with the `DirectoryEntry` class, you don't need to supply a path for binding if you know that you are within a directory context in the network and the `defaultNamingContext` will be retrieved from `LDAP://rootDSE` to provide a default path. However, it is good practice to supply a known path via custom configuration.

Retrieving a Directory Entry Example

We are now ready to show you how to retrieve an entry from the directory provider. Retrieving an entry from a directory service using `System.DirectoryServices` is effortless because any object in a directory service is considered to be an entry. As we have already discussed, to retrieve an entry from a directory service, you must supply a path, credentials, and the type of authentication. When using the default constructor of the `DirectoryEntry` class, binding will default to the server that is in the client's context.

Here is the most basic example:

```
using System;
using System.DirectoryServices;

class RetrieveEntryExample
{
    static void Main()
    {
        DirectoryEntry de = new DirectoryEntry();
        try
        {
            Console.WriteLine(de.Name);
        }
        catch(Exception e)
        {
            Console.Write(e.Message);
        }

    }
}
```

The output of this example should be similar to the following:

DC=ADSERVER

The output is the Domain DNS server that holds the directory service. Note that no path was actually sent out to the server; consequently, the DirectoryEntry instance was bound to the defaultNamingContext as explained earlier.

Building a Directory Browser

In this section you are going create an application named Directory Browser to implement and illustrate the functionality found in the System.DirectoryServices namespace; as you learn new things, these will be added to this application. A directory browser is a very common type of application to use for browsing and performing operations in a directory.

You will be able to use the directory browser you build for the following:

- ❏ Adding a new entry
- ❏ Deleting an entry
- ❏ Moving the location of an entry
- ❏ Property handling
- ❏ Connect to different providers (IIS, WinNT)

The directory browser will consist mainly of .NET controls on a form. The control that will be most used is the TreeView, which is the best control for navigating through a hierarchy.

The application consists of three forms:

- ❑ **FrmMain**, for viewing and performing tasks
- ❑ **FrmMove**, for moving entries
- ❑ **FrmAdd**, for adding a new entries

We are also going to show you how to create a Singleton class called `DirectoryUtil` to centralize most functionality that will be used by the application. This class in particular will have functionality added as you discover new features in `System.DirectoryService`.

In the application, you are going to use the following controls:

tvwDirectory: A `TreeView` control for browsing the directory.

TabMain: A `TabControl` for grouping other controls.

lstProperties: A `ListBox` for displaying the properties of an entry.

lstPropertyValue: A `ListBox` for showing the value(s) for a particular property.

btnAddUpdatePropertyValue: A `Button` to add or update a property value.

btnRemovePropertyValue: A `Button` for removing (deleting) a property value.

txtPropertyValue: A `TextBox` for entering a new property value.

imgList: An `ImageList` that will contain icons that represent the objects in `tvwDirectory`.

lblPath: A `Label` that sits above `tvwDirectory` showing the current node's path.

Some of these controls and small forms will be constructed in different sections of this chapter. The layout of the application will look like this:

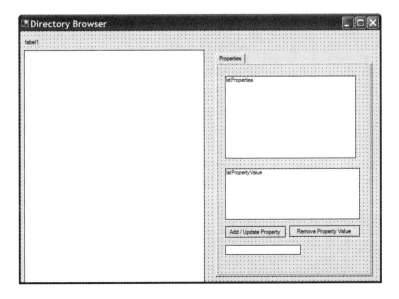

Let's get started with the `DirectoryUtil` class. The `DirectoryUtil` is a Singleton class, meaning you are going to build it using the Singleton design pattern. The *Singleton* pattern ensures that only one instance of the class will be created, and it is used to share other objects and methods throughout the application. Another important aspect of a Singleton is that it ensures that random code does not instantiate that class as well. In order to create a Singleton, you must create a private constructor and also make sure that the class is thread safe, meaning that only one thread will be able to instantiate the class. Furthermore, the class will create a static instance of itself, which will be the one to which all callers will have access.

One of the reasons for following this Singleton approach here is to reuse `DirectoryEntry` objects. You can't avoid binding to the directory object, but you can save the overhead of creating new `DirectoryEntry` objects by reusing the objects you've already created.

The following code shows the beginning of the class definition, consisting of the following:

- ❑ A private string named _path to hold the path to the root container object (the object that will load the entire `TreeView`)

- ❑ A `DirectoryEntry` object named _rootContainer to bind to the _path string

- ❑ A static reference variable named _directoryUtil for holding the only instance of the class

- ❑ Another `DirectoryEntry` named _sharedDirectryEntry, which will represent different nodes in the `TreeView`

- ❑ A static object, _lockObject, which will be used to protect the part of the code from multiple threads calling the first instantiation of the object

- ❑ A delegate called `DirectoryUtilEventHandler` and a public event, OnBind, for notification of a binding request from a caller

```
public delegate void DirectoryUtilEventHandler(object sender, string path);
public class DirectoryUtil
{
    //Global instance of the singleton
    private static DirectoryUtil _directoryUtil;
    //Top of the directory to be handled globally.
    private static DirectoryEntry _rootContainer;
    //Shared instance
    private static DirectoryEntry _sharedDirectorEntry;
    //Path for loading directory entry
    private string _path;
    //Used to create a lock on the process of new objects
    private static object _lockObject = "For locking";
    //Event for binding notification
    public event DirectoryUtilEventHandler OnBind;

    . . .
```

Next you have the private constructor that will create the shared `DirectoryEntry` instance as well as the rootContainer. As we mentioned before, the default constructor of `DirectoryEntry` binds to the defaultNamingContext via LDAP; this is the main task for the _rootContainer object because you are going to load the `TreeView` from this instance.

At the moment, it doesn't matter which path the sharedDirectoryEntry binds to—you just want to create it, here is the constructor section.

```
...
private DirectoryUtil()
{
    //bind to the rootDSE {DirectoryEntry("LDAP://rootDSE");}
    _rootContainer = new DirectoryEntry();
    //Instantiate shared instance
    _sharedDirectorEntry = new DirectoryEntry();
}
...
```

Because you have a private constructor you must instantiate the class implicitly, so you create a read-only property to get the single instance of the class. The following code shows a static property Instance that will return the instance of the DirectoryUtil class, creating it if it does not already exist. You wrap the creation code with a lock statement, to ensure that only one thread can create the new instance.

```
public static DirectoryUtil Instance
{
    get
    {
        lock(_lockObject)
        {
            if(_directoryUtil == null)
                _directoryUtil = new DirectoryUtil();
        }
        return _directoryUtil;
    }
}
```

Now you are going to define a way to recycle the _rootContainer object. We have mentioned before that you can reuse a DirectoryEntry instance by changing the value of the path and calling the RefreshCache() method. Initially the root container is going to be bound to the defaultNamingContext, but if you want to change the path for some reason (such as changing providers, from LDAP to IIS), you can just call your RefreshDirectoryStructure() method. This method will reassign the value of the Path property to the current _path value and bind the object by calling the RefreshCache() method. Once this occurs, it will notify all subscribers of the OnBind event by raising the it here.

```
...
private void RefreshDirectoryStructure()
{
    _rootContainer.Path =_path;
    _rootContainer.RefreshCache();
    _sharedDirectorEntry.Path =_path;
    _sharedDirectorEntry.RefreshCache();
    if(OnBind != null)
        OnBind(this,_path);
}
...
```

You are also going to make this binding mechanism public so that callers will be able to refresh the structure of the root container after any changes. Rather than expose `RefreshDirectoryStructure()` itself, you have a public `Bind()` method that calls `RefreshDirectoryStructure()`.

```
. . .
public void Bind()
{
    //Bind root container.
    RefreshDirectoryStructure();
}
. . .
```

You can now define a way for callers to change the path by creating a `Path` property for the `DirectoryUtil` class. Furthermore, when clients change the value of the `Path` property, you call the `RefreshDirectoryStructure()` to rebind instantly.

```
. . .
public string Path
{
    get
    {
        return _path;
    }
    set
    {
        _path = value;
        RefreshDirectoryStructure();
    }
}
. . .
```

Lastly, you expose `SharedEntry` and `RootContainer` as read-only properties. These will be used to represent the top root container of the directory (`RootContainer`) and the children (`SharedEntry`).

```
. . .
public DirectoryEntry SharedEntry
{
    get
    {
        return _sharedDirectorEntry;
    }
}

public DirectoryEntry RootContainer
{
    get
    {
        return _rootContainer;
    }
}
. . .
```

Now it's time for you to jump into the FrmMain code. In the private declarations for the form, you initially define a reference variable for the DirectoryUtil instance, then, in the form's constructor, you subscribe to the OnBind event of the DirectoryUtil object, and finally you call the InitTree() method, which loads the TreeView.

```
...
//Reference to the Instance of the Directory utility class
private DirectoryUtil util;

public FrmMain()
{

    InitializeComponent();
    //Singleton reference
    util = DirectoryUtil.Instance;
    util.OnBind += new DirectoryUtilEventHandler(RefreshedDirectoryHandler);
    InitTree();
...
```

The handler for the OnBind event merely refreshes the TreeView and updates the label displaying the path:

```
private void RefreshedDirectoryHandler(object sender, string path)
{
    this.lblPath.Text = path;
    this.InitTree();
}
```

In the InitTree() method, you clear any existing nodes in the TreeView and add a top TreeNode, passing the RootContainer property of the util object—this contains the top of the directory structure. The TreeNode that you add contains the name of the root container obtained from the DirectoryEntry.Name property.

```
...
private void InitTree()
{
    this.tvwDirectory.Nodes.Clear();
    this.tvwDirectory.Nodes.Add(new TreeNode(util.RootContainer.Name,0,0));
}
...
```

Now you are ready to run the application for the first time:

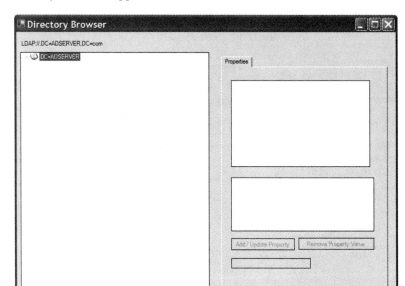

As far as System.DirectoryServices is concerned, you've not really learned anything new yet. Basically, all you've done is performed serverless binding with a directory entry and held an instance of a top-level container of Active Directory, in this case LDAP://DC=ADSERVER, DC=COM. In the next section, you are going to navigate through the directory by drilling down in the tree.

Retrieving Entries from a Directory—Linear Navigation

The easiest way to retrieve more than one entry from a directory requires you to use the parent-child relationship that is defined in the directory hierarchy. We have already discussed how a DirectoryEntry can be either a container or non-container object; container entries can hold references to other objects, allowing us to organize the entries into groups. The DirectoryEntries class in the System.DirectoryServices namespace is able to maintain references to several DirectoryEntry objects.

DirectoryEntries implements the IEnumerable interface, and consequently must implement the GetEnumerator() method; this means that you can iterate through it using a foreach statement, or simply increasing the indexer with MoveNext(). The Children property of the DirectoryEntry object returns a DirectoryEntries instance that contains a DirectoryEntry for each child.

A directory is based on a hierarchical model that can make it confusing to identify directory elements in an object-oriented context, mostly because of the DirectoryEntry abstraction. For example, the root of a directory context (LDAP://DC=ADSERVER,DC=COM) is represented by a DirectoryEntry instance that can contain other DirectoryEntry objects in the Children property; these, in turn, hold further DirectoryEntry objects that can each hold further DirectoryEntry objects in their Children property as well.

The following diagram represents this relationship from the root container to users in the CN=Users directory entry, and also shows the relationship as it appears in the Microsoft Management Console (MMC) for Active Directory administration.

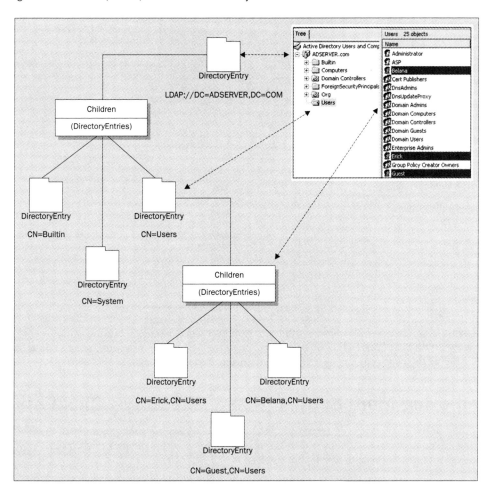

As you can see from this diagram, the DirectoryEntry instance exposes the Children property revealing a DirectoryEntries instance (a collection of DirectoryEntry objects), which gives access to other DirectoryEntry objects. In CN=Users, you can clearly see that the Children property gives access to all users and groups in the directory.

Now you are ready to populate the TreeView of the Directory Browser application. Going back to your application, you'll remember that you have only established the top TreeNode of the TreeView with the name of the root container exposed by the Name property of the util.RootContainer DirectoryEntry instance.

Now it is time to use the Children property of that DirectoryEntry instance and iterate through the contained DirectoryEntry objects with a foreach loop. As you iterate through the collection, you get each child reference's Name and add it to a node in the TreeView as a child node of the top-level node:

```
private void InitTree()
{
   this.tvwDirectory.Nodes.Clear();
   this.tvwDirectory.Nodes.Add(new TreeNode(util.RootContainer.Name,0,0));

   foreach(DirectoryEntry child in util.RootContainer.Children)
   {
      this.tvwDirectory.Nodes[0].Nodes.Add(new TreeNode(child.Name,3,4));
   }
   //Expand tree.
   this.tvwDirectory.ExpandAll();
}
```

On your server, this result should be similar to the following:

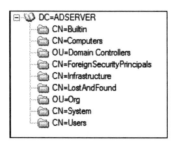

In this example, you already know that the root container is merely binding to the defaultNamingContext and iterating through the Children property, which contains all child entries of the root container—in this case, the root of the directory.

Retrieving More Entries from a Directory—ClickPerView

In the previous section, you retrieved the child entries from the root container of the directory; now you are going to retrieve entries that are deeper in the tree. This means that you can explore the directory from the root to any leaf in the tree.

However, rather than retrieving information about the whole catalog at once, you will request entries from the directory as the user clicks a particular node in the TreeView. We like to call this approach ClickPerView. When you click a particular TreeNode in the TreeView, only then will the application request the directory for more directory entries, consequently populating the clicked TreeNode with other child TreeNodes (if the DirectoryEntry has children).

When you click a TreeNode, you need to solve a couple of problems:

❑   Getting a reference to the current TreeNode in the directory

❑   Determining if the TreeNode was already clicked and already loaded with children

Finding out if a `TreeNode` was already clicked is not a difficult task. You can use a few different approaches, but here you are going to use one called *stamping*; nowadays, many developers call it *tagging* because it uses the `Tag` property found in the `TreeView` control.

Here you will use tagging by assigning a value to the `Tag` property of a `TreeNode` when the user clicks the node. In this case, the value assigned is an object with the `DirectoryEntry.Path` value and a value that indicates if that entry was previously called; this way you can meet the requirement discussed earlier. The object you'll be storing in the `Tag` property will be an instance of a class called `TreeNodeInfo` that we define now:

```
class TreeNodeInfo
{
    private bool _isLoaded;
    private string _ldapPath;

    public TreeNodeInfo(string Path, bool isLoaded)
    {
        _ldapPath = Path;
        _isLoaded = isLoaded;
    }

    public string Path
    {
        get
        {
            return _ldapPath;
        }
    }
    public bool IsLoaded
    {
        get
        {
            return _isLoaded;
        }
        set
        {
            _isLoaded = value;
        }
    }
}
```

As you can see, this is a very simple structure. When you add a new node from a child, you will store the instance of this class in the `Tag` object.

Before going ahead and populating more nodes, you must go back to the `InitTree()` method in the `FrmMain` and add instances of the `TreeNodeInfo` to the top level `TreeNodes`:

```
private void InitTree()
{
    this.tvwDirectory.Nodes.Clear();
    this.tvwDirectory.Nodes.Add(new TreeNode(util.RootContainer.Name,0,0));
    //Tag TreeNode
    this.tvwDirectory.Nodes[0].Tag = new TreeNodeInfo(util.Path,true);
    int index = 0;
```

```
        foreach(DirectoryEntry child in util.SharedEntry.Children)
        {
            index = this.tvwDirectory.Nodes[0].Nodes.Add(new
                            TreeNode(child.Name,3,4));
            //Tag TreeNode
            this.tvwDirectory.Nodes[0].Nodes[index].Tag =
                                        new TreeNodeInfo(child.Path,false);
        }
        this.tvwDirectory.ExpandAll();
    }
```

Note that you also must use an integer index to keep track of the `TreeNode`s you've created. The `Add()` method of the `TreeNodeCollection` returns an integer to the newly created `TreeNode`, so you can index the current instance to tag that `TreeNode`. You have now tagged both the root container level and its children, so go ahead and implement that for subsequent hierarchical levels in the directory.

Now you are going to handle the navigation using the ClickPerView approach. You need to add a handler for the `AfterSelect` event of the `TreeView`, which fires after the user selects a `TreeNode`.

The event handler will take as parameters the `TreeView` as the `sender` and a `TreeViewEventArgs` object, which contains very important object references, such as the reference to the `TreeNode` that fired the event, from which we can get the `Tag` property and hence the `TreeNodeInfo` object.

```
    private void tvwDirectory_AfterSelect(object sender,
                    System.Windows.Forms.TreeViewEventArgs e)
    {
        //TreeNodeInfo from current clicked TreeNode
        TreeNodeInfo nodeInfo = (TreeNodeInfo)e.Node.Tag;
        int index = 0;
        //Bind to an instance of the current node entry in the TreeView
        util.SharedEntry.Path = nodeInfo.Path;
        //Only Rebind the SharedEntry.
        util.SharedEntry.RefreshCache();
        //Add current path on the label
        this.lblPath.Text = nodeInfo.Path;
        //Check if the TreeNode was previously loaded
        if(!nodeInfo.IsLoaded)
        {
            try
            {
                //Iterate throughout the child nodes
                foreach(DirectoryEntry child in util.SharedEntry.Children)
                {
                    //Add node to the current node's TreeNodeCollection
                    index = e.Node.Nodes.Add(new TreeNode(child.Name,3,4));
                    //Tag node
                    e.Node.Nodes[index].Tag =
                            new TreeNodeInfo(child.Path,false);
                }
                //Set value to loaded
                nodeInfo.IsLoaded = true;
```

```
        e.Node.Tag = nodeInfo;
        this.tvwDirectory.SelectedNode.Expand();
    }

    catch (Exception ex)
    {
        //Trace errors
    }

  }
}
```

In the code, you first get a reference to the `TreeNodeInfo` stored in the `TreeNode.Tag` property:

```
//TreeNodeInfo from current clicked TreeNode
TreeNodeInfo nodeInfo = (TreeNodeInfo)e.Node.Tag;
```

Then, you reuse the `SharedEntry DirectoryEntry` object by setting the `Path` property to the string stored in the `nodeInfo.Path` property. Then you rebind the `SharedEntry` by calling its `RefreshCache()` method directly. You will use the `SharedEntry` shortly.

```
//Bind to an instance of the current node entry in the TreeView
util.SharedEntry.Path = (nodeInfo.Path);
//Only Rebind the SharedEntry.
util.SharedEntry.RefreshCache();
```

Now, you test the `nodeInfo.IsLoaded` property. If it's `true`, you won't bother loading again; otherwise you continue to the body of the `if` statement:

```
//Check if the TreeNode was previously loaded
if(!nodeInfo.IsLoaded)
{
```

Finally, you iterate through the children of the `SharedEntry` using a `foreach` statement. For every child, you add a `TreeNode` to the current node. You should also assign a new `TreeNodeInfo` object to the `Tag` property. This `TreeInfo` object contains the path and a value of `false` to show that we haven't yet loaded it. Note that we have previously bound the `SharedEntry` to the currently collected `TreeNode`, so it is now the parent of the loading `TreeNode`.

```
foreach(DirectoryEntry child in util.SharedEntry.Children)
{
    //Add node to the current node's TreeNodeCollection
    index = e.Node.Nodes.Add(new TreeNode(child.Name,3,4));
    //Tag node
    e.Node.Nodes[index].Tag = new TreeNodeInfo(child.Path,false);
}
```

After all is said and done, you change the value of IsLoaded to true so that this current node doesn't get asked to load again, which saves the application from querying the server unnecessarily.

```
//set value to loaded
nodeInfo.IsLoaded = true;
e.Node.Tag = nodeInfo;
this.tvwDirectory.SelectedNode.Expand();
```

Now you can test the functionality—just run the application and click a tree node; this shows a result like the following:

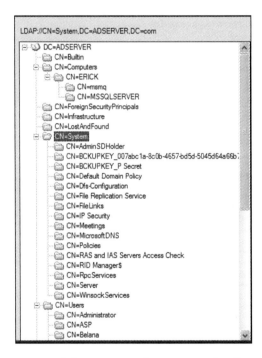

If the user clicks any TreeNode and the corresponding entry in the directory has children, then he will be added to the current TreeNode. Note that because you are using the ClickPerView approach, the same nodes are not reloaded, but the SharedEntry is rebound. You can test the performance of the ClickPerView approach by commenting out the if statement that checks to see whether the nodes have already been loaded, and seeing the effect of reloading them again.

Adding an Entry in the Directory Service

Adding an entry in the directory is not difficult, but finding out where to put the entry is. In other words, you need to know which DirectoryEntry is going to be the parent of the entry. You have already put a great deal of work toward getting that part resolved, but now you need to follow these basic steps before you add a new entry in the directory:

1. Locate the new entry.

2. Check to see if the location can be a parent.

3. Set values for the mandatory properties and also any optional properties you wish to use.

4. Check to see if the entry already exists, and if it does, remove it.

5. Update changes.

Before you consider adding entries from your Directory Browser application, take a look at this very simple example that demonstrates the basic code required first.

```
using System;
using System.DirectoryServices;

class AddDirectoryEntryExample
{
    static void Main()
    {
```

Suppose you want to add a new user in the CN=Users container; you first need to get the DirectoryEntry object reference to it as the parent:

```
//Get the container entry (Parent)
DirectoryEntry entry = new
    DirectoryEntry("LDAP://CN=Users,DC=ADSERVER,DC=COM");
```

The next step is to add a child entry to this directory entry. However, first you need to check to see if this is possible; in other words, you need to make sure the entry is actually a container. You can use the SchemaEntry property of DirectoryEntry to do this. This property holds a DirectoryEntry object that contains the schema information about your directory object, and if the object is a container, the object holding its schema has a Name of container:

```
//Test if the entry object is a container
if(entry.SchemaEntry.Name == "container")
{
```

As we have already mentioned, a DirectoryEntry object has a Children property that allows us to access all the children of the DirectoryEntry container. This Children property is nothing more than a reference to a DirectoryEntries object, which has an Add() method that takes two string arguments. The first argument represents the name of the new entry and the second is the SchemaClassName that represents the type of object it is (user, group, organization unit, etc.). In this case, you are adding a new User type.

```
DirectoryEntry childEntry = entry.Children.Add("CN=Gary
Archer","User");
```

Unlike `Add()` methods found in other collections, the `Add()` method of `DirectoryEntries` basically creates a new `DirectoryEntry` in the collection and returns a `DirectoryEntry` reference that represents that new object. The main reason for this is that when you add new objects to a directory, you often need to manipulate the object further before you can commit it into the directory, such as when you are setting up mandatory properties or customizing the values of the optional properties.

Thus, the `Add()` method returns a new instance of a `DirectoryEntry` that represents the new entry, and then you can assign the mandatory and optional properties to that instance:

```
//Mandatory properties
childEntry.Properties["sAMAccountName"].Add("garyArcher");
//Optional properties
childEntry.Properties["description"].Add("Useful description");
childEntry.Properties["displayName"].Add("Gary Archer");
childEntry.Properties["givenName"].Add("Gary");
childEntry.Properties["userPrincipalName"].Add("gary");
childEntry.Properties["mail"].Add("archerg@federation.universe");
childEntry.Properties["sn"].Add("Archer");
```

In the previous chapter, you saw two types of properties: mandatory and optional. These properties are reinforced by the schema of the object's class. We are going to look at schemas later in the chapter.

As far as Active Directory is concerned (which we are using in these examples), when you add a user, you must at least define the mandatory `sAMAccountName` property of the underlying object, otherwise a `COMException` is thrown, notifying you that a constraint has been violated. The `sAMAccountName` must be unique within the domain. When you are working with ADSI, we advise you to search the domain for that string before you add an account. However, when you are working with `DirectoryEntry`, putting your code inside a `try...catch` block will suffice to alert you of any naming conflicts. You can catch the `COMException` that bubbles from the underlying native object; this provides useful details about the underlying ADSI object's error (most of the errors will occur in this ADSI object).

After assigning the property values, in the case of a `User` object you should add a further property to enable the account. The `userAccountControl` property takes values from the ADSI `ADS_USER_FLAG` enumeration, which defines values for user logon features such as **Account Disabled**, or **User Password Not Required**. We will look at user management in more detail in Chapter 6.

```
//Pass flag to enable the account.
childEntry.Properties["userAccountControl"].Add(0x0200);
```

> **It is a good idea to encapsulate all values in the ADS_USER_FLAG in an enum type, especially when adding users and groups.**

Even though you used the `Add()` method to create a new entry in the `Children` property, you have not added this new entry to the *directory*. To create this new entry to the directory effectively, you must update the changes. But before you do that, you must check to see if the entry already exists in the directory.

You do this with the `DirectoryEntry.Exists()` static method, to which you pass your newly created `DirectoryEntry` object.

If your new entry already exists, you should remove it first with the `Remove()` method of `DirectoryEntry`. The `Remove()` method takes an actual `DirectoryEntry` object, so we first retrieve the entry by passing the path into the `DirectoryEntry` constructor:

```
if(DirectoryEntry.Exists(childEntry.Path))
{
    Console.WriteLine("Entry already exists");
    entry.Children.Remove(new DirectoryEntry(childEntry.Path));
}
```

If the object exists in the directory, then your attempt to add a new object with the same path will fail. Remember, the directory path is similar to a primary key in a relational database, and using the schema of the directory, it enforces rules and constraints to ensure that the integrity of the data within the directory is maintained.

The final step (updating changes) is to call the `CommitChanges()` method of the child `DirectoryEntry` object, which performs all pending updates in the directory server. If you do not call `CommitChanges()`, the directory is not updated, and the object remains in the property cache on the client. Caching will be discussed later in this chapter in the "Getting and Setting Properties" section.

```
            childEntry.CommitChanges();
        }
    }
}
```

As mentioned before, `CommitChanges()` updates the directory with all the information that was changed on the client cache; it does this by simply calling `SetInfo()` from the native object, thus flushing the cache to the directory.

Back to the Directory Browser

In the Directory Browser application, you will now introduce the functionality to add users and groups, which use the process you saw earlier. First, you should add a context menu to `FrmMain` and associate it with the `TreeView` to allow users to add an entry:

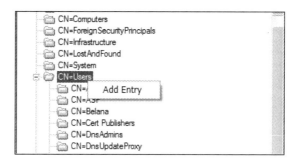

Add the following code to the handler for the **Add Entry** context menu entry's Click event. This code checks to see if the object you wish to add to actually is a container by checking to see if its SchemaClassName has the value container; if it does, you will reveal the form for adding objects as shown here:

```
private void AddEntry_Click(object sender, System.EventArgs e)
{
    //Check if parent is a container
    if(util.SharedEntry.SchemaClassName == "container")
    {        //Show form for adding new entry
        FrmAdd frm = new FrmAdd();
        frm.ShowDialog();
    }
    else

    {
        MessageBox.Show("Current Entry is not a container",
            "Error adding new Entry",
            MessageBoxButtons.OK,MessageBoxIcon.Error);
    }
    //Refresh structure.
    util.Bind();
}
```

The last line calls the Bind() method in the DirectoryUtil class, which rebinds the _rootContainer and triggers the event to fire in the client, forcing the TreeView to refresh.

The form for adding new entries, FrmAdd, looks like this (this image shows two copies of the form):

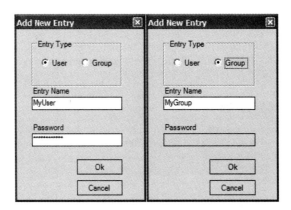

This form allows you to add either a User or a Group type of entry. When you choose Group, the **Password** box is disabled, but for a User entry, the box is enabled, allowing you to enter a password. A password is not a mandatory property for a Group type of entry.

You can view the results of newly added entries by looking at results in the CN=Users (where CN=MyUser was created) node of the Directory Browser application, as shown here:

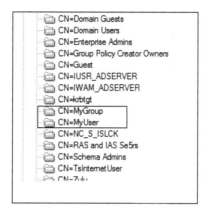

In the next section, you are going perform some further manipulation with these newly created objects.

Moving an Entry Object

Moving an object in a directory is equivalent to changing its parent. In ADSI, the method that is often used is the MoveHere() method; in fact, this is the method that is used behind the scenes by the MoveTo() method of the DirectoryEntry object so that it can perform the same functionality. There are two overloads for the MoveTo() method, both of which require a DirectoryEntry object that specifies the new parent of the object to be moved. The overload with only the DirectoryEntry parameter moves the entry to a new location, preserving the entry's name. The other overload has an extra string parameter that specifies a new name for the entry once it has been moved. Here is a typical example of their usage:

```
//Moves to a new location keeping the current name
entry.MoveTo(new DirectoryEntry("new path"));

//Moves to a new location with a new name
entry.MoveTo(new DirectoryEntry("new path"), "newName");
```

Now you are going to use this method to add some extra functionality to the Directory Browser in order to move objects between containers.

The FrmMove form has a similar TreeView to FrmMain, but it only displays directory entries that are containers (in other words, the objectClass property has the value "container"). We won't show the code that does this here, as it uses techniques that we'll cover in the next chapter. However, you can access it in the full code download (available from the Downloads section of the Apress web site at http://www.apress.com), or else you can piece it together yourself from the code for searching directories that you will learn in Chapter 3.

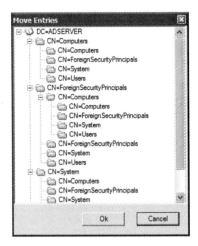

The code for the **Ok** button's `Click` event handler looks like this:

```
try
{
    TreeNodeInfo nodeInfo = (TreeNodeInfo)this.tvwContainer.SelectedNode.Tag;
    //Validate

    //Check if any TreeNode is selected
    if(!(this.tvwContainer.SelectedNode.Index > 0))
        throw new Exception("Please Select a Destination");
    else
    {
        //Do moving
        new DirectoryEntry(util.SharedEntry.Path).MoveTo(
                        new DirectoryEntry(nodeInfo.Path));
    }
    //Go back to FrmMain
    this.Dispose();

}
catch(Exception ex)
{
    MessageBox.Show(ex.Message,
            this.Text.ToString(),
            MessageBoxButtons.OK,
            MessageBoxIcon.Stop);
}
...
```

This code uses the `MoveTo()` method of the `DirectoryEntry` class to move the entry from the selected `TreeNode` in FrmMain's `TreeView` (represented by `SharedEntry`) to the new location specified by the path of the selected node in the `TreeView` in FrmMove.

This screen shows the process in action:

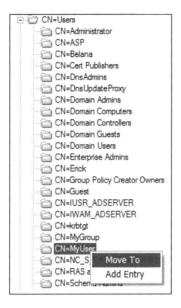

After you choose **Move To** from the context menu for an entry, the `FrmMove` form opens and you just select the destination and press OK:

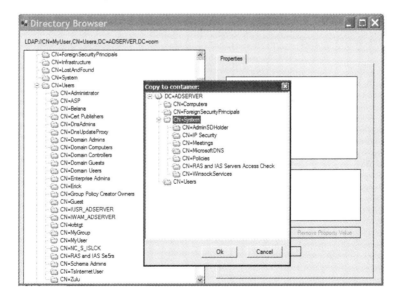

Finally, FrmMove is disposed of and FrmMain refreshes the TreeView by calling the InitTree() method to rebuild the directory structure, which shows the moved object in the chosen destination.

Renaming an Entry Object

You have already flagged that the path of a DirectoryEntry uniquely determines its location in the directory. Thus if you change the path, you can, in principle, move the object. The DirectoryEntry.Rename() method does this for you—if you pass in a string to this method, the name of that DirectoryEntry instance will be changed to this string.

For example, renaming the entry with the following path:

    LDAP://**CN=Belana**,CN=Users,DC=ADSERVER,DC=com

to:

    LDAP://**CN=Modeski**,CN=Users,DC=ADSERVER,DC=com

moves the first DirectoryEntry from one location to another. By understanding this, you can accept what really happens when you call the Rename() method in the DirectoryEntry object—the arguments are basically taken and passed to a call to the two-parameter MoveTo() method.

Getting and Setting Properties

All objects in a directory have properties; they define relationships to other objects and make them unique. In this section, we are going to describe some general uses of properties and show you how to enumerate, modify, and add these properties.

The System.DirectoryServices namespace contains the following classes, which you must have to handle properties:

> **PropertyCollection:** Defines a collection of properties that can be found in a DirectoryEntry that wraps the properties exposed by the native object.

PropertyValueCollection: Contains the values of a property in a PropertyCollection item.

The System.DirectoryServices property-accessing functionality creates a comfortable wrapper around the old ADSI property access methods: the PropertyCollection uses the IAdsPropertyList interface to organize access to the collection.

The properties of a directory entry are exposed through the Properties property of the DirectoryEntry instance, which is of type PropertyCollection. PropertyCollection has a PropertyNames property, through which you can get the names of the entry's properties, and a Values property, through which you can get the values of a property. Since a property can be single valued or multivalued, each directory property has a PropertyValueCollection collection to represent the values.

The native ADSI methods (GetEx(), GetInfoEx(), and GetInfo()) are called from the DirectoryEntry object to retrieve the property information, and this is passed to the collections. Fortunately you don't need to deal with these methods on a daily basis because the processes of dealing with these properties occur implicitly and are handled by the DirectoryEntry instance. We'll look more at these ADSI methods in Chapter 4.

Listing the DirectoryEntry Properties and Values

You'll now learn how to incorporate the functionality that allows you to list directory entry properties and values into your Directory Browser application. First you'll retrieve the property names from the selected TreeNode representing a directory entry and populate the lstProperties list box. To proceed, add an entry to the context menu for the property-loading functionality:

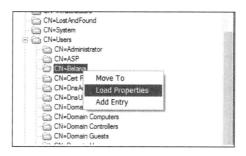

Then, in the `Click` event-handler of the **Load Properties** context menu entry, add the following code:

```
...
private void LoadProperties_Click(object sender, System.EventArgs e)
{
    this.lstProperties.Items.Clear();
    foreach(string propertyName in util.SharedEntry.Properties.PropertyNames)
    {
        this.lstProperties.Items.Add(propertyName);
    }
}
...
```

This clears the `lstProperties` list box and gets the currently selected entry from the `TreeNode`, which is the `SharedEntry DirectoryEntry` object. After this is finished, simply iterate through the collection by adding the `string` array retrieved from the `PropertyNames` property and adding each string to the `lstProperties` list box.

Here is the result for the **CN=Belana** user:

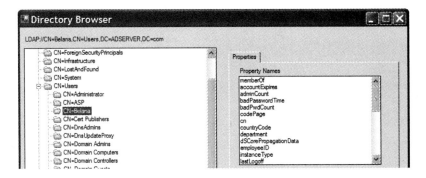

You now have all the property names displayed in the `lstProperties` list box; great! However, they don't really mean much to you without their values. As we mentioned earlier, a directory entry property is used to return value(s) that have a meaning in the directory, so you now need to go one step further and retrieve these values.

For each property name selected from the `lstProperties` list box, you need to load the value(s) into the `lstPropertyValues` list box located underneath `lstProperties`. First, you have to get the name of the property from the currently selected `TreeNode`.

In the `SelectedIndexChanged` event handler of `lstProperties`, add the following:

```
private void lstProperties_SelectedIndexChanged(object sender,
System.EventArgs e)
{
    string propertyName = this.lstProperties.Items[
                this.lstProperties.SelectedIndex
                     ].ToString();
    ReloadPropertyValues(propertyName);
}
```

This simply gets a `string` representing the selected item in `lstProperty`; this is the property name from which you want to view the value(s). Then pass this `string` to the `ReloadPropertyValues()` method, which has the following definition:

```
...
private void ReloadPropertyValues(string propertyName)
{
    this.lstPropertyValue.Items.Clear();
    PropertyValueCollection values = util.SharedEntry.Properties[propertyName];
    foreach(object propValue in values)
    {
        this.lstPropertyValue.Items.Add(propValue);
    }
}
...
```

This method takes the name of the property as a string argument, `propertyName`, and gets the `PropertyValueCollection` from the relevant property of the `SharedEntry` object, which is the directory entry represented by the currently selected `TreeNode`. The relevant property is simply obtained from the `Properties` indexer by passing in the string `propertyName`. To get the values of the property, just iterate through the `PropertyValueCollection` and add the values to the `lstPropertyValue` list box.

As you know, a property can be single valued or multivalued. As you iterate through the collection, you don't need to keep track of whether you have a single value or more, because the `foreach` statement will loop until it exhausts the items in the collection. Here is an example that shows the values for the `cn` property of the user Belana:

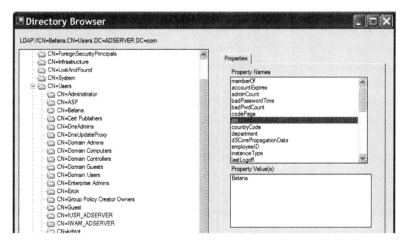

As you can see, there is a single value **Belana** in the property value list. Now here is an example of a multivalued property:

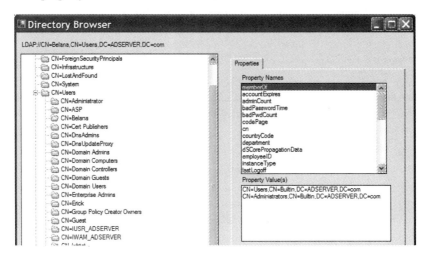

Note that some of the properties cannot be read by casting them to a string value; this is the case with the `System.Byte` array that is returned by the `objectGUID`, which would need further processing in order to get readable values. You can determine these values by testing the type, or more efficiently, by knowing what properties you are going to view. `System.DirectoryServices` still lacks many enumerations and types that can be found in ADSI mapping to native directory structures. For example, the `lastLogon` is a `LargeInteger` type that is not found in .NET. You need to either cast it to an `IADsLargeInteger` using COM interop, or else perform further undocumented processing!

Modifying Properties

Directory Services is typically used for reading rather than writing, but sometimes you need to write further information or remove obsolete information, such as phone numbers, addresses, or e-mail addresses, for example.

The most difficult parts of modifying properties in a `DirectoryEntry` is finding out what the name of the property is and determining the index of the value that you want to modify. As you have already seen, the value of a single-valued property always can be accessed by the first index of the collection, but it can also be accessed through the `Value` property, which will return the value of the first index of the `PropertyValueCollection`.

Let's begin our example by displaying the values in the url property:

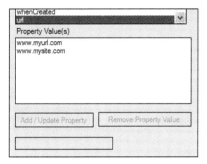

You can see that this is a multivalued property; you can also see some controls on the form that are currently disabled; these include a button for adding a new property value, a button for removing a value from the property, and a text box for inserting a new value.

Here is the code you need to define in the Click event handler of the **Add / Update Property** button:

```
private void btnAddPropertyValue_Click(object sender, System.EventArgs e)
{

    //Get Current property name
    string propertyName =
        this.lstProperties.Items[this.lstProperties.SelectedIndex].ToString();
    //Check if we can add multiple values to the property
    try
    {
        util.SharedEntry.Properties[propertyName].Add(
                        this.txtPropertyValue.Text);
        //Update directory
        util.SharedEntry.CommitChanges();
    }
    catch(Exception ex)
    {
        util.SharedEntry.Properties[propertyName].Value =
                        (object)this.txtPropertyValue.Text;
        //Update directory
        util.SharedEntry.CommitChanges();
    }
    //Reload property value list
    ReloadPropertyValues(propertyName);
}
...
```

Here you can see that we tried to add the new value on the basis that the property is multivalued. If the property is only single valued, then the call to CommitChanges() fails, and an exception is thrown. In this case, you need to add the value as a single-valued property using the Value property in the PropertyValueCollection. After all that, refresh the list of values.

For example, double-clicking the **Property Value(s)** list box enables the buttons, and then you can add a new URL in the text box:

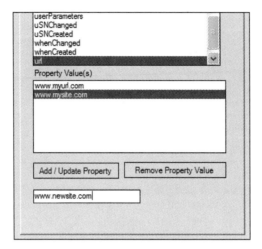

Upon entering the URL and clicking the **Add / Update Property** button, you will get the following output:

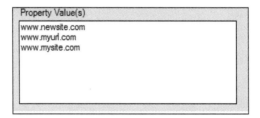

You can also remove property values using the Remove() method from the PropertyValueCollection; this is done in the Click event handler of the **Remove Property Value** button:

```
private void btnRemovePropertyValue_Click_1(object sender, System.EventArgs e)
{
    string theValue = this.lstPropertyValue.Items[
            this.lstPropertyValue.SelectedIndex].ToString();
    string propertyName = this.lstProperties.Items[
            this.lstProperties.SelectedIndex].ToString();
    util.SharedEntry.Properties[propertyName].Remove(theValue);
    util.SharedEntry.CommitChanges();
    //Reload property value list
    ReloadPropertyValues(propertyName);
}
...
```

Here the code gets the currently selected item in the lstPropertiesValue list box and calls the Remove() method of the PropertyValueCollection, using the Properties indexer to retrieve the appropriate property. A call to CommitChanges() ensures that the changes are made before you refresh the list of property values.

To actually carry this out, you only need to select the value from the list of property values and press the **Remove Property Value** button to remove a particular value of a property. Note that if you remove all but one value of a multivalued property, the property does not become single valued. A property being multivalued or single valued is determined by the schema of that object and does not depend on how many values are actually stored in the object.

When dealing with multivalued properties, you can use different methods of PropertyValueCollection to insert values or even arrays of objects in the property.

Inserting by index with the Insert() method: Pass the index to insert into and an object as the value to insert.

```
entry.Properties["telephoneNumber"].Insert(3,"(425)555-1166");
```

Inserting a range of values with the AddRange() method: Simply pass an array of objects.

```
entry.Properties["operator"].AddRange(new string[] {"Gary","Dary"})
```

Inserting to a collection index:

```
entry.Properties["wwwHome"][0] = "http://www.myspaceship.com";
```

The PropertyValueCollection inherits from CollectionBase, and as a result, it possesses various inherited properties and methods such as List, OnInsert(), and OnRemove(), which are very useful for performing data conglomeration.

Switching Providers

Now that you have done some work using Active Directory, we'll introduce you to a new functionality in the program that will also help you in the next section when you learn how to view schemas. So far we have being using the default naming context (hardcoded in the DirectoryEntry), which is fine if your application is bound by one provider, but what if you want to view entries in IIS or from a local network using the WinNT provider, or what if you want to use LDAP to connect to external LDAP providers?

All the information about a directory entry in your application is kept in a TreeNodeInfo object stored in the Tag of the nodes; the TreeView does not care what Directory Service we are using.

Now you need to add another context menu to the FrmMain form. This menu should produce an input box when you click on it that asks for a new path. Unfortunately no input box is defined in C# or in the .NET Framework for quick and dirty inputs (everybody does it!), so we are going to use the one that is available for Visual Basic .NET, which works fine for quick data input.

Here is the code defined in the new context menu:

```
private void ChangePath_Click(object sender, System.EventArgs e)
{
    //Pop up a new inputbox and return the string.
    string newPath =
        Microsoft.VisualBasic.Interaction.InputBox(
            "Enter a new Path:",

            "Change Path","",
            this.tvwDirectory.Location.X,this.tvwDirectory.Location.Y);
    //Only change path if new path is returned.
    if(newPath.Length > 0)
    {
        //Change current rootContainer path
        util.Path = newPath;
        //Re-Bind
        util.Bind();
    }
}
```

The code is very simple, it calls for the input box and checks to make sure that the text entered is not empty, then it changes the Path property of the util (DirectoryUtil) object, and then it binds to the new path, forcing a refresh of the entire TreeView. It is up to the client to ensure that she enters a sensible path into the input box.

Let's enter paths from some different providers to see the outcome:

❑   WinNT Provider:

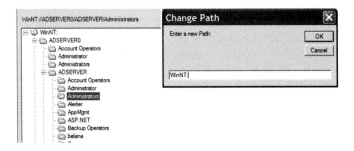

❑   IIS Provider:

In the previous chapter, you used Internet Explorer (IE) to open an LDAP link in Microsoft Address Book; let's now see how this link looks in your Directory Browser application:

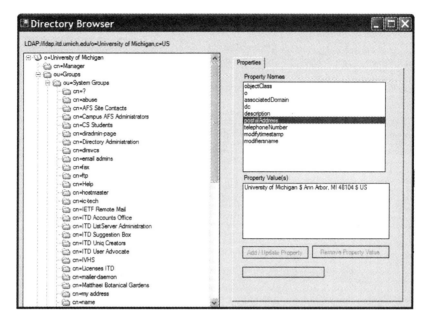

As you can see, the generic nature of `System.DirectoryServices` allows you to create applications that can connect to different providers. Bear in mind that the `TreeView` in your Directory Browser application will load and display properly for different providers, but the properties may not load for some providers such as X.500 because ADSI may not support that property type.

Caching

A common problem many developers encounter when they first work with ADSI and `System.DirectoryServices` is that they find that their entries don't get updated when changes are made to the object. The reason for this is, of course, because they don't flush the local cache in order to update their changes to the directory.

Caching data on the client is purely for performance and convenience: for performance because it can be very tough to update several properties and entries at once, and for convenience because when the user feels that the output is right, he calls the `CommitChanges()` method, updating the provider with changes made to the directory object.

When using `DirectoryEntry` you should keep caching in mind. Caching can definitely give you some performance advantages, especially because when you call the `CommitChanges()` method, you are asking the underlying object to call the `SetInfo()` ADSI method, which sends data across the network. Minimizing this will increase the performance of the application greatly.

Calling `CommitChanges()` after each property modification is a poor approach for saving the object, because it increases network traffic and leads to a possible performance decrease:

```
entry.Properties["telephoneNumber"].Insert(3,"(425)555-1166");
entry.CommitChanges();

entry.Properties["operator"].AddRange(new string[] {"Gary","Dary"})
entry.CommitChanges();

entry.Properties["wwwHome"][0] = "http://www.myspaceship.com";
entry.CommitChanges();
```

Calling CommitChanges() after all property modifications have taken place is a better way to go because this minimizes the amount of network activity; This way, the underlying ADSI object saves trips back to the server, minimizing network traffic and increasing the application's performance.

```
entry.Properties["telephoneNumber"].Insert(3,"(425)555-1166");

entry.Properties["operator"].AddRange(new string[] {"Gary","Dary"})

entry.Properties["wwwHome"][0] = "http://www.myspaceship.com";
//Update Directory.
entry.CommitChanges();
```

The .NET Framework already applies the caching approach in working with Directory Services; for example, if you call the NativeGUID property, the DirectoryEntry calls an internal method called FillCache(), which takes a string denoting the property to be retrieved. The internal FillCache() method tests to see if the cache is already filled, and if it is, it returns the property name from the local cache (NativeGUID); otherwise it retrieves the single property from the directory and updates the local cache.

This is basically how you should be thinking. You can make good use of caching by updating the local cache with the properties that you need to update; you perform this by using the RefreshCache() method. This method takes a string array containing the names of the properties you need to retrieve from the directory to the local cache, instead of retrieving all of the properties:

```
entry.RefreshCache(new string[] {"memberOf", "department"});
```

This line of code only retrieves the memberOf and department properties instead of retrieving every single property in the directory.

An important thing to note about using RefreshCache() without any parameters is that it will erase all of the data in the local cache and retrieve new values from the directory. Thus, if you have made changes to the local cache and want to keep them, you should not call RefreshCache() prior to calling the CommitChanges() method, or else these changes will be lost. In the following example, we demonstrate how values can be lost when you do not update the cache back to the server. Here, we call read properties from an object and modify one of these properties' values; before we call the CommitChanges() methods, we call the RefreshCache(), which results in the modified value being discarded by the original one from the remote server.

```
Console.WriteLine("Username: " + entry.Properties["cn"].Value);
Console.WriteLine("Department: " + entry.Properties["department"].Value);

Console.WriteLine("....Changed value in local cache");
entry.Properties["department"].Value = "Kitchen";

Console.WriteLine("Department: " + entry.Properties["department"].Value);

Console.WriteLine("....Discarding changes by refreshing cache");
entry.RefreshCache();

entry.CommitChanges();

Console.WriteLine("Department: " + entry.Properties["department"].Value);
```

The output of this example would be as follows:

As soon as you call `RefreshCache()` the local cache is wiped out, and all changes are purged. This means that `RefreshCache()` can also be viewed as a canceling mechanism.

In contrast to this approach, you can call the `RefreshCache(string[])` overload and safely pass in only the properties that you want to be refreshed.

```
Console.WriteLine("....Discarding changes by refreshing cache");
entry.RefreshCache(new string[]{"memberOf"});
```

This modification to the example produces the following:

In fact, the only property that was retrieved when you called the `RefreshCache()` was `memberOf`, and it was safely updated in the local cache without disturbing any other values.

The Schema

When talking about a directory service and the process of creating new users, groups, or containers, we should ponder how these objects are created and where their structures are kept. A directory object is a data structure whose "blueprint" is kept in the schema of the directory itself.

The schema is the definition of classes and attributes that are used in the directory and it can be found in the `CN=Schema,CN=Configuration` path.

For example, the `User` class definition is kept in

```
CN=User,CN=Schema,CN=Configuration,DC=ADSERVER,DC=com
```

and it is defined as type `classSchema`. If you look at the `department` class, it is located at

```
CN=Department,CN=Schema,CN=Configuration,DC=ADSERVER,DC=com
```

and this is defined as an `attributeSchema` type.

Now that you are aware of the schema location, we'll show you how to use it with the Directory Browser application. Just run the Directory Browser and set a new path as `LDAP://CN=Schema,CN=Configuration,DC=ADSERVER,DC=com` (using your server path instead of `ADServer.com`):

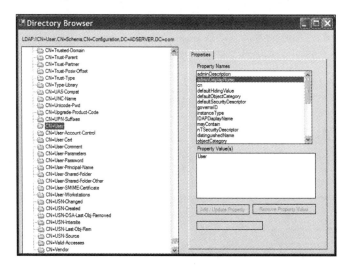

This screen shows the result of what happens when you click CN=User, which is a class defined in the schema. Now you understand the second `string` parameter in the `DirectoryEntries.Add()` method:

```
DirectoryEntry newEntry = new DirectoryEntry.Children.Add("CN=MyUser",
"User");
```

This second parameter refers to the schemaClassName and specifies from which class the new object should draw its schema.

Furthermore, note that the SchemaClassName property of a DirectoryEntry object holds the name of that object's schema class. With this, you can make a final modification to the Directory Browser application, so that it recognizes which class each entry belongs to, and displays a different icon. Here is the new code for the AfterSelect event handler of the TreeView:

```
private void tvwDirectory_AfterSelect(object sender,
                                      System.Windows.Forms.TreeViewEventArgs e)
{
    ...
    if(!nodeInfo.IsLoaded)
    {
    ...
        foreach(DirectoryEntry child in currentEntry.Children)
        {
            switch(child.SchemaClassName)
            {
                case "user"://User
                    index = e.Node.Nodes.Add(new TreeNode(child.Name,1,1));
                    break;
                case "group"://Group
                    index = e.Node.Nodes.Add(new TreeNode(child.Name,2,2));
                    break;
                case "computer"://Computer
                    index = e.Node.Nodes.Add(new TreeNode(child.Name,5,5));
                    break;
                case "mS-SQL-SQLServer"://Sql Server
                    index = e.Node.Nodes.Add(new TreeNode(child.Name,6,6));
                    break;
                case "printQueue"://Sql Server
                    index = e.Node.Nodes.Add(new TreeNode(child.Name,6,6));
                    break;
                default://Generic folders
                    index = e.Node.Nodes.Add(new TreeNode(child.Name,3,4));
                    break;
            }
            e.Node.Nodes[index].Tag = new TreeNodeInfo(child.Path,false);
        }
    }
    ...
}
```

Here you are basically identifying the schema type of each entry and assigning a different icon from the `ImgLst` image list. Here is the result:

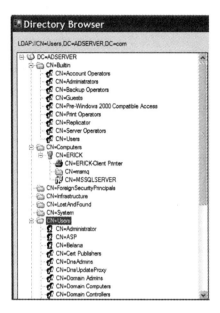

This provides a much better visual effect by showing whether a node is a group, a user, or a printer. You can also extend this approach for switching image lists if you change providers–for example, if you connect to an IIS provider, you can detect that and change the type of visual effect.

The concept of creating data structures from a schema is a strong one for many reasons, especially when you are extending business requirements. In directories, the schema ensures that you can maintain data integrity and at the same time provide a powerful mechanism for extensibility.

Modifying the Schema

Even though directories possess several default objects defined in the schema, there are times when you need to store different information in a certain object. Suppose that you have user objects that require an attribute such as `yearsOfService`, or `preferredTvShow`, that is not found in the current schema–you can define a new `attributeSchema` and add it to the user object. Or perhaps you want to define a completely new type of object in the directory; for instance, suppose there is a `Computer` class definition but you want to create a new one called `Laptop`. You would complete each of these tasks by extending the schema.

> Be aware that once you extend a schema, you cannot go back—other than to demote the entire domain controller (DC) and start from scratch again. In particular, this is a warning for developers who tend to modify functionality on the fly to overcome immediate issues: extending schemas in directories should not be used as workarounds!

Even though you cannot delete new schema extensions, you can disable them to prevent new instances of that class from being created, but you must also disable all classes that implement this extension.

Remember that an application won't stay around forever, but the business will (hopefully), so it is a better design decision to extend the schema based on business requirements rather than on a particular application's needs.

Extending the Schema—Adding New Properties

In this section, we are going to show you how to add a new property to the class schema User of the Active Directory. You should look at a few things before you go ahead and extend the schema. This is mostly because whatever you add or change in the schema will affect the entire directory structure, so it would be nice to get it right the first time!

Attributes in the schema are of the type attributeSchema, and attributes themselves also have attributes. The attributes that are mandatory for creating a new attributeSchema using a DirectoryEntry are as follows:

> **attributeID or Object Identifier (OID):** A unique value issued by several authorities to identify distinct data for distributed applications. OIDs are normally used in the Open System Interconnection (OSI) Application level in the X.500 standard. As part of the legacy that LDAP inherits from X.500, RFC 2251 denotes the need for this attribute, so it is included in the LDAP specification.

> **oMSSyntax:** An integer that represents the syntax of the object. An object is accessed by querying its type and value; in conjunction with the attributeSyntax, the object can define the syntax for accessing the attribute.

> **attributeSyntax:** In conjunction with oMSSyntax, this attribute determines what kind of data type can be stored in the attribute.

> **isSingleValued:** A Boolean value that determines if the new attribute is to be single or multivalued.

> **searchFlags:** A Boolean value that determines whether or not the attribute is to be indexed.

> **schemaIDGUID:** Uniquely identifies the object to the system. This element is essential for controlling access to the object on the system (access control entries).

> **lDAPDisplayName:** This is the name that identifies the object to LDAP clients and uniquely identifies the object in the directory; it is much easier to use than the schemaIDGUID.

> **isMemberOfPartialAttributeSet:** A Boolean representation that indicates whether the attribute can be published globally in the Global Catalog.

Before you get into the implementation code, take a look at the appropriate values for each one of these attributes:

Attribute Name	Value	Description
attributeID	1.2.840.113556.1.4.7000. 233.28688.28684.8.498378 .1433773.1438157.352141	Generated by oidgen.exe
isSingleValued	True	Only carries a single value
searchFlags	True	Indexed
schemaIDGUID	System.Guid	GUID generated by .NET Framework
lDAPDisplayName	CN=LevelOfPatience	Identifier for LDAP
IsMemberOfPartial AttributeSet.	True	Globally known
attributeSyntax	2.5.5.4	Case-insensitive string
oMSSyntax	20	Case-insensitive string

The two values that are of most interest to you are attributeID and lDAPDisplayName. The attributeID must be unique, and it is generated by the oidgen.exe tool, which is found on the Windows Server 2000 Resources disc. This utility generates an object identifier that you can use in the attributeID value of the property. You can run the tool from the command line to get a different object identifier each time.

The lDAPDisplayName must be unique within the DC structure of your directory. It should be a name that is relevant to the functionality it is providing. For instance, we have an attribute that we'd like to add for all users of our DC called CN=levelOfPatience; we believe it will be very helpful to determine when users are not willing to perform some tasks!

This code will not produce any output, only a new attribute in the User object.

```
using System;
using System.DirectoryServices;

class ExtendingSchemaExample
{
    static void Main(string[] args)
    {
        try
        {
```

First, you'll create the GUID for the `schemaIDGUID` by creating a new `Guid` object and converting it to a `byte` array, which is the type of data that the `schemaIDGUID` accepts:

```
byte[] byteGuidArray;
Guid guidID = new Guid();

guidID = Guid.NewGuid();
byteGuidArray = guidID.ToByteArray();
```

Now create a new `DirectoryEntry` representing the schema, which is returned by ADSI when you call the `schemaNamingContext` of the `rootDSE` context. Note that you are getting the CN=User context.

```
DirectoryEntry rootDSE = new
    DirectoryEntry("LDAP://rootDSE");
DirectoryEntry root = new DirectoryEntry("LDAP://CN=User," +

rootDSE.Properties["schemaNamingContext"].Value.ToString());
```

Now instantiate a new `DirectoryEntry` by adding a child object to the schema entry of the `User` class of type `attributeSchema` and by adding the LDAP identifier as `CN=LevelOfPatience`.

```
DirectoryEntry schemaAttribute = root.Children.Add(
                    "CN=LevelOfPatience","attributeSchema");
```

Once you get the reference to the `DirectoryEntry` representing the new `attributeSchema`, you can add all the values specified in the table that we defined before.

```
schemaAttribute.Properties["lDAPDisplayName"].Add("levelOfPatience");
schemaAttribute.Properties["isSingleValued"].Add(true);
schemaAttribute.Properties["attributeID"].Add(

"1.2.840.113556.1.4.7000.233.28688.28684.8.498378.1433773.1438157.352141");
schemaAttribute.Properties["attributeSyntax"].Add("2.5.5.4");
schemaAttribute.Properties["oMSyntax"].Add(20);
schemaAttribute.Properties["searchFlags"].Add(1);
schemaAttribute.Properties["schemaIDGUID"].Add(byteGuidArray);

schemaAttribute.Properties["isMemberOfPartialAttributeSet"].Add(true);
```

Finally, you can update the directory with the new schema attribute.

```
schemaAttribute.CommitChanges();
        }
        catch(System.Runtime.InteropServices.COMException ex)
        {
            Console.WriteLine(ex.Message);
        }
    }
}
```

Now there is a new property in the Global Catalog, levelOfPatience. One way to test it is by getting a reference to an existing user, accessing the property through Properties["levelOfPatience"], and modifying its value.

```
using System;
using System.DirectoryServices;

class TestNewAttribute
{
    static void Main(string[] args)
    {
        DirectoryEntry entry = new  DirectoryEntry(
                        "LDAP://CN=Belana,CN=Users,DC=ADSERVER,DC=com");

        Console.WriteLine(entry.Properties["levelOfPatience"].Value);

        entry.Properties["levelOfPatience"].Value = "Very High";
        entry.CommitChanges();
        Console.WriteLine("..Changed property value");

        Console.WriteLine(entry.Properties["levelOfPatience"].Value);
    }
}
```

The output of this example is the following:

In your Directory Browser, the new property looks like this:

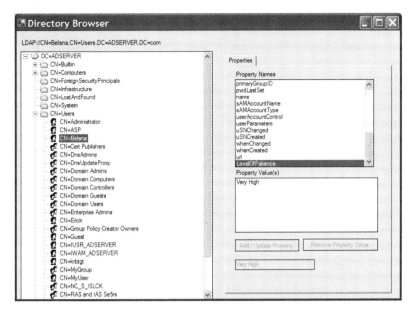

As you can see, we've created a new attribute in the schema that can be used from now on by any User objects in the directory.

Summary

In this chapter you had a quick tour of the System.DirectoryServices namespace, and you saw its major classes in action performing the key tasks for working with Directory Services, and in particular, Active Directory.

You built a simple Directory Browser application using classes from the System.DirectoryServices namespace to illustrate the relevant functionality. While developing this application, you saw how to perform the following:

- ❑ Bind to a directory service.
- ❑ List entries in a directory using the Children collection from a DirectoryEntry.
- ❑ Move directory entries between locations.
- ❑ Retrieve and list properties from a DirectoryEntry object.
- ❑ Retrieve and list property values from a DirectoryEntry object.
- ❑ Bind the application to different providers and locations.
- ❑ List entries in the schema of Active Directory.
- ❑ Extend the schema using System.DirectoryServices classes.

In this chapter you've seen the basics of retrieving information from Directory Services. In the next chapter, we'll move on to more sophisticated information retrieval, as we show you how to search Directory Services.

3

Searching Directory Services

In the last chapter, you studied the `System.DirectoryServices` namespace and some of its key classes. In this chapter, you'll see the `DirectorySearcher` class from within this namespace and see how to use it to perform searches on the Active Directory. We'll also cover other supporting classes that can be used with the `DirectorySearcher` class and techniques you can use to search the Active Directory.

In particular, we'll focus on the following:

- ❑ Basics of searching the Active Directory
- ❑ Searching the Active Directory in .NET, and the key classes this requires
- ❑ The `DirectorySearcher` class in detail
- ❑ Various search techniques like paging, sorting, and so on
- ❑ Searching with ADO.NET and the ADSI Provider
- ❑ Remote searching

Searching Directory Services—The Basics

The ability to search a directory service and retrieve information is one of the key feature of Active Directory. Suppose you have a complex network of computers and you want to find out which users have mobile or pager numbers, or what person is located in a specific area. A search operation lets you find such requirements using selection criteria or a query.

As we discussed in the previous chapters, the Active Directory tree represents a hierarchy of directory objects like user, organizational unit (OU), or computer, each of which is uniquely identified by its distinguished name. The *hierarchy* provides the basis for defining the scope of the search query. The *schema* contains the definitions for objects and enforces the rules that govern the structure and the content of the directory tree. The schema consists of a set of classes, attributes, and syntax that represent an instance of the class in the schema. An *attribute* describes the characteristics of an object and defines the type of information it can hold. The attributes can be optional or mandatory.

For example, the following figure shows the hierarchy for an Apress domain, which has some OUs like Editor and Reviewer, and users like Doug, Jeff, and Shawn. The User is the class in the Active Directory, whereas Tony and Jack are the objects of the class User. Note that we will be referencing a similar structure in the examples of this chapter.

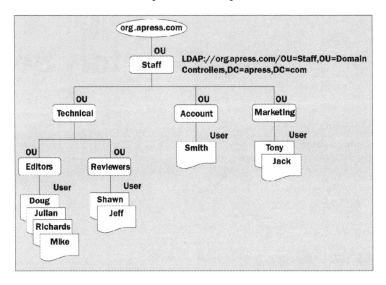

When you perform a search in a directory service, all the objects specified by the scope of the search are examined, and those that do not match the criteria of your search are filtered out. The search also returns various associated properties of the objects, and your results can be sorted to obtain even more control over the final result.

Now let's look at the searching support in the System.DirectoryServices namespace.

Searching the Active Directory in .NET

The .NET Framework has provided strong support for searching the Active Directory with the DirectorySearcher class. Like the rest of System.DirectoryServices, the DirectorySearcher class sits on top of the Active Directory Services Interface (ADSI), this time to provide easy search functionality from managed code. The class has various methods and properties to define the specific search and can be used with or without the DirectoryEntry class depending on overloads.

A number of other classes in `System.DirectoryServices` support the `DirectorySearcher` in its search activities. You can use `SearchResult` and `SearchResultCollection` to store a search result, whereas you can use the `ResultPropertyCollection` and `ResultPropertyValueCollection` classes to collect and manipulate properties and values. You can then sort the returned results with the `SortOption` class. We'll look at these after you've seen the basics of `DirectorySearcher`.

Principal Classes for Searching the Active Directory

The following table summarizes the principal classes used for searching the Active Directory.

Class	Purpose
DirectorySearcher	This is the main class used for searching the Active Directory. The enumerations SearchScope, SortDirection, and ReferralChasingOption help to define the search.
SearchResult	The FindOne() method of the DirectorySearcher class returns the SearchResult instance when it performs a search.
SearchResultCollection	The DirectorySearcher returns the SearchResultCollection instance when it performs a search with the FindAll() method.
SortOption	The SortOption class defines how to sort the results of a search.
ResultPropertyCollection	The Properties property of the SearchResult class returns the ResultPropertyCollection.
ResultPropertyValueCollection	This class contains the values found in the SearchResult property.

The Four Ingredients of a Search

Before you jump into the details of how to implement an Active Directory search, you'll first need to look at the four ingredients that every search requires:

- ❏ A search root
- ❏ A filter
- ❏ A list of properties to retrieve
- ❏ A search scope

With these ingredients, all the objects specified by the scope of the search are examined (starting with the search root), those that do not match the criteria of your search are filtered out, and various properties of the objects that remain are returned.

Now we'll talk about each of these ingredients in turn.

Search Root

The search root determines where in the directory the search should start.

The search root is specified through the `DirectorySearcher.SearchRoot` property, which is of type `DirectoryEntry`. We described the `DirectoryEntry` class in detail in the previous chapter, and you saw that it encapsulates a node in a directory service.

The search root plays an important role in performing an efficient search. By specifying an appropriate root, you can improve the performance of your query, since you will be starting your search near where you believe your target can be found.

For example, if you look back at the Apress structure, you will see that the Reviewer OU is the ideal root to use to search for all the reviewers. To start the search any higher in the hierarchy would mean extra iteration through the hierarchy to get to the Reviewer OU, which actually contains the reviewers.

Filter

A *filter* is a Lightweight Directory Access Protocol (LDAP) string that allows you to search objects in a directory with specified criteria for greater control and more efficient searches. The LDAP query syntax is a combination of attribute, relational operator, and value. The general syntax looks like this:

```
(<attribute><operator><value>)
```

The relational operator can be one of the following:

Relational Operator	Meaning
=	Equal to
~=	Approximately equal to (The exact meaning of "approximately equal to" is determined by the directory service itself.)
<=	Lexicographically less than or equal to
>=	Lexicographically greater than or equal to

Note that the LDAP search filter does not recognize the > (greater than) or < (less than) symbols. If you want to use this functionality in your filter, it is advisable to rephrase your filter using >= or <=. For example, instead of `YearsOfService < 10` try `YearsOfService <= 9`.

The * character acts a wildcard. For example, you could have the following simple filters:

❑ To get all users whose surname starts with C

```
(sn = C*)
```

❑ To get all objects

```
(objectClass = *)
```

❑   To find all computers

```
(objectCategory = computer)
```

You can combine statements to form compound queries using logical operators:

Logical Operator	Meaning
&	AND
|	OR
!	NOT

The LDAP syntax makes use of Polish notation, so the logical operator comes before the condition:[1]

```
(&(objectCategory = person)(objectClass = user))
```

which would be more familiar to you as

```
(objectCategory = person) AND (objectClass = user)
```

If the search filter has any special characters, then they need to be replaced with the relevant escape sequence:

ASCII Character	Escape Sequence Substitute
NULL	\00
*	\2a
\	\5c
(	\28
)	\29

With all this in place, you can create complex filters, such as the following:

❑   To get all users who have mobile numbers

```
((&(objectCategory = person)(objectClass = user)(mobile = *))
```

❑   To get users who have pagers but not mobile numbers

```
((&(objectCategory = person)(objectClass = user)(pager = *)(!mobile = *))
```

You can set the filter for a search using the `DirectorySearcher.Filter` property.

---

[1] Polish Notation: A method for expressing a sequence of calculation in which each operator precedes its operands. This notation was developed by the Polish logician Jan Lukasiewicz in 1929. For example, A (B + C) would be expressed as * A + B C.

List of Properties to Load

Suppose that you want to retrieve all the names and surnames of every user in a complex network. If you set the filter to get all the user objects in the directory, then when you perform the search, it will return the objects (users) you are after, but it will also return all the properties of each of these objects, of which there could be many. This way of returning all properties, of course, is likely to decrease the network performance because of the large amount of unwanted information being transported. To ensure that you only retrieve specific properties of an object from a search, you can specify a list of properties to load.

While constructing a `DirectorySearcher` object, you can pass in a string array containing the names of the properties that you want to retrieve before you begin the search. You can also use the `PropertiesToLoad` property of the `DirectorySearcher` class to create the list of properties to load similar to the following:

```
searcher.PropertiesToLoad.Add("name");
searcher.PropertiesToLoad.Add("sn");
```

Search Scope

The search scope determines the extent of the search within the directory, starting from the search root.

Three search scopes defined by values from the `System.DirectoryServices.SearchScope` enumeration can be specified for searching the Active Directory; these are

> **Base:** Limits the search to the base object and therefore returns only one object.
>
> **OneLevel:** Searches one level of the immediate children excluding the base object.
>
> **Subtree:** Searches the whole subtree, including all children and the base object.

The following figure illustrates these three possible search scopes:

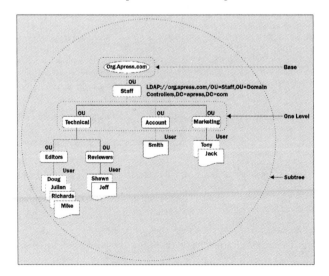

The search scope is set through the SearchScope property of the DirectorySearcher class, and as we mentioned, it takes values from the System.DirectoryServices.SearchScope enumeration. (Yes, the name of the enumeration is the same as the name of the property here!)

The DirectorySearcher Class

The DirectorySearcher class is an important component class from the System.DirectoryServices namespace that you can use to query an Active Directory. The DirectorySearcher class performs its queries using LDAP, the system-supplied provider used for performing searches.

With its constructor overloads, a DirectorySearcher object can be created that specifies the search root, filter string, the properties to be retrieved, or the search scope. The overload can be the default constructor or a combination of SearchRoot, Filter, SearchScope, and PropertiesToLoad. In the following section, you will see how to create instances of the DirectorySearcher class in different ways, depending on the basic search requirements. After that, you'll look at some important properties and methods of the DirectorySearcher class.

Creating an Instance of DirectorySearcher

You can create an instance of a DirectorySearcher object in one of several ways, depending on the constructor overload; each of these reflects a different intended use for the object.

Default Constructor

You can create an instance of the DirectorySearcher without passing any parameters. When you use such an instance to perform a search on a directory, the following default values are assigned to the properties of that instance.

Property	Default Value	Description
SearchRoot	null	The search root is set to the root of the domain.
Filter	(objectClass=*)	The search retrieves all objects.
PropertiesToLoad	An empty string array	The search retrieves all properties.
SearchScope	Subtree	This property searches the entire subtree.

You can use the default constructor if you want to retrieve all objects of a domain or if you wish to set the values yourself at some point later in your code.

Specifying the Search Root

By providing a `DirectoryEntry` object that represents a search path or root to the `DirectorySearcher` constructor, you can create an instance like the one shown here. When you create such an instance, the other properties are set to their default values as shown in the previous table. This is useful if you want to retrieve all objects for a known path.

```
//Create DirectoryEntry instance specifying root or path.
DirectoryEntry entry = new DirectoryEntry("LDAP://apress");
//Create DirectorySearcher instance using a root.
DirectorySearcher mySearcher = new DirectorySearcher(entry);
```

Note that you cannot pass a string to the `DirectorySearcher` constructor to specify the root or path—this will be interpreted as a filter, as you shall now see.

Specifying the Filter Only

By passing only a single `string` to the `DirectorySearcher` constructor, you can specify filter criteria while creating the object itself. This is useful when you don't know the exact location of an object in the entire domain. The created instance takes all other default properties as shown in the previous table.

```
//Searches for the last name Patterson in entire domain
DirectorySearcher mySearcher = new DirectorySearcher("(sn=Patterson)")
```

Specifying the Search Root and the Filter

This constructor is useful when you want to search for objects with specific filter criteria at a specific location. The following example would search for the name `Douglas` in the OU `Editor`:

```
//Create root object
DirectoryEntry entry = new DirectoryEntry ("LDAP://org.apress.com/OU=Editor,"+
                                           "OU=Technical,OU=Staff,OU=Domain "+
                                           "Controllers,DC=apress,DC=com");

//Create DirectorySearcher by specifying filter criteria
DirectorySearcher mySearcher = new DirectorySearcher (entry,
                                                  "(givenname = Douglas)");
```

Specifying the Filter and a List of Properties to Load

With this overload, you can retrieve search results using specific properties and a specific filter. In the following example, the `DirectorySearcher` returns all objects from a domain whose name starts with `J`, along with their country. Here you pass the properties to load as a `string` array.

```
//Create set of properties to retrieve during the search
string[] prop = new string[2];
prop[0] = "name";
prop[1] = "co";
//DirectorySearcher object with Filter and properties to load
DirectorySearcher searcher = new DirectorySearcher("(CN=J*)", prop);
```

Specifying Search Root, Filter, and Properties to Load

Here we pass a DirectoryEntry object, a string, and a string array. This constructor is useful for retrieving a specific node with specific filter criteria and properties. In the following example, a DirectorySearcher object is created in such a way that it returns the names and countries of all objects whose common name (CN) starts with J from the Reviewer OU.

```
//Create set of properties to retrieve during the search
string[] prop = new string[2];
prop[0] = "name";
prop[1] = "co";

//Create Root object to get all objects from OU - Reviewer
DirectoryEntry root = new DirectoryEntry("LDAP://org.apress.com/" +
    "OU=Reviewer,OU=Technical,OU=Staff,OU=Domain Controllers," +
    "DC=apress,DC=com");

//DirectorySearcher object with Root, Filter, and Properties To Load
DirectorySearcher searcher = new DirectorySearcher(root,"(CN=J*)",prop);
```

The Remaining Constructors

The two remaining constructor overloads allow us to specify

❏   A filter, a list of properties to load, and a search scope

❏   A search root, a filter, a list of properties to load, and a search scope

By now, you should be very familiar with the syntax for this constructor, so we won't go into any more detail on these.

Public Properties of the DirectorySearcher Class

The properties of the DirectorySearcher class allow you to further control the behavior of the search. In the following table all the important properties of the DirectorySearcher class that we haven't already met are summarized:

Property	Description
CacheResults	This property returns or sets a Boolean value that indicates whether or not the search results are to be cached. By setting this property to true, the searched result is cached on the local computer. For better performance, set this property to false if the search result is large.
	The default value is true.

Property	Description
ClientTimeout	The ClientTimeout property gets or sets the maximum amount of time that the client waits for the server to return results. The search is aborted without any results if the server does not respond within the specified time. A System.TimeSpan instance is used to specify the time period.
	The default timeout is -1, which means the client will wait indefinitely until the server responds. The maximum time limit value is 120 seconds.
ServerTimeLimit	This property gets or sets the maximum amount of time the server spends searching. The time is represented in the form of an instance of the TimeSpan structure. The server stops and returns results found only up to the specified time.
	The default value is -1. If the time limit is the default or a negative value, then it uses a server-determined default time of 120 seconds.
PageSize	This property gets or sets the page size in a paged search. This property is useful while you are processing large amounts of directory data. The specified value of this property indicates the maximum number of objects the server can return in a paged search. The server processes and returns results when a client request results.
	The default value is zero, which indicates no paged search.
ServerPageTimeLimit	The ServerPageTimeLimit gets or sets the maximum amount of time the server spends on searching an individual page. The PageSize property must be set to a proper value to use this property.
	The default is -1, which means that the search is to be conducted without a time limit.
SizeLimit	This property gets or sets the maximum number of objects the server returns in a search.
	The default value is zero, which means the server-determined page size of 1,000 objects is used. The server-determined time limit is also used if the specified value is more than 1,000.
PropertyNamesOnly	This property gets or sets a Boolean value that decides whether to retrieve values or not. By setting this property to true, the search results contain only the names of attributes.
	The default value is false which retrieves both the attribute names and values.

Property	Description
ReferralChasing	With ReferralChasing, the search can be controlled in a multidomain network. Referral chasing is the action taken by a client to contact the referenced server to continue the directory search. This property can be set in four different ways from the System.DirectoryServices.ReferralChasing enumeration:
	ReferralChasing.None: The search does not continue from the client to the other servers.
	ReferralChasing.Subordinate: Causes the search to go on to the child domains. Thus if the root is DC=Apress, DC=COM the server can return the results and a referral to DC=Germany, DC=Apress, DC=COM where DC=Germany is the child domain.
	ReferralChasing.External: The default option that causes the server to refer the client to an independent server that is not in the subdomain.
	ReferralChasing.All: The client chases both external and subordinate referrals.
Sort	The Sort property determines how the results will be sorted. This property takes an instance of the SortOption class. We will look at sorting in a moment.
Filter	As discussed earlier, the Filter property of DirectorySearcher can be used to set criteria for searching the Active Directory.

Searching with the DirectorySearcher

Now that you've seen the constructor and the properties of the DirectorySearcher, and you've seen how to set up your queries, it's time to start executing them.

The DirectorySearcher class has two methods for executing searches on the Active Directory:

FindOne(): Performs a search and returns only the first object found.

FindAll(): Performs a search and returns a SearchResultCollection consisting of all objects that are found during the search.

The following section describes both methods with examples to explain how to implement them.

The FindOne Method

The FindOne() method executes the search on the Active Directory and returns only the first entry in the search result as an instance of SearchResult. If no entries are found, then it returns null. By processing the SearchResult, you can get the required information.

This code shows how you would retrieve all the reviewers by specifying a cn = * filter.

```
public static void FindOne()
{
    DirectoryEntry root = new DirectoryEntry(
        "LDAP://org.apress.com/OU=Reviewer, OU=Technical,OU=Staff," +
        "OU=Domain Controllers,DC=apress,DC=com");
    DirectorySearcher searcher = new DirectorySearcher(root);

    searcher.Filter = "(cn=*)";

    searcher.PropertiesToLoad.Add("name");
    searcher.PropertiesToLoad.Add("telephonenumber");
    searcher.PropertiesToLoad.Add("co");

    SearchResult resEnt = searcher.FindOne();
    ResultPropertyCollection myResultPropColl;
    myResultPropColl = resEnt.Properties;

    // Process properties of the retrieved object
    foreach (string myKey in myResultPropColl.PropertyNames)
    {

        foreach (Object myCollection in myResultPropColl[myKey])
        {
            Console.WriteLine(myKey + " = " + myCollection);
        }
    }
}
```

And here is the output of this example, which shows properties for only one object:

The FindAll Method

The FindAll() method executes a predefined search on the Active Directory and returns results in the form of a SearchResultCollection object.

The FindAll() method throws an InvalidOperationException exception if the SearchRoot property is not set, and if searching by the provider is not supported, then it throws a NotSupportedException exception.

In the following code the `SearchAndPopulateResult` method is used to demonstrate the use of the `FindAll()` method. The rest of the examples in this chapter use this same method to search the objects and then process the searched result. This method takes the `DirectorySearcher` object as a parameter and processes the result to print the properties and values of the searched objects. Here you iterate through the `SearchResultCollection` returned by the `FindAll()` method, and process each individual `SearchResult` exactly as you did in the previous example:

```
//The SearchAndPopulateResult method
public static void SearchAndPopulateResult(DirectorySearcher searcher)
{
    //Get all objects for a searcher with predefined criteria
    foreach(SearchResult resEnt in searcher.FindAll())
    {
        //Process the result
        foreach (string propName in resEnt.Properties.PropertyNames)
        {
            foreach (object val in resEnt.Properties[propName])
            {
                Console.WriteLine(propName + " = " + val);
            }
        }
        Console.WriteLine ("");
    }
}
```

Performing a Paged Search

You use a paged search when you want to retrieve only a certain number of objects from the directory, rather than all the possible results.

The code for your paged search example is the same as the one you saw in the `FindAll()` method example, except you assign a page size to the `DirectorySearcher` object with its `PageSize` property. In this example, you will be retrieving the first ten objects:

```
//Create DirectoryEntry object
DirectoryEntry root = new DirectoryEntry(
    "LDAP://org.apress.com/OU=Reviewer, OU=Technical,OU=Staff," +
    "OU=Domain Controllers,DC=apress,DC=com");
DirectorySearcher searcher = new DirectorySearcher(root);

//Assign Page size
searcher.PageSize = 10;
```

Sorting the Results with the SortOption Class

The `SortOption` class specifies how to sort the results of a search. This class allows you to specify the direction of the search (ascending or descending) and the property name by which to sort. The class can be created either using the default constructor or by passing in the property name and sort direction as parameters. If you use the default constructor, then you have to specify both parameters explicitly through the `Direction` and `PropertyName` properties.

Thus you can either create a `SortOption` object like this:

```
//Create object
SortOption sorter = new SortOption();
//need to set properties to sort accordingly
sorter.PropertyName = "givenname";
sorter.Direction = SortDirection.Ascending;
```

or like this:

```
//Create object by using overload
SortOption sorter = new SortOption("givenname",SortDirection.Ascending);
```

Sorting the Search Result

As we mentioned earlier, the `SortOption` class orders the results based on a given property and in a particular direction. Note that the sorting can only involve one property, which is assigned through `SortOption.PropertyName`. The final step is to set the `Sort` property of your `DirectorySearcher` object to the required `SortOption` object, and then perform the search.

To see how the `SortOption` works, take a look at this simple example. In the following code, you'll retrieve all the objects with e-mail IDs and sort the names into ascending order.

```
public static void SortResults()
{
    DirectoryEntry root = new DirectoryEntry("LDAP://apress");
    DirectorySearcher searcher=new DirectorySearcher(root);
```

The `Filter` property specifies that you will filter out all objects having mail IDs, and the `PropertiesToLoad` property will specify which properties of the object are to be retrieved during the search.

```
searcher.Filter = "(mail=*)";
searcher.PropertiesToLoad.Add("name");
searcher.PropertiesToLoad.Add("mail");
searcher.PropertiesToLoad.Add("co");
```

Now comes `SortOption`. The `PropertyName` is set to `"name"` and `Direction` is set to `SortDirection.Ascending`, which will sort all the names into ascending order. (The other possible value for the sort direction is `SortDirection.Descending`.)

```
SortOption sorter = new SortOption();
//need to set properties to sort accordingly
sorter.PropertyName = "name";
sorter.Direction=SortDirection.Ascending;
```

Finally, you set the SortOption object to the Sort property of the DirectorySearcher object and then search and process the result with your own SearchAndPopulateResult() method.

```
    searcher.Sort = sorter;
    //The function is already written
    SearchAndPopulateResult (searcher);
}
```

Here is the output of the sorted result against the Active Directory:

The SearchResult Class

The SearchResult class consists of the first entry returned during a search. The SearchResult retrieves the data from the SearchResultCollection, which is available when the DirectorySearcher executes a query. This collection only contains properties that were explicitly requested through the PropertiesToLoad property of the DirectorySearcher class. The FindOne() method of the DirectorySearcher class returns an instance of the SearchResult class.

The instances of SearchResult are similar to the instances of DirectoryEntry. However, DirectoryEntry retrieves data each time a new object is accessed, whereas the data for SearchResult is already present in the SearchResultCollection returned from a query performed with DirectorySearcher. Therefore, SearchResult is more efficient than DirectoryEntry. The DirectoryEntry retrieves all objects and their properties specified in root, whereas SearchResult retrieves only the properties that are specified using DirectorySearcher.PropertiesToLoad property's collection.

The SearchResultCollection Class

The SearchResultCollection class has a collection of SearchResult instances returned during a search, and it can be used to get at the properties and values of objects returned from a search.

This class has a few important properties. The Count property returns the number of objects in the collection. The Item property acts as an indexer for the SearchResultCollection. The PropertiesLoaded property returns a string array that contains the names of the properties loaded for the original search.

The ResultPropertyCollection Class

The SearchResult class has a Properties property of type ResultPropertyCollection. This collection contains the properties that you asked to load for a particular entry retrieved from the search, and can be used to access their values.

ResultPropertyCollection has an Item property that acts as an indexer for the collection. This takes a string index and retrieves the value(s) of the property with the specified name as a ResultPropertyValueCollection. PropertyNames returns the names of the retrieved properties, and Values is used to get the values of these properties.

In the following code, the ResultPropertyCollection is used to get the property collection:

```
public static void GetPropertiesFromSearchedResult()
{
    //Create DirectoryEntry object
    DirectoryEntry ent = new DirectoryEntry("LDAP://apress");

    //Create DirectorySearcher by specifying filter criteria
    DirectorySearcher searcher = new DirectorySearcher
                        (ent,"(givenname=Douglas)");

    //retrieve the search result
    SearchResult searchResult = searcher.FindOne();
    //get the properties in collection
    ResultPropertyCollection searchResultPropColl = searchResult.Properties;


    //populate collection
    foreach (string prop in searchResultPropColl.PropertyNames)
    {
        foreach (Object propval in searchResultPropColl[prop])
        {
            Console.WriteLine(prop + "--" + propval);
        }
    }
}
```

Here is the output of this code, showing the values from the ResultPropertyCollection for a User object. We didn't specify the properties we wanted to load, so all properties for the entry are returned:

```
■ F:\Apress\resultPropColl.exe                                    _ □ X
wwwhomepage--www.apress.com                                            ▲
whencreated--8/5/2003 1:41:32 PM
badpasswordtime--0
distinguishedname--CN=Douglas Patterson,OU=Editors,OU=Techni
DC=apress,DC=com
objectclass--top
objectclass--person
objectclass--organizationalPerson
objectclass--user
c--GB
name--Douglas Patterson
pwdlastset--1238850527
userprincipalname--doug@org.apress.com
givenname--Douglas
adspath--LDAP://org.apress.com/CN=Douglas Patterson,OU=Edito
taff,DC=org,DC=apress,DC=com
objectguid--System.Byte[]
instancetype--4                                                    °
homephone--292292292
codepage--0
whenchanged--8/8/2003 3:26:18 PM
co--UNITED KINGDOM
cn--Douglas Patterson
usncreated--3586
sn--Patterson
accountexpires---1
badpwdcount--0
telephonenumber--35355909
lastlogoff--0
usnchanged--3849
company--Apress
useraccountcontrol--512                                            ▼
◄                                              ►           //
```

The ResultPropertyValueCollection Class

This class contains all the values for an individual property of a search result. As we saw above, a
ResultPropertyValueCollection is returned when we access an individual property of a
search result through the indexer of the ResultPropertyCollection. This class has Count
(inherited from ReadOnlyCollectionBase) and Item properties that can be used to get the total
number of elements, and as an indexer, respectively.

In the following code, the ResultPropertyValueCollection class is used to get the surname
(the sn property) from the search results.

```
public static void DisplayPropertyValueColl()
{
    //Create DirectoryEntry object
    DirectoryEntry ent = new DirectoryEntry("LDAP://apress");


    //Create DirectorySearcher by specifying filter criteria
    DirectorySearcher dirSearcher = new DirectorySearcher (ent,"(name=Doug*)");

    //retrieve the search result
    SearchResult searchResult = dirSearcher.FindOne();
```

```
//get the value in ResultPropertyValueCollection
ResultPropertyValueCollection searchResultPropColl1 =
                        searchResult.Properties["sn"];

//print value
Console.WriteLine(searchResultPropColl1[0].ToString());
}
```

Here is the output of this search, showing the surname of the sought-after individual:

Searching with ADO.NET and the ADSI Provider

In the previous discussion, you studied how to use the `DirectorySearcher` object to search the Active Directory. In this section, you'll see how to search Active Directory using ADO.NET. The first step is to add proper namespaces for working with ADO.NET and the Object Linking and Embedding Database (OLE DB) provider:

```
using System;
using System.Data.OleDb;
```

In the second step, you create a `Connection` object and then assign it a proper provider:

```
OleDbConnection con = new OleDbConnection("Provider=ADsDSOObject");
```

`ADsDSOObject` is the name of the OLE DB provider for Directory Services. Note that the OLE DB provider `ADsDSOObject` is a read-only OLE DB provider, which means that you cannot actually use this provider to update data in the directory, only to read data.

Creating a Query to Search

This is the core of the entire code where you have to specify the query for the search result. A query can be written in two formats: a SQL-based format, or in the standard LDAP format.

SQL Dialect

This is a simple way to write a query using the Structured Query Language (SQL), much as you would for databases such as SQL Server. You select properties from a directory entry just as you would columns from a table in a database:

Here is an example:

```
string sql= "SELECT Name, Company, Telephonenumber FROM 'LDAP://apress' " +
             "WHERE Company <>'apress' AND givenname= '*' ORDER BY NAME ASC";
```

The drawback of this method is that you can't specify the search scope.

LDAP Dialect

As well as the SQL dialect, the ADSI OLE DB provider supports query statements in the LDAP format that we saw at the start of the chapter.. The advantage of using the LDAP dialect is that it allows the search scope to be specified. The query string consists of four parts separated by semicolons (;):

❑   Base distinguished name

❑   Search filter

❑   Attributes such as AdsPath, name, and company

❑   Search scope, which can be base, one-level, or subtree

The same query that you wrote in the SQL dialect example can be written in LDAP dialect as follows:

```
<LDAP://org/DC=apress,DC=com>;(&(!company=Apress)(givenname=*);name, company;
subtree
```

where:

❑   `<LDAP://org/DC=apress,DC=com>` is the distinguished name.

❑   `(&(!company=Apress)(givenname=*)` is the filter.

❑   `name, company` is the list of attributes.

❑   `subtree` is the scope.

Your next step is to create a command object using the existing connection and SQL, and then open the existing connection.

```
OleDbCommand cmd = new OleDbCommand(sql ,con);con.Open ();
```

To read the data, you use the data reader object, which actually gets the data when you call the `ExecuteReader()` method of the command object.

```
OleDbDataReader adReader  ;
adReader  = cmd.ExecuteReader();
```

Now you simply have to read the data and output the results:

```
while(adReader.Read())
{
```

```
Console.WriteLine("Name = " +
        adReader.GetValue(adReader.GetOrdinal("name")));
Console.WriteLine("Company = " +
        adReader.GetValue(adReader.GetOrdinal("company")));
Console.WriteLine("Telephone = " +
    adReader.GetValue(adReader.GetOrdinal("telephonenumber")));
Console.WriteLine("");
}
```

Finally, close the opened objects:

```
adReader.Close();
con.Close ();
```

Here is the entire code for searching Active Directory using ADO.NET:

```
using System;
using System.Data.OleDb ;;

public class AdodbLdap
{
    static void Main()
    {
        AdodbSearch();
    }

    public static void AdodbSearch ()
    {
    //create connection object
    OleDbConnection con = new OleDbConnection("Provider=ADsDSOObject");

    //create SQL
    string sql= "select name, company, telephonenumber " +
        "from 'LDAP://apress' where Company <>'apress' and givenname= '*'" +
        "order by name ASC";

    //create command object using SQL and connection and open
    OleDbCommand cmd = new OleDbCommand(sql ,con);
    con.Open ();
    //create datareader and get the data
    OleDbDataReader adReader;
    adReader = cmd.ExecuteReader();

    //populate result
    while(adReader.Read())
    {
        Console.WriteLine("Name = " +
            adReader.GetValue(adReader.GetOrdinal("name")));
        Console.WriteLine("Company = " +
            adReader.GetValue(adReader.GetOrdinal("company")));
        Console.WriteLine("Telephone = " +
            adReader.GetValue(adReader.GetOrdinal("telephonenumber")));
        Console.WriteLine("");
```

```
        }
        //close objects
        adReader.Close();
        con.Close ();
    }
}
```

And here is the output:

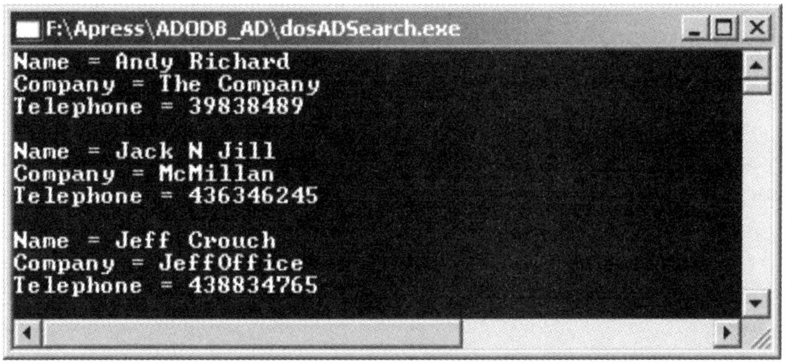

The ADSearcher Windows Application

To help you understand the practical use of the `DirectorySearcher` class let's create a real world application—ADSearcher, which searches Active Directory for custom criteria. In this example, you will also see how to create and bind search results to a `DataGrid` for easy display. You can extend this example to make directory changes with an editable `DataGrid`.

The user interface is shown in the following screenshot. You can add buttons and labels and label them accordingly, and you can add a `DataGrid` to display the search results. The **AdsPath** and **Filter** text boxes accept custom criteria for where to search and what to search for, respectively. A blank field causes the default setting to be used and performs the search accordingly. The **Authentication** check box allows the user to enter a user ID and password, enabling the associated group box. The **Load Properties** button displays all available properties for a given filter. With the >> and << buttons, the user can add or remove the properties for searching. Finally, the **Search** button executes the query for the selected criteria and populates the `DataGrid`.

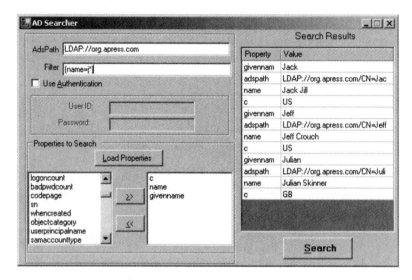

Now take a look at the code part. The GetProperties() method populates properties into listbox1 depending on the **Filter** criteria. At the start of the application the filter is empty, and therefore, listbox1 is populated with all the properties. The **Load Properties** button also calls the same method to refresh the list box.

```
private void GetProperties()
{
    //clean the list boxes for new entry
    listBox1.Items.Clear ();
    listBox2.Items.Clear ();
    try
    {
```

The DirectoryEntry object is created with the specified user credentials if the **Authentication** check box is checked; otherwise, no user information is supplied:

```
DirectoryEntry ent;
if (chkAuth.Checked)
{
    ent = new DirectoryEntry (txtAdsPath.Text,
                              txtUID.Text,
                              txtPwd.Text);
}
else
{
    ent = new DirectoryEntry (txtAdsPath.Text);
}
```

The `DirectorySearcher` object is created using the `DirectoryEntry` instance. Note that specifying no path means you'll be using the default root and a null filter and all properties will be retrieved by default.

```
DirectorySearcher propSearch = new DirectorySearcher(ent);
propSearch.Filter = txtFilter.Text;
```

Next, the code searches the directory using the `FindAll()` method and populates the list box as shown here:

```
foreach(SearchResult resEnt in propSearch.FindAll())
{
    foreach (string propName in resEnt.Properties.PropertyNames)
    {
        listBox1.Items.Add(propName);
    }
}
}
catch (Exception eR)
{
    MessageBox.Show(eR.Message);
}
}
```

The code for adding and removing the properties is simple—you just add the selected item to the other list box and then remove it from the one it's in:

```
private void txtAdd_Click(object sender, System.EventArgs e)
{
    try
    {
        listBox2.Items.Add (listBox1.SelectedItem);
        listBox1.Items.RemoveAt(listBox1.SelectedIndex);
    }
    catch(Exception eR){}
}
private void txtRemove_Click(object sender, System.EventArgs e)
{
    try
    {
        listBox1.Items.Add(listBox2.SelectedItem);
        listBox2.Items.RemoveAt(listBox2.SelectedIndex);
    }
    catch(Exception eR){}
}
```

The **Search** button actually searches the directory for user-entered criteria. The creation of the `DirectoryEntry` and the `DirectorySearcher` objects is the same as you have seen in the `GetProperties()` method.

```
private void txtSearch_Click(object sender, System.EventArgs e)
{
    try
    {
        DirectoryEntry root;
        if (txtUID.Text.Length > 1)
        {
            root = new DirectoryEntry(txtAdsPath.Text, txtUID.Text,
                                      txtPwd.Text);
        }
        else
        {
            root = new DirectoryEntry (txtAdsPath.Text);
        }

        DirectorySearcher searcher = new DirectorySearcher(root);
        searcher.Filter = txtFilter.Text;
```

The user-selected properties from `listbox2` are loaded with the `PropertiesToLoad` property of the `DirectorySearcher` class as shown here:

```
//Assign user selected properties
for (int i=0; i<listBox2.Items.Count; i++)
{
    searcher.PropertiesToLoad.Add(listBox2.Items[i].ToString());
}
```

Finally, the `SearchAndBind()` method is called to search the directory for the criteria entered, and then to bind the result to a `DataGrid`.

```
//call method to search and bind the result to Data Grid
        SearchAndBind(searcher);
    }
    catch (Exception eR)
    {
        MessageBox.Show(eR.Message);
    }
}
```

The `SearchAndBind()` method takes a `DirectorySearcher` instance and executes the search. In the first part of the method, a `DataTable` is created and added to a new `DataSet` object. The `DataTable` has two columns added to it: `Property` and `Value`. The first column will hold the property name and the second column will hold its value.

```
private void SearchAndBind(DirectorySearcher searcher)
{
    DataSet propValDS = new DataSet();
    DataTable propValTable = new DataTable ("propVal");
    propValTable.Columns.Add("Property", System.Type.GetType("System.String"));
    propValTable.Columns.Add("Value", System.Type.GetType("System.String"));
    propValDS.Tables.Add(propValTable);
```

In the second part of the method, the `DirectorySearcher` instance passed into the method executes the directory query using `FindAll()`. You can then loop through each property held in the `Properties` collection, and for each property, you can loop through all of its values and create a new `DataRow` holding the name of the property and the particular value. (Remember that properties can be multivalued.)

```
foreach(SearchResult sRes in searcher.FindAll())
{
    foreach (string pName in sRes.Properties.PropertyNames)
    {
        foreach (object val in sRes.Properties[pName])
        {

            DataRow dR = propValDS.Tables["propVal"].NewRow();

            dR["Property"] = pName;
            dR["Value"] = val;

            propValDS.Tables["propVal"].Rows.Add(dR);
        }
    }
}
```

Finally, you can assign the `DataTable` to the `DataSource` property of the `DataGrid`, and then you are ready to display your records.

```
dataGrid1.DataSource = propValDS.Tables["propVal"];

}
```

The remaining code for this application can be downloaded from the Downloads section of the Apress web site (`http://www.apress.com`), although we have covered the most important parts of the Active Directory search functionality here.

Searching Remotely

Suppose that a network administrator from a complex networked organization is working from a remote place and wants to perform a search. The following example shows how he would search the Active Directory across the Web. The example is divided into two pages. On the first page all the search parameters are taken from the user and the second page performs the search based on the selected criteria.

Here is a screenshot of the first page of the application—inputting the search criteria:

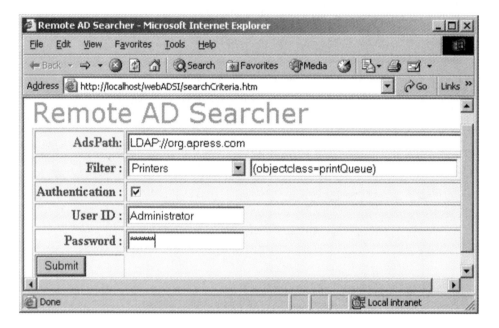

The **AdsPath** text box is used to accept the search root. For setting the filter, the user can select a fixed filter or create her own by selecting the **Custom** option. When the user selects a fixed criterion, such as **Printers**, the code uses the default filter for that object; in the case of **Printers**, this is (objectClass=printQueue).

The **Authentication** check box controls whether or not authentication is used. Using authentication wrongly will return the following error: The authentication mechanism is unknown.

When the user submits her criteria, the adSearchResult.aspx page is loaded, and the search begins. The Page_Load event fires when the page loads, and this is where we implement the search:

```
private void Page_Load(object sender, System.EventArgs e)
{
```

We start by displaying the selected criteria for the user's information:

```
Response.Write ("<STRONG><FONT color=red size=6 >Search
                Result</FONT></STRONG>");

Response.Write ("<HR>");
Response.Write ("The AdsPath is :" + Request.Form["adsPath"]);
Response.Write ("<P></P>The Filter is set for :" +
                Request.Form["txtFilter"]);
Response.Write ("<HR>");
```

In the main part of the code, the `DirectorySearcher` object is created with the specified criteria and passed to the `SearchAndPopulateResult()` method to process the search and display the results on the web page.

```
try
{
    DirectoryEntry ent;
    if (Request.Form["Checkbox1"] == "on")
    {
        ent = new DirectoryEntry(
                Request.Form["adsPath"], Request.Form["UID"],
                Request.Form["PWD"]);
    }
    else
    {
        ent = new DirectoryEntry(Request.Form["adsPath"]);
    }
    DirectorySearcher searcher = new DirectorySearcher(ent);

    searcher.Filter =Request.Form["txtFilter"];
    SearchAndPopulateResult(searcher);
}
catch (Exception eR)
{
    Response.Write(eR.Message);
}
}
```

The `SearchAndPopulateResult()` method is next; its core functionality is the same as you saw earlier when the results were displayed to a Windows Form. You can use the `StringBuilder.Append()` method to create an output string that you can dump to a server-side `div` tag for display.

```
public void SearchAndPopulateResult(DirectorySearcher searcher)
{
    StringBuilder Sb = new StringBuilder();
    foreach(SearchResult resEnt in searcher.FindAll())
    {
        Response.Write("<TABLE border=1>");
        Sb.Append("<tr>");
        Sb.Append("<td  bgColor=buttonface " +
                "align=center><STRONG>Property</STRONG></td>");
        Sb.Append("<td  bgColor=buttonface " +

                "align=center><STRONG>Value</STRONG></td>");
        Sb.Append("</tr>");
        foreach (string pN in resEnt.Properties.PropertyNames)
        {
            foreach (object va in resEnt.Properties[pN])
            {
                Sb.Append("<tr>");
                Sb.Append("<TD bgColor=#ccffcb align=right>");
                Sb.Append(pN);
                Sb.Append("</TD>");
```

```
            Sb.Append("<TD bgcolor=#ffffcc>");
            Sb.Append(va);
            Sb.Append("</TD></tr>");
        }
    }
    Sb.Append("</TABLE>");
    Sb.Append("<hr>");
    divOutput.InnerHtml = Sb.ToString();
  }
}
```

And here is the output of the search result:

Search Result

The AdsPath is :LDAP://org.apress.com

The Filter is set for :(objectclass=printQueue)

Property	Value
location	printLoc
printcollate	True
printspooling	PrintAfterSpooled
distinguishedname	CN=ORG-IBM 2390 PS/1,CN=ORG,OU=I Controllers,DC=org,DC=apress,DC=com
objectclass	top
objectclass	leaf
objectclass	connectionPoint
objectclass	printQueue
printbinnames	Manual Paper Feed
printbinnames	Auto
printbinnames	Tractor Feed

Exposing Directory Searching As a Web Service

Active Directory can be accessed using a web service. In this section, you'll see how to use a web service to search directory objects. The example is divided into two parts: the web service client and the actual web service. The web service will need several parameters from the client, such as a user ID, password, search root, and filter; in this upcoming example you will be using an XML-formatted string and string array to pass information from the client to the service. The client creates an XML-formatted string using the System.Xml.XmlTextWriter class and passes it to the service. The string array is used to pass the list of properties to load to the web service. In response, the web service executes the query based on parameters received and sends an XML-formatted result to the client. You'll first see the service-side code and then client code.

The `GetADDetails()` web method takes the XML-formatted string and a string array as parameters and returns the result in an XML-formatted string.

```
[WebMethod]
public string GetADDetails(string xmlParams, string[] propToLoad)
{
```

You can then use a `System.Xml.XmlDocument` object to load the XML and get the values. The `DirectoryEntry` object is created using the received parameters as shown here:

```
//create XmlDocument object
XmlDocument doc = new XmlDocument();
//load xml formatted string
doc.LoadXml(xmlParams);
//create DirectoryEntry object by extracting XML
DirectoryEntry root = new DirectoryEntry (
            doc.GetElementsByTagName("ROOT")[0].InnerXml,
            doc.GetElementsByTagName("ID")[0].InnerXml,
            doc.GetElementsByTagName("PWD")[0].InnerXml);

DirectorySearcher searcher=new DirectorySearcher(root);
```

In the same way, you can extract the filter from the XML string and assign it to the `Filter` property of your `DirectorySearcher`.

```
//Assign filter
searcher.Filter = doc.GetElementsByTagName("FILTER")[0].InnerXml;
```

The string array, which you receive as one of the parameters, consists of the properties that you want to load. You loop through this array and add each of these properties to the `PropertiesToLoad` collection.

```
//Add properties to load from string array
for (int i = 0; i< propToLoad.Length; i++)
   searcher.PropertiesToLoad.Add(propToLoad[i]);
return SearchAndPopulateResultInXML(searcher);
}
```

The `SearchAndPopulateResultInXML()` method retrieves the `DirectorySearcher` object and creates the XML using an `XmlTextWriter` as shown here:

```
private static string SearchAndPopulateResultInXML(DirectorySearcher searcher)
{
   StringWriter w =new StringWriter();
   XmlTextWriter xw = new XmlTextWriter(w);
   xw.Formatting = Formatting.Indented;
   //create XML using properties and values
   xw.WriteStartDocument();
   xw.WriteStartElement("ADSearchData");
```

```
    foreach(SearchResult resEnt in searcher.FindAll())
    {
        foreach (string pN in resEnt.Properties.PropertyNames)
        {
            foreach (object val in resEnt.Properties[pN])
            {
                xw.WriteElementString(pN, val.ToString() );
            }
        }
    }
    xw.WriteEndElement();
    xw.WriteEndDocument();
    xw.Flush ();
    xw.Close ();
    return w.ToString();
}
```

The client is simple; just create an XML formatted string using XmlTextWriter:

```
private void button1_Click(object sender, System.EventArgs e)
{

    //create XmlTextWriter
    StringWriter w = new StringWriter();
    XmlTextWriter xw = new XmlTextWriter (w);
    xw.Formatting = Formatting.Indented;
    xw.WriteStartDocument();
    xw.WriteStartElement("ADSearchData");
    //create xml
    xw.WriteElementString("ROOT","LDAP://apress");
    xw.WriteElementString("ID","UserId");
    xw.WriteElementString("PWD","Password");
    xw.WriteElementString("FILTER","(objectClass=*)");

    xw.WriteEndElement();
    xw.WriteEndDocument();
    xw.Flush();
    xw.Close();

    string xmlParams = w.ToString();
```

The string array is used to collect all the properties that you will want to load during the search.

```
//create string array for 'properties to load'
    string[] sb = new string[3];
    sb[0] = "objectclass";
    sb[1] = "co";
    sb[2] = "mail";
```

Finally, you can call the web service method and pass in your parameters.

```
        //call web service by passing created xml string and string array.
        localhost.Service1 s = new localhost.Service1();
        MessageBox.Show(s.GetADDetails(xmlParams, sb));
    }
```

Thus the web service returns an XML-formatted string; an example of this is shown in the following screenshot. You can use this XML to fill a `DataTable` within a `DataSet` and bind to a control like a `DataGrid` for easy display.

```
<?xml version="1.0" encoding="utf-16"?>
<ADSearchData>
 <objectclass>top</objectclass>
 <objectclass>domain</objectclass>
 <objectclass>domainDNS</objectclass>
 <adspath>LDAP://org.apress.com/DC=org,DC=apress,DC=com</adspath>
 <objectclass>top</objectclass>
 <objectclass>organizationalUnit</objectclass>
 <adspath>LDAP://org.apress.com/OU=Staff,DC=org,DC=apress,DC=com</adspath>
 <objectclass>top</objectclass>
 <objectclass>organizationalUnit</objectclass>
 <adspath>LDAP://org.apress.com/OU=Technical,OU=Staff,DC=org,DC=apress,DC=com</adspath>
 <objectclass>top</objectclass>
 <objectclass>organizationalUnit</objectclass>
 <adspath>LDAP://org.apress.com/OU=Editors,OU=Technical,OU=Staff,DC=org,DC=apress,DC=com</adspath>
 <adspath>LDAP://org.apress.com/CN=Julian Skinner,OU=Editors,OU=Technical,OU=Staff,DC=org,DC=apress,DC=com</adspath>
 <objectclass>top</objectclass>
 <objectclass>person</objectclass>
 <objectclass>organizationalPerson</objectclass>
 <objectclass>user</objectclass>
 <co>UNITED KINGDOM</co>
 <mail>doug@apress.com</mail>
 <adspath>LDAP://org.apress.com/CN=Douglas Patterson,OU=Editors,OU=Technical,OU=Staff,DC=org,DC=apress,DC=com</adspath>
 <objectclass>top</objectclass>
 <objectclass>person</objectclass>
 <objectclass>organizationalPerson</objectclass>
 <objectclass>user</objectclass>
 <co>UNITED KINGDOM</co>
 <objectclass>top</objectclass>
 <objectclass>organizationalUnit</objectclass>
 <adspath>LDAP://org.apress.com/OU=Reviewers,OU=Technical,OU=Staff,DC=org,DC=apress,DC=com</adspath>
 <adspath>LDAP://org.apress.com/CN=Jeff Crouch,OU=Reviewers,OU=Technical,OU=Staff,DC=org,DC=apress,DC=com</adspath>
 <objectclass>top</objectclass>
 <objectclass>person</objectclass>
 <objectclass>organizationalPerson</objectclass>
 <objectclass>user</objectclass>
 <co>UNITED STATES</co>
 <objectclass>top</objectclass>
 <objectclass>organizationalUnit</objectclass>
 <adspath>LDAP://org.apress.com/OU=Marketting,OU=Staff,DC=org,DC=apress,DC=com</adspath>
 <objectclass>top</objectclass>
 <objectclass>person</objectclass>
 <objectclass>organizationalPerson</objectclass>
 <objectclass>user</objectclass>
 <adspath>LDAP://org.apress.com/CN=Tony Clinton,OU=Marketting,OU=Staff,DC=org,DC=apress,DC=com</adspath>
 <adspath>LDAP://org.apress.com/CN=Jack Jill,OU=Marketting,OU=Staff,DC=org,DC=apress,DC=com</adspath>
```


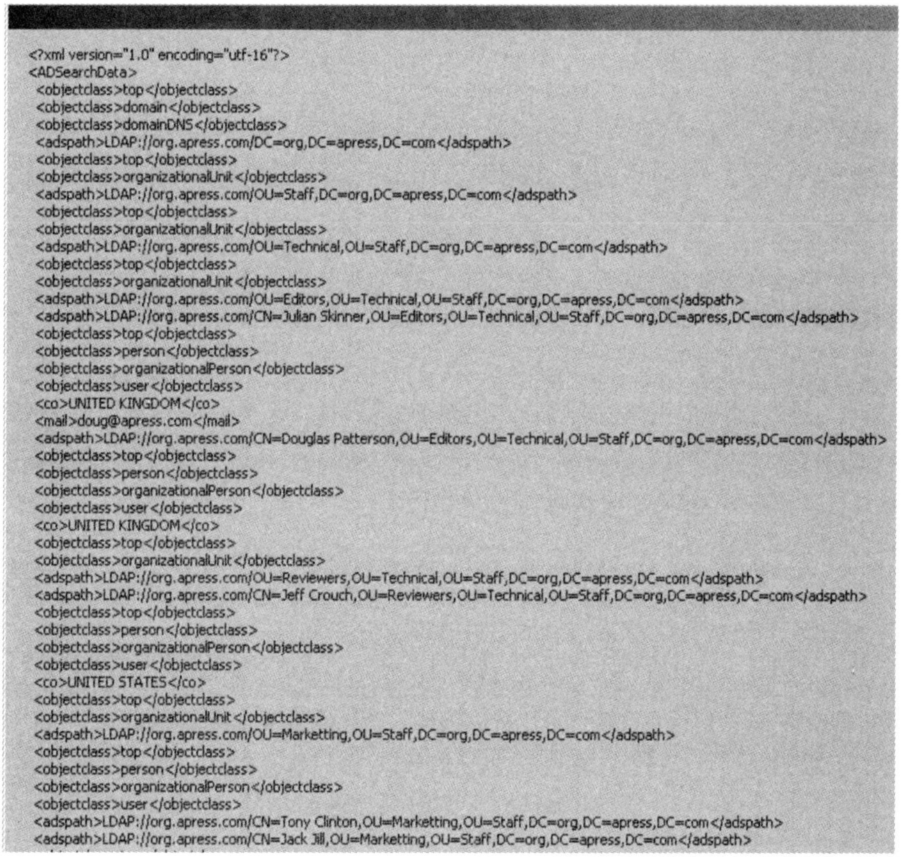

Searching Other Providers

As we discussed previously, LDAP is the only provider that supports searching through a search query–you can browse with the other providers as you saw in the Chapter 2, but you can't return objects based on filter-style criteria. You can manually loop through all the properties returned and check these individually against some criteria, but there is no built-in directory functionality for this with providers such as IIS or WinNT.

However, you can use the `Find()` method of the `DirectoryEntries` class to return the object in that collection with a specified name, or an object with a specified name and belonging to a certain class.

Here we search the IIS metabase to retrieve a virtual directory called `FoodMart`. A limitation of `Find()` is that it returns only a single object and can't be used to return all the objects of a particular class rather than of a particular name.

```
public static void IisSearch()
{
    DirectoryEntry eRes;
    // Create DirectoryEntry object
    DirectoryEntry ent = new DirectoryEntry(
                            "IIS://localhost/W3SVC/1/Root");
    DirectoryEntries myEntries = ent.Children;


    eRes = myEntries.Find("FoodMart", "IIsWebDirectory");
    Console.WriteLine(eRes.Name + " is found");
}
```

Summary

In this chapter you looked at various techniques for searching Directory Services–the LDAP provider is the only provider that currently supports searching, so the chapter's examples were based on Active Directory. The `DirectorySearcher` is the key class for searching, and it has a rich set of features for selecting the scope of the search, filtering the results, and working with the returned results.

In this chapter you learned the following:

❑   How to use the ADO.NET and the ADSI OLE DB provider to search Active Directory

❑   How to specify the query in an SQL format or an LDAP format using the ADSI OLE DB provider; the SQL dialect is simpler, but does not allow us to specify a scope for the search

❑   How to build Windows-based and web-based applications for searching

❑   How to expose directory searching as a web service

ADSI in .NET

In the previous chapters, you saw the various classes the .NET Framework provides for performing various operations in Directory Services. Despite the power of System.DirectoryServices, some situations require you to go beneath this layer, into the underlying Active Directory Service Interfaces (ADSI) object itself. You were introduced to ADSI briefly in Chapter 1, and in this chapter, you'll get a better picture of how you can use ADSI and System.DirectoryServices together. In this chapter, we'll cover the following topics:

❑   ADSI in .NET

❑   Some key interfaces, including IADs

❑   Using ADSI interfaces in .NET

❑   Working with Windows Services and ADSI

Note that this chapter isn't intended to be a comprehensive guide to ADSI–instead you'll see some of its main interfaces and how you can use these in conjunction with the System.DirectoryServices classes.

ADSI Interfaces

ADSI is a set of COM interfaces that present a single programming model for accessing and managing network resources through various Directory Services providers.

You can use the ADSI interfaces to perform tasks on a directory such as adding new users, managing printers, and locating resources.

Like `System.DirectoryServices`, ADSI provides support for different providers:

❑ The Lightweight Directory Access Protocol (LDAP) provider, as used by Active Directory

❑ The WinNT provider

❑ The Internet Information Services (IIS) provider, for accessing the IIS metabase

ADSI has plenty of interfaces that work with users, computers, the property cache, and other functionalities such as Windows Services. The following table shows the various categories of ADSI interfaces (you were introduced to these briefly in Chapter 1) and some examples that belong to each category.

Category	Interface Examples	Description
Core	IADS, IADSContainer, IADSNamespaces, and IADSOpenDSObject	These are the most important interfaces. Basic object management can be performed with these objects. The core functions let you load properties into the property cache, enter a directory store, and commit changes to the underlying directory.
Schema	IADsClass, IADsProperty, and IADsSyntax	These interfaces provide a mechanism for managing and extending Active Directory schema.
Property cache	IADsPropertyEntry, IADsPropertyList, IADsPropertyValue, and IADsPropertyValue2	These interfaces define methods that can be used to manipulate the properties in the property cache.
Persistent object	IADsFileService, IADsFileShare, IADsGroup, IADsLocality, IADsComputer, IADsDomain, IADsCollection, IADsMembers, IADsO, IADsOU, IADsPrintjob, IADsPrintQueue, IADsService, and IADsUser	These interfaces can be used to manage persistent data like file shares and job listings in print queue.

Category	Interface Examples	Description
Dynamic object	IADsComputerOperations, IADsFileService Operations, IADsPrintJobOperations, IADsPrintQueueOperations, IADsResource, IADsServiceOperations, and IADsSession	These interfaces work with dynamic data in a directory service (e.g., the commands issued over a network).
Security	IADsAccessControlEntry, IADsAccessControlList, and IADsSecurityDescriptor	This category provides interfaces an ADSI client can use to establish connections and use security features supported by the directory.
Non-automation	IDirectoryObject, and IDirectorySearcher	These interfaces are for non-automation clients like C or C++. These are much faster and can be used to optimize performance. In addition, they provide VTable access to methods for managing and searching directory service objects.
Extension	IADsExtension	This interface is used to extend the functionality of existing ADSI classes.
Utility	IADsDeleteOps, IADsObjectOptions, and IADsPathname	These interfaces provide functions for managing ADSI objects.
Data type	IADsNetAddress, IADsOctetList, IADsPath, IADsPostalAddress, IADsReplicaPointer, IADsTimestamp, IADsTypedName, IADsAcl, IADsBackLink, IADsCaseIgnoreList, IADsEmail, IADsFaxNumber, IADsHold, and IADsLargeInteger	This category provides interfaces that can access ADSI data types.

Although there are more than 50 interfaces, only a few of them are widely used. The core interfaces `IADs` and `IADsContainer` can cover most of the day-to-day work that is required in directory manipulation.

Now we'll move on to work with some of the most important ADSI interfaces in .NET.

ADSI and .NET

Although .NET provides a rich set of classes to work with directories in the `System.DirectoryServices` namespace, sometimes you may need to get your hands dirty with ADSI interfaces. With ADSI, programming at a lower level is possible. The `System.DirectoryServices` classes do not have the rich functionality that you can achieve through ADSI programming. Note, however, that when you work with ADSI interfaces in managed code, you are using COM interop, and it will cause the overhead of creating the runtime-callable wrapper, data marshaling, and so on.

To use ADSI in your projects, first add a reference to the ADSI COM library. In VS.NET, you do this by selecting **Add Reference** from the **Project** menu, and selecting **Active DS Type Library** from the COM tab.

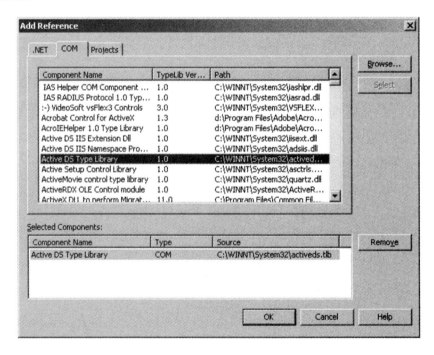

For command-line compilation, use the `TlbImp.exe` utility to create a managed wrapper for this type library:

```
> TlbImp C:\Windows\System32\ActiveDs.dll
```

You will need to reference this DLL with the `/r:ActiveDs.dll` compilation option when you compile .NET code that uses the ADSI interfaces.

Next, add a `using` directive for this library:

```
using ActiveDs;
```

The advantage of working with ADSI is that you now have objects that directly represent different types of directory entries. Rather than the generic `DirectoryEntry` object of `System.DirectoryServices`, with ADSI, you can have objects that represent users, computers, and printers, with methods and properties that are available *before* compile time, thanks to early binding with the ADSI library. For example, the following screenshot shows an IntelliSense drop-down for some of the methods and properties available to `IADsService`, an interface used to configure Windows Services:

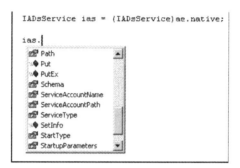

Accessing the Native Object

You can access the underlying ADSI object wrapped by a `DirectoryEntry` instance through the `DirectoryEntry.NativeObject` property. This returns an object, which you can cast to your desired ADSI interface. For example, here you cast to an `IADs` interface:

```
DirectoryEntry entry = new DirectoryEntry();

IADs iads = (IADs)entry.NativeObject;
```

Accessing Native Methods

The `DirectoryEntry` class has an `Invoke()` method with which you can call methods on the underlying ADSI object. This is a straightforward and fast way to manipulate objects in a directory. The `Invoke()` method takes two parameters: a `string` for the name of the method to invoke, and an `object` array. If the return value of the native method implements the `IADs` interface, then a corresponding `DirectoryEntry` object is returned. You can then use the returned `DirectoryEntry` object to further manipulate it in the managed code.

A disadvantage of this approach when compared with working with the raw interfaces and calling methods directly on them is that you have to know the methods available beforehand. Working with concrete instances of ADSI interfaces means that you can take advantage of VS.NET's IntelliSense as you saw earlier, provided that you are working in VS.NET, of course.

The following code shows how to use Invoke() to call methods on the native Active Directory. In the code, the Invoke() method is used to change SAMAccountName of user by calling native methods—Put and SetInfo. The SAMAccountName (Security Account Manager-Account-Name) property is a unique logon name used to support clients and servers from a previous version of Windows (such as Windows NT 4.0/95/98).

The DirectoryEntry object is created using the appropriate ADsPath.

```
public static void usingInvoke()
{
    DirectoryEntry e = new DirectoryEntry("LDAP://org.apress.com/" +
        "CN=Mix Char,OU=Staff,OU=Domain Controllers,DC=apress,DC=com");
```

In the second step, create an object array to hold the parameters for the call to Put (the name of the property you want to set, and the value you want to set it to). Next, call the DirectoryEntry's Invoke() method, passing in the name of the native method and the parameter array you've just created. Finally, use the Invoke() method to call SetInfo to save the changes.

```
    Object[] parArray = new Object[2]{ "samAccountName", "suchi" };

    e.Invoke("Put",parArray);
    e.Invoke("SetInfo");
    Console.WriteLine("Changes are made!!");
}
```

We'll see more of Invoke() in Chapter 6.

In the next sections, you'll see various ADSI interfaces and how to use them in .NET. Let's start with the IADs interface.

The IADs Interface

The IADs interface is the most important core interface. It defines the basic object features—namely the properties and methods of any ADSI object—and most ADSI interfaces implement IADs.

IADs Properties

The following table shows the properties of the IADs interface:

Property	Description
Name	Gets the relative name of the object
AdsPath	A read-only property used to get the ADsPath of the object
Class	Gets the name of the schema class
GUID	Returns the globally unique identifier (GUID) of the directory object
Parent	Returns the ADsPath string of the parent container
Schema	Gets the ADsPath string of the schema class

The following code, in the IADsPropPrinting() method, shows you how to print all the properties of a directory object with the IADs interface. You can use the DirectoryEntry object to create a root and then convert it to an IADs implementation using its NativeObject property.

```
public static void IADsPropPrinting()
{
    IADs iads;
```

The IADs interface requires a root object that you can obtain by using the NativeObject property of DirectoryEntry object. Note that NativeObject returns an object, so you have to cast this to an IADs implementation to access the IADs properties.

```
DirectoryEntry e = new DirectoryEntry("LDAP://apress");
iads = (IADs)e.NativeObject;
```

Once you assign the object, the next task is just to print the available properties:

```
Console.WriteLine ("Name :" + iads.Name);
Console.WriteLine ("Class :" + iads.Class);
Console.WriteLine ("GUID :" + iads.GUID);
Console.WriteLine ("ADsPath :" + iads.ADsPath);
Console.WriteLine ("Parent :" + iads.Parent);
Console.WriteLine ("Schema :" + iads.Schema);
}
```

The printed output should look something like this:

```
Name :DC=apress
Class :domainDNS
GUID :b9e0ae9f97fefa4199b75aa40f110f2e
ADsPath :LDAP://apress/DC=apress,DC=com
Parent :LDAP://apress/DC=com
Schema :LDAP://apress/schema/domainDNS
```

Note that since the properties displayed are properties of the managed wrapper object for IADs, hence .NET properties, you could use Reflection to enumerate all the properties, as shown in following code. The Reflection namespace provides a managed view of loaded types, methods, and fields, with the ability to dynamically create and invoke types.

```
using System.Reflection;

public static void IADsPropPrinting()
{
    DirectoryEntry e = new DirectoryEntry("LDAP://apress");
    IADs iads = (IADs)e.NativeObject;

    Type t = typeof(IADs);

    PropertyInfo[] props = t.GetProperties();

    foreach (PropertyInfo pi in props)
    {
        try
```

```
        {
            string name = pi.GetValue(iads, null).ToString();
            Console.WriteLine(pi.Name + ": " + name);
        }
        catch (Exception exc)
        {
            Console.WriteLine(pi.Name+ ": Value not obtainable");
        }
    }
}
```

Here you see that we used the `System.Type.GetProperties()` method to obtain a collection of properties, and then we retrieved the value of a particular property with the `System.Reflection.PropertyInfo.GetValue()` method, passing in the object instance and a `null` parameter for indexing purposes.

IADs Methods

The following table shows the methods of the IADs interface:

Method	Description
Get()	This method retrieves a property of a given name from the property cache. The returned property can be single valued or multivalued. If the property is not found in the cache, then an implicit call to GetInfo() is made, which refreshes the cache. Also, when a property is not initialized, calling this method also invokes an implicit call to the GetInfo() method.
GetInfo()	This method loads the values in the property cache and can be used to refresh this cache.
GetEx()	This method retrieves property cache values for a given attribute. The returned value is of type Array; a single value is represented as a one-dimensional array.
GetInfoEx()	This method refreshes only those property values in the cache that are specified in attributes; GetInfo() refreshes the whole cache and is, therefore, more expensive than GetInfoEx().
Put()	This method sets a new value to a specified property in the property cache.
PutEx()	This method is more flexible than Put() and performs operations on a single property value or an entire property value set. It also allows you to specify whether you are updating, appending, clearing, or deleting existing values.
SetInfo()	You can use this method to save the cached property values of the ADSI object to the underlying directory store. This method is called by System.DirectoryServices.CommitChanges().

Manipulating Properties with the Get() and Put() Methods

The Get() and Put() methods respectively retrieve properties from and set properties in the property cache. You must use the SetInfo() method to make physical changes to the directory after you assign it new values using the Put() method. The Get() method takes one parameter—the name of the property—whereas the Put method takes two parameters—the name of the property and the values to set.

The following code snippet shows how to use both methods to manipulate Active Directory properties. The first Get method returns multiple values; the second method only returns a single value.

In the first part of the code, the root object is created and assigned to the IADs interface.

```
public static void IADsGetAndPut()
{
    DirectoryEntry e = new DirectoryEntry("LDAP://org.apress.com/" +
                          "CN=Jeff Crouch,OU=Reviewer,OU=Technical," +
                          "OU=Staff,OU=Domain Controllers,DC
                                            ➥ =apress,DC=com");

    IADs iads = (IADs)e.NativeObject;
```

The Get() method returns an array of objects if the property has multiple values. The OtherHomePhone property has multiple values; therefore, an array is created and assigned to the Get() method. Next the values from the array are printed using a foreach loop.

```
//Get Method call that returns multiple values
Array propvals = (Array)iads.Get("OtherHomePhone");
foreach (object propval in propvals)
{
    Console.WriteLine(propval);
}
```

If the Get() method returns a single value, then you can print it directly with the following:

```
//Get Method call that returns single value
Console.WriteLine("Old Home Page : " + iads.Get("wWWhomePage").ToString());
```

Next you'll see how to use the Put() method to update the property value. Here we are changing the wWWhomepage property to a new value.

```
//Put
iads.Put("wWWhomepage","www.apress.com\\crouch");
Console.WriteLine("New Home Page : " + iads.Get("wWWhomePage").ToString());
```

Now you need to make sure you call the SetInfo() method to commit the changes, just as we saw in Chapter 2 that we needed to call DirectoryEntry.CommitChanges() to save any changes to a DirectoryEntry object:

```
    //Commit the result
    iads.SetInfo();
}
```

Manipulating Properties with GetEx() and PutEx()

The GetEx() method returns an array of objects that represents the values of a single-valued or multivalued property. The method takes one parameter—a string holding the name of the property.

You can use PutEx() to update the values of a property; it is more flexible than the Put() method. This method takes three parameters. The first is a control code that indicates the mode of modification—such as clear, update, append, or delete—with the value for the mode coming from the ADS_PROPERTY_OPERATION_ENUM enumeration of ActiveDs.

The following table shows control code value and its description:

Value	Description
ADS_PROPERTY_CLEAR	Removes the property values from the object
ADS_PROPERTY_UPDATE	Replaces the current value with the passed values
ADS_PROPERTY_APPEND	Appends new values to existing one(s)
ADS_PROPERTY_DELETE	Deletes specified values of a property

The second parameter is a string that holds the name of the property, and the third parameter is a VARIANT array. Since .NET does not have a VARIANT type, you can use an object array instead:

```
public static void PutExAndGetEx()
{
    DirectoryEntry e = new DirectoryEntry("LDAP://org.apress.com/" +
        "CN=Jeff Crouch,OU=Reviewer,OU=Technical,OU=Staff," +
        "OU=Domain Controllers,DC=apress,DC=com");
    IADs iads = (IADs)e.NativeObject;

    //Get the old numbers
    Console.WriteLine("Printing old numbers");
    Array propvals = (Array)iads.GetEx("OtherHomePhone");
    foreach (Object propval in propvals)
    {
        Console.WriteLine(propval);
    }
```

Now you can create an array of new telephone numbers and update them with the PutEx() method, remembering, of course, to call SetInfo() to make your changes from the local cache permanent.

```
        Console.WriteLine("Updating new numbers");
        //new numbers
        Object[] obArray = new Object[3] {280212,220520,5433318};
        //update the numbers
        iads.PutEx(ADS_PROPERTY_OPERATION_ENUM.ADS_PROPERTY_UPDATE,
                "OtherHomePhone",obArray);
        iads.SetInfo();

        Console.WriteLine("Printing changed numbers....");

        propvals = (Array)iads.GetEx("OtherHomePhone");

        foreach ( object phone in propvals )
        {
            Console.WriteLine(phone);
        }
    }
```

The output of this looks like the following:

Working with Schema in ADSI

In this section, you'll develop a simple example that will output the mandatory and optional properties of a directory entry using the IADsClass interface. First of all, you'll use the Schema property of IADs. This will return the path that holds the schema of the class of your directory entry. You can see that the IIS provider has been used in this example.

```
using System;
using System.DirectoryServices;
using ActiveDs;

class ViewSomeSchema
{
    static void Main(string[] args)
    {

        DirectoryEntry e = new DirectoryEntry(
                "IIS://localhost/Logging/Custom Logging/Extended Properties");
```

Now you can cast the native object to an instance of IADs, and retrieve the Schema property. Note that this value is the same as e.SchemaEntry.Path. Set the path of your existing DirectoryEntry object to the path of its schema, and then rebind the DirectoryEntry object, as shown here:

```
IADs iads = (IADs)e.NativeObject;

e.Path = iads.Schema;
e.RefreshCache();
```

Now you can cast the native object to an instance of IADsClass.

```
IADsClass iac = (IADsClass)e.NativeObject;
```

IADsClass has two properties of interest to you here: MandatoryProperties and OptionalProperties, which respectively contain the collections of mandatory and optional properties for the class schema. In the following example, first you'll obtain the mandatory properties. You'll then cast this collection to an Array, and then iterate through it, simply displaying the value of each element in the Array:

```
Console.WriteLine("MANDATORY PROPERTIES");

Array mandatoryProps = (Array)iac.MandatoryProperties;

foreach (object o in mandatoryProps)
{
    Console.WriteLine(o);
}
```

Next, display the optional properties using the same approach:

```
Console.WriteLine("OPTIONAL PROPERTIES");

Array optionalProps = (Array)iac.OptionalProperties;
foreach (object o in optionalProps)
{
    Console.WriteLine(o);
}
    }
}
```

The output of this simple example is as follows:

Here there is an absence of mandatory properties, and a number of optional properties.

Interestingly, if you use your Directory Browser application from Chapter 2 to try and load the properties for

```
IIS://localhost/Logging/Custom Logging/Extended Properties
```

the System.DirectoryServices approach throws an exception, claiming that the number of properties cannot be returned.

Working with Containers and IADsContainer

The IADsContainer interface allows you to create, delete, and manage contained ADSI objects. The Container object is any ADSI object that can contain other ADSI objects. The Container property can be used to check whether or not the object is a container. One example of a container object is Computer, which has other objects such as User and Group.

The IADsContainer object has a few properties and methods; we list some of them in the following tables:

Property	Description
Count	Returns the number of directory objects in container
Filter	Gets or sets a filter

Method	Description
GetObject()	Gets the interface on the named object
Create()	Creates a new object
Delete()	Deletes a specified object
CopyHere()	Copies objects within directory service
MoveHere()	Moves objects within directory service

Creating and Deleting Objects Using IADsContainer

You can use the IADsContainer to create or delete the objects in the directory with the Create() and Delete() methods. These methods both take two parameters: the name of the schema class object to create or delete, and the relative name of the object. The changes take effect when you call the SetInfo method.

The following code shows you how to use the Create() and Delete() methods to create a new user—note that we have to provide the mandatory sAMAccountName property—and then delete the unfortunate individual.

```
public static void CreateAndDeleteUser()
{
    IADsContainer cont;
    IADsUser usr;
```

125

```
        DirectoryEntry e = new DirectoryEntry(
            "LDAP://org.apress.com/OU=Editor,OU=Technical,OU=Staff," +
            "OU=Domain Controllers,DC=apress,DC=com");
        cont = (IADsContainer)e.NativeObject;
        usr = (IADsUser)cont.Create("user", "CN=James Cook");
        usr.Put("sAMAccountName", "jcook");
        usr.SetInfo();
        Console.WriteLine("Press any key to delete newly created object");
        Console.ReadLine();
        cont.Delete("user", "CN=James Cook");
    }
```

Note the difference between the `Create()` method and the `DirectoryEntries.Add()` method; although this code specifies the same information, the distinguished name and the schema class, the schema class comes first in the `Create()` method. In fact, `DirectoryEntries.Add()` uses `Create()` to do its work.

Working with Users and IADsUser

This interface helps manipulate all user-related information such as the name, home phone, and address of a user. This interface inherits from `IADs` and is designed to represent and manage an end-user account on a network.

The next example quickly shows you how to get user-related information using the `IADsUser` interface:

```
public static void GetUserDetails()
{
    IADsUser user;
    DirectoryEntry e = new DirectoryEntry("LDAP://org.apress.com/" +
        "CN=Jeff Crouch,OU=Reviewer,OU=Technical,OU=Staff," +
        "OU=Domain Controllers,DC=apress,DC=com");
    user = (IADsUser)e.NativeObject;
    Console.WriteLine(user.Get("EmailAddress").ToString());
    Console.WriteLine(user.Get("HomePage").ToString());
}
```

You'll see more about working with users in Chapter 6, there, you'll see native methods like `SetPassword()`, which is used to set the password for the user account.

Working with Computers and IADsComputer

You can use the `IADsComputer` interface to accumulate information about computers on a network. Using the properties provided by this interface, you can get such things as the computer name, the operating system, processor details, and other information. Note that the WinNT provider does not support all of the `IADsComputer` properties—only some of them appear here:

```
public static void GetCompProp()
{
    IADsComputer cp;
    DirectoryEntry e = new DirectoryEntry("WinNT://ORG");
    cp = (IADsComputer)e.NativeObject;
```

```
        Console.WriteLine("Name :" + cp.Name);
        Console.WriteLine("Class :" + cp.Class);
        Console.WriteLine("GUID :" + cp.GUID);
        Console.WriteLine("ADsPath :" + cp.ADsPath);
        Console.WriteLine("Parent :" + cp.Parent);
        Console.WriteLine("Schema :" + cp.Schema);
        Console.WriteLine("Owner :" + cp.Owner);
        Console.WriteLine("Division :" + cp.Division);
        Console.WriteLine("OperatingSystem :" + cp.OperatingSystem);
        Console.WriteLine("OperatingSystemVersion :" + cp.OperatingSystemVersion);
        Console.WriteLine("Processor :" + cp.Processor);
        Console.WriteLine("ProcessorCount :" + cp.ProcessorCount);
    }
```

The output of this code should look like the following:

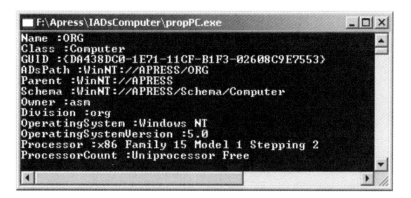

Sadly, `Processor` is a read-only property; you can't upgrade your processors that easily!

Working with Windows Services

The final application we will discuss in this chapter is an ADSI Windows Services Controller. It's a simple Windows Form application that uses the WinNT ADSI provider; it lists all the Windows Services on a particular machine and allows the user to start, stop, pause, or continue the service:

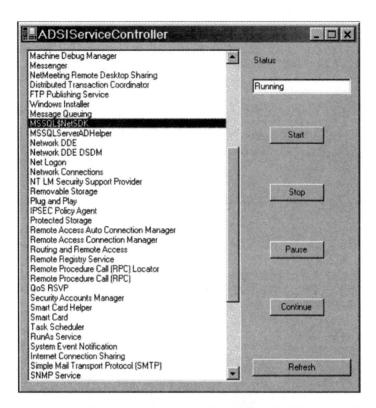

The application consists of a single form, with a list box that displays the full name of the service, a text box to display the status of the service selected in the list box, and buttons to control the service or refresh the list.

The key ADSI interfaces that you can make use of in this example are IADsContainer, IADsService, and IADsServiceOperations. You've already seen IADsContainer earlier in the chapter, and IADsService and IADsServiceOperations are interfaces for working with Windows Services. You'll be getting the full name of the service from the IADsService.DisplayName property and controlling the service with IADsServiceOperations. IADsServiceOperations has a Status property, which returns the status of the particular service (running, stopped, etc.), and four methods of interest to us: Start(), Stop(), Pause(), and Continue(). If we tell you that the Start() method starts a service running, then it's not too hard to work out what the other three methods do!

First of all, take a look at the private variables you'll be using:

```
private string rootPath = "WinNT://ORG";
private string[] serviceStatus = new string[] {
    "Error!!", "Stopped",
    "Starting", "Stopping",
    "Running", "Continuing",
    "Pausing", "Paused" };
private ArrayList serviceNames;
```

The rootPath string holds the path for binding to the root of the WinNT directory. At various points, you'll bind to the path of the chosen Windows Service, and to refresh your list of services, you will need to retrieve the root.

The serviceStatus string array holds the values that report the status of a particular Windows Service. A number representing the status will be extracted from the Status property of IADsServiceOperations in due course.

The serviceNames ArrayList will hold the ADsPath for each particular service–this means you will be able to use the selected index from the list box to easily retrieve the corresponding path for binding to the chosen service.

Now you have your private Directory Services variables:

```
private DirectoryEntry entry;

private IADs iads;
private IADsServiceOperations iadsService;
private IADsContainer iadsContainer;
```

In your form's constructor, you can create the DirectoryEntry object, bind it to rootPath, and then call the GetServices() method, which will fill the list box with the names of the services.

```
public Form1()
{
    InitializeComponent();
    entry = new DirectoryEntry(rootPath);

    GetServices();
}
```

In the GetServices() method, the first thing you should do is store the item selected in the list box. This item will then be reselected after the list is refreshed.

```
public void GetServices()
{
    int selected = this.lstServices.SelectedIndex;
```

Now rebind to rootPath, and refresh the cache to recycle your DirectoryEntry object. GetServices() will be called after the status of a service is changed, and so entry.Path will be pointing to that particular service rather than to the root, hence your need to restore the original path. After refreshing the cache, clear the list box and the ArrayList:

```
    entry.Path = rootPath;
    entry.RefreshCache();

    this.lstServices.Items.Clear();
    serviceNames.Clear();
```

You can cast the underlying native object of entry to your IADsContainer instance and then set its Filter property. The Filter property will restrict the objects to those that are of a certain class–in this case, the Service class. The Filter property takes an object array; if you include more than one class in the array, this will include objects from the union of the classes. Thus filtering with User and Group would return all objects that are a User or a Group:

```
iadsContainer  = (IADsContainer)entry.NativeObject;

iadsContainer.Filter = new object[] {"Service"};
```

Now you can iterate through the IADsContainer object, which contains an assortment of IADs objects. You can use IADs in your foreach loop, rather than the traditional object that you've seen in many examples in this chapter. As you iterate through, you add the display name of the service to the list box. You can obtain this by casting the IADs object to an IADsService and using its DisplayName property. Then, you can simply add the ADsPath value of the service to your ArrayList, so that you can easily bind to the service on demand.

```
foreach (IADs io in iadsContainer)
{
    this.lstServices.Items.Add(((IADsService)io).DisplayName);
    serviceNames.Add(io.ADsPath);
}
```

Finally, reselect the item that was selected before the refresh and call the UpdateStatus() method, which displays the status of the currently selected service.

```
if (selected>0)
    this.lstServices.SelectedIndex = selected;
else
    this.lstServices.SelectedIndex = 0;

UpdateStatus();
}
```

UpdateStatus() begins by checking to see if you do actually have an item selected:

```
public void UpdateStatus()
{
    if (this.lstServices.SelectedIndex<0)
        return;
```

Next, set the path of your DirectoryEntry object to that of the selected service—retrieved from the serviceNames ArrayList—and rebind.

```
entry.Path = serviceNames[this.lstServices.SelectedIndex].ToString();
entry.RefreshCache();
```

To get at the service status, cast the native object to an IADsServiceOperations object and then use the Status property. Take a logical AND of this value since only the first three bits of the number hold this information (see the ADSI documentation for information about the other bits).

```
iadsService = (IADsServiceOperations)entry.NativeObject;

this.textBox1.Text = serviceStatus[iadsService.Status & 7];
}
```

The `UpdateStatus()` method is called from the `SelectedIndexChanged` event handler for the list box:

```
private void lstServices_SelectedIndexChanged(object sender,
                         System.EventArgs e)
{
    UpdateStatus();
}
```

So now you can display all the services on the machine and the status of the selected service. Now you will add the code to control the services. First look at starting the service with the code from the Start button's `Click` handler:

Before you begin, make sure that a service has been selected and then get its display name from the list box:

```
private void btnStart_Click(object sender, System.EventArgs e)
{
    if (this.lstServices.SelectedIndex<0)
        return;
    string serviceChosen = this.lstServices.Items
    [this.lstServices.SelectedIndex].ToString();
```

Using a `try...catch` block, you can get the ADsPath of the selected service and rebind it.

```
try
{
    entry.Path = serviceNames[this.lstServices.SelectedIndex].ToString();
    entry.RefreshCache();
```

Now cast the native object to an `IADsServiceOperations` and attempt to start the service with `Start()`. If you have a problem starting the service, the `catch` block will handle it.

```
    iadsService = (IADsServiceOperations)entry.NativeObject;
    iadsService.Start();
```

Now refresh the list of services and the status of this particular service. When the list is refreshed, this service will still be selected:

```
    GetServices();
}
```

Finally, in your `catch` block, display a message box to indicate that there has been a problem with starting this service:

```
catch(Exception exc)
{
    MessageBox.Show("Error starting service " +
                    serviceChosen,exc.ToString());
}

}
```

Not surprisingly, the code for the **Stop**, **Pause**, and **Continue** buttons is almost identical, except for the call to `iadsService.Start()`, which is replaced by a call to the respective `Stop()`, `Pause()`, or `Continue()` method of `iadsService`.

The code for the **Refresh** button is simply a call to `GetServices()` to refresh the list box display.

This completes your ADSI Windows Services Controller application; you can access the complete application from the Downloads section of the Apress web site (`http://www.apress.com`).

Summary

In this chapter, you looked at some of the key ADSI interfaces, and how to work with them in managed code. ADSI has a rich collection of interfaces, but it brings the inevitable problems of COM interop, such as dealing with the non-.NET data types returned by the methods or properties. However, with ADSI, you do have the advantage of early binding, which means that you can use IntelliSense in VS.NET to see the methods and properties that you can use on the ADSI object—remember that this object directly represents an entry in a directory, such as a user or computer.

In this chapter you studied

❑ How to use the `NativeObject` property of the `DirectoryEntry` class to access the underlying ADSI object, and how to use the `Invoke()` method

❑ How to work directly with the ADSI interfaces in managed code

❑ How to use the `IADs` interface to obtain schema information

❑ How to create a simple ADSI Windows Form Controller application using the `IADsServiceOptions` and `IADsService`

5

Directory Service Security

In the last couple of chapters, we investigated how to use the `System.DirectoryServices` classes to access and manipulate Directory Services objects. In this chapter, you will see how you can apply security to objects in the Active Directory. We will begin by revising some security concepts that are important for using Directory Services. We'll then identify some of the Directory Services security functionality that is not accessible from the `System.DirectoryServices` classes, develop a few classes that can give you access to this functionality from your managed code, and finally show you how you can integrate this functionality into the example Directory Browser application that you constructed in Chapter 2.

This chapter will look at the following:

- ❑ Authentication and authorization
- ❑ Authentication with `System.DirectoryServices`
- ❑ Adding authentication support to the Directory Browser application
- ❑ Managing permissions with Access Control Lists (ACLs) and Access Control Entries (ACEs)
- ❑ Using the ADSI security interfaces
- ❑ Creating managed wrappers for the ADSI interfaces

Security Overview

We often think of security as only pertaining to preventing malicious users or code from gaining unauthorized access to an application or data. However, the process of implementing security includes designing applications in such a way that they ensure that certain procedures are always followed. For example, a well designed application should make sure that user passwords are of a certain length and complexity. More generally, applications should be designed only to expose the functionality that specific users require. For instance, although you might want to let all users access information about a particular type of Directory Services object—a `User` object, for instance—you might only want a few users to be able to change or delete `User` objects.

Initially, we're going to take a quick look at some basic security concepts.

Authentication

Authentication is nothing more then the process of verifying identity. When you answer the telephone, for instance, you expect to be able to authenticate the caller, usually when the caller gives her name. But just her name would probably not be enough by itself; you *authenticate* that the person is who she says she is by identifying her voice. Once she has been authenticated, you may grant her certain permissions, such as the permission to talk to you: in other words, you *authorize* the caller to speak to you. If the person on the other end of the line fails the authentication—for instance, she refuses to divulge a name or any other clues to her identity—you would probably not grant her any such permission (i.e., you'd hang up on her). The same thing happens when a user is authenticated against Active Directory Service Interfaces (ADSI): she is challenged to provide a username with a corresponding password.

Many applications implement custom authentication with Lightweight Directory Access Protocol (LDAP) providers such as Active Directory. Once a user is authenticated, permissions or authorization for certain resources may be granted or denied.

Authorization

Once a user is authenticated, he is granted particular rights and permissions to allow or prevent him from doing certain things: he is *authorized* to access certain resources. For example, if a water pipe in the kitchen bursts, and you successfully authenticate a plumber at the front door, you then authorize him to investigate the pipes; however, you would probably not authorize him to help himself from your liquor cabinet.

This process is parallel to what happens when a user is authenticated against an LDAP provider with a set of permission attributes. You may authorize this user so that she can access certain directories, but not others, and you may allow her read permissions but deny her write permissions for a particular directory.

Windows and .NET Security

Windows security and .NET security are very different: one is an unmanaged environment and the other is managed. Prior to .NET, you would program the Windows application programming interface (API) directly, or you would program it via Object Linking and Embedding (OLE); now you generally don't have to because you can access most functionality via the .NET classes. However, .NET does not support managed New Technology File System (NTFS) security access in .NET, so you cannot directly access and use certain aspects of NTFS security functionality. Nonetheless, you can still exploit NTFS functionality using the .NET Interoperability services.

> *The .NET framework makes available code access security that is not related to the Windows security model. For more information about .NET security, see* .NET Security *by Jason Bock, Tom Fischer, Nathan Smith, and Pete Stromquist (Apress, 2002).*

> *For a detailed investigation of .NET interoperability, try* COM and .NET Interoperability *by Andrew Troelsen (Apress, 2002).*

Authentication Using System.DirectoryServices

Although you might trust all users to be able to add a new user or change a property such as a phone number or address, you might well want to restrict access to more sensitive information. That's why you need to control access to your system by knowing who is trying to access which object, and by being able to grant or refuse authorization, as appropriate.

In this section, we are going to investigate how to authenticate a user using the `DirectoryEntry` object. The type of authentication we use here is specified through the `DirectoryEntry.AuthenticationType` property and takes it values from the `AuthenticationTypes` enumeration.

Let's start by showing you how you can bind to a `DirectoryEntry` object by passing the appropriate credentials to the constructor in the following way:

```
DirectoryEntry entry = new DirectoryEntry(path, username, password,
                                          AuthenticationTypes.Secure);
```

The credentials you use to be authenticated consist of the username and password. You also pass the *type* of authentication you wish to be performed; in this instance, you indicate that you want `Secure` authentication. Note that Active Directory does not perform any authentication itself. What actually performs the authentication is the *Authentication Service (AS)*. The AS manages operations involving authentication protocols such as Kerberos version 5 or Windows NT/LAN Manager (NTLM). By specifying that you want `Secure` authentication, you ensure that the AS is used for authentication (we look at the other options very shortly in the `AuthenticationTypes` enumeration).

The AS will check whether the object with which you are binding has valid credentials, and it will create a *security context* (token) for the client that is performing the binding. This token is a representation of the user credentials that are provided to the AS. Once the security token has been created, another object can impersonate the user and can perform any tasks that are permitted for that security context.

If the AS fails to create a security context, it means that the credentials provided do not match up with those that should have been provided for the user; in this case, Active Directory will refuse the binding. If this happens, and the authentication type is `AuthenticationTypes.Secure`, an exception should be thrown. This means that you can use a `DirectoryEntry` object as a way to authenticate a user, but not to perform the authentication itself. You'll see shortly (in the section entitled "Adding Authentication Support to the Directory Browser") how this works in practice—you simply bind to a `DirectoryEntry` object, passing in the user's credentials, and if an exception is thrown, you know that the authentication has failed.

The eleven types of authentication that a `DirectoryEntry` can perform are as follows:

Anonymous: Performs no authentication. This is the same as binding the "everyone" security context.

Delegation: Specifies that ADSI can delegate the user's security context. This is required if your application moves objects across trusted domains.

Encryption: Requests that ADSI use encryption when communicating with the server.

FastBind: With this method, only the base ADSI interfaces are exposed. This option can have the effect of boosting performance, because ADSI does not query the `objectClass` property to determine what interfaces it supports. The drawback is that ADSI does not actually determine if the object exists on the server.

None: Passes a `null` reference. In Active Directory domains, ADSI will attempt to authenticate to the domain controller with the security context of the user who's currently logged in.

ReadonlyServer: Using a serverless binding provider, this authentication type specifies that a writable server is not required. You use this authentication type if the operation you are performing does not need to make changes to a directory object.

Sealing: Data is *encrypted* with Kerberos. You must also set the `Secure` flag. Note that this accomplishes encryption only. The `Secure` flag accomplishes authentication.

Secure: ADSI requests that *authentication* be performed by Kerberos or NTLM. If the username and password are `null`, then ADSI uses the security context of the user account under which the application is running.

SecureSocketsLayer: With this method, a Microsoft Certificate Server must be installed, because messages are signed with a certificate. This provides integrity and authentication using the Secure Sockets Layer (SSL). This does not encrypt the message; it just guarantees that it is from the intended sender and has not been modified in transit.

ServerBind: Tells ADSI to bind to a specific server (the server name in your LDAP path). This flag reduces network traffic.

Signing: Ensures that the data has not been modified in transit. If you set this flag, you must also set the `Secure` flag.

To achieve different types of binding, you must use a combination of these flags. In order to combine these flags, use the | operator to define multiple values. For example, the following combination is useful:

```
entry.AuthenticationType = AuthenticationTypes.Secure |
                           AuthenticationTypes.Sealing;
```

This ensures that AS performs authentication and data is encrypted.

Where Are Credentials Stored?

As you have already seen, a user supplies appropriate credentials to access (bind to) an object. This type of user is often called a *trustee*. A trustee can be trusted to perform various operations, such as reading from or writing to a particular object.

In some ways, Active Directory security is very similar to the NTFS security model. Active Directory objects store credentials and related permissions in an *Access Control List (ACL)*, a container that can hold one or more *Access Control Entries (ACEs)*. Each ACE in an ACL contains a trustee and defines the permissions that can or cannot be granted to the trustee.

You can use the ADSI Edit utility that ships with Windows 2000 Server and Windows Server 2003 to view these security entries by right-clicking a User, then Properties, then the Security tab, and then Advanced. Here is an example of entries for a user called Belana:

As you can see, the user Administrator has full control over this user, and any user who is a member of the Authenticated Users group can read properties from this User object, such as phone number, address, home page, and so on.

We will explore the ACL and ACE in detail later in this chapter.

Adding Authentication Support to the Directory Browser

In this section, you will build on the Directory Browser application that you started developing in Chapter 2 by adding functionality to enable the authentication of a user. In some parts of this chapter, we will assume that you have a rough idea of what this application does, and how it is put together.

The full code for this application may be downloaded from the Downloads section of the Apress web site (http://www.apress.com).

The easiest way to authenticate a user is to bind to the RootDSE of Active Directory, passing the user's credentials and the Secure flag for the authentication type.

In the DirectoryUtil call, you can add a new method called Authenticate(). First, define a signature to take a username and password and check to see whether the private variable path is null. If it is null, it means you are trying to bind to the directory for the first time, so bind to the default naming context:

```
public bool Authenticate(string username, string password)
{
   if (path == null)
   {
      path = "LDAP://";
      path += new DirectoryEntry("LDAP://rootDSE").Properties
                     ["defaultNamingContext"].Value.ToString();
   }
```

Then try to bind to the rootDSE (the default naming context) passing the username and password and three authentication types: Secure, Sealing, and Signing.

```
   try
   {
      DirectoryEntry entry = new DirectoryEntry(path, username,
                           password,
                           AuthenticationTypes.Secure |
                           AuthenticationTypes.Sealing |
                           AuthenticationTypes.Signing);
```

Once you've created the object, you must rebind to the entry to enforce authentication. You can do this by calling RefreshCache() on the DirectoryEntry object:

```
      entry.RefreshCache();
```

If no exception is thrown by Active Directory, the following lines are executed, which saves the username and password in local variables and rebinds the root container object. Here, you also added a Boolean property isAuthenticated. This is also exposed as a property so that you can check the authentication status from various other parts of the application.

```
      this.password = password;
      this.username = username;
      RefreshDirectoryStructure();
      this.isAuthenticated = true;
      return true;
   }
```

If an exception has been thrown, catch it and return a message, as shown here:

```
catch(UnauthorizedAccessException e)
{
    throw new Exception(e.Message);
}
return false;
}
```

Now you just need to create a login form to take a username and password. It will look something like this:

Behind the click event of the Login button, you need to add the following code (note that you can also add the DirectoryUtil object in the FrmLogin, as shown here):

```
private void btnLogin_Click(object sender, System.EventArgs e)
{
    try
    {
        FrmMain.isAuthenticated = true;

        util.Authenticate(this.txtUsername.Text.Trim(),
                          this.txtPassword.Text.Trim());
        this.Dispose();
    }
    catch(Exception ex)
    {
        MessageBox.Show(ex.Message);
    }
}
```

In this code you merely have to call the Authenticate() method of the DirectoryUtil object and pass the username and password.

Finally, add an instance of the FrmLogin form in the Load method of the FrmMain form in order to show the FrmLogin form. After the FrmLogin form is disposed, check for the isAuthenticated property, which exposes the isAuthenticated private bool. If it is not authenticated, it will dispose of the current form and exit the application; otherwise it will bind to the directory and load the application.

```
private void FrmMain_Load(object sender, System.EventArgs e)
{
    FrmLogin frm = new FrmLogin();
    frm.ShowDialog();
    if (!isAuthenticated)
    this.Dispose();
    util.Bind();
}
```

Note that if you wish to use the AuthenticationTypes.Sealing value, you must enable Kerberos so that it can encrypt the responses and requests. You can enable Kerberos by going to **Domain Controller Security Policy, Kerberos Policy,** checking the **Define this policy setting** check box, and selecting **Enabled:**

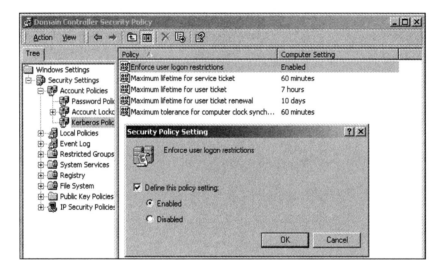

Testing the Authentication

Now you are ready to log in using a specific set of credentials. Take a look at the permissions set for the user called Erick for the trustee Belana in Active Directory.

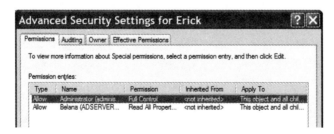

As you can see, the user called Belana (a trustee in this case) is only allowed to read properties. So log in as Belana and test these permissions. You can start by opening the login form (FrmLogin):

Before you enter the appropriate credentials, you can test the functionality by entering a username that does not existing in Active Directory. You should be presented with the following message:

This shows that authentication is working–the message in the exception is brought up from the underlying ADSI object.

If the user *is* authenticated, the AS creates a security token, Active Directory is allocated a thread impersonating that user, and the application can load the children of the directory.

At this stage, you should be able to load the application since the security principal Authenticated Users was added to the RootDSE of the directory.

Once the application has loaded, try to delete the user Erick:

When you try this, you're presented with the following message:

Because you are not authorized to delete this object, an exception was thrown in
CommitChanges(). Your application responded to this exception by showing an access denied
message.

In order to catch such exceptions, you must add exception handling in the method that changes or
adds properties in the FrmMain form. In the following code, you can see that we've added this
exception handling to the btnAddPropertyValue_Click() event:

```
...
try
{
    // Get Current property name
    string propertyName = this.lstProperties.Items
                    [this.lstProperties.SelectedIndex].ToString();
    // Check if we can add multiple values to the property
    try
    {
        util.SharedEntry.Properties[propertyName].Add(
                                this.txtPropertyValue.Text);
        // Update directory
        util.SharedEntry.CommitChanges();
    }
    catch(Exception ex)
    {
        util.SharedEntry.Properties[propertyName].Value =
                            (object)this.txtPropertyValue.Text;
        // Update directory
        util.SharedEntry.CommitChanges();
    }

}
catch(System.UnauthorizedAccessException exy)
{
    MessageBox.Show(exy.Message);
}
...
```

As you have seen, the user Belana can only read properties from the user Erick, so any attempt to
modify any properties will result in the **Access Denied** message box.

Authorization Fundamentals

Since the introduction of Windows NT, administrators or services have been able to grant users and groups authorization so that they can access system resources such as files or programs. In this context, before they can gain access to resources, users must provide a username and password for authentication. Groups can also be granted the same type of authorization, but they don't supply any credentials; users, on the other hand, are authorized depending on the groups they belong to, but unlike groups, they need, at some point, to present credentials.

Every ADSI object in Active Directory (or underlying `DirectoryEntry` object) has a property called `ntSecurityDescriptor`. This property is used as a pointer to the security descriptor of a directory entry. The `SecurityDescriptor` is the object that manages and maintains the ACE objects. These objects define what each trustee is allowed or not allowed to do, so they're central to the Active Directory security model. Let's take a more detailed look at these.

Access Control Entry (ACE)

An *Access Control Entry (ACE)* specifies access rights related to a trustee. There are four elements of an ACE that are evaluated by the system:

- ❏ Trustee
- ❏ Permission
- ❏ Target object
- ❏ Behavior

When a user opens a file, the operating system looks into the ACE to see whether the trustee corresponds to a valid directory entity. The trustee represents an entity in the directory that can denote a user, a group, or even a service. An ACE object has a property called `Trustee`. This is related to a specific directory entry.

If the trustee is a valid user, the operating system will check what permissions it should apply to this user, including whether it should allow or deny access (we detail permission types in the following section). If authorization is granted, it will look up the target object. This could be a single property of the object (phone number), or the whole object (again, we will look at how the target object is specified in a subsequent section). Lastly, the behavior specifies whether the ACE may or may not be inherited by all child objects of the ACE owner.

Permissions

A *permission* specifies the type of actions a trustee can or cannot perform. In an ACE, these permissions are defined in two different properties, `AccessMask` and `AceType`.

AccessMask

`AccessMask` is used to define the type of authorization a user requires. It does not specify whether access should be granted or denied; it simply defines what actions should be evaluated. These actions are described in an ADSI enumeration called `AD_RIGHTS_ENUM`. The possible values are as follows:

Enumeration	Hex Value	Description
ADS_RIGHT_DELETE	0x10000	The right to delete the object.
ADS_RIGHT_READ_CONTROL	0x20000	The right to read data from the security descriptor of the object.
ADS_RIGHT_WRITE_DAC	0x40000	The right to modify the ACL.
ADS_RIGHT_WRITE_OWNER	0x80000	The right to take ownership of an object.
ADS_RIGHT_SYNCHRONIZE	0x100000	The right to use the object for synchronization.
ADS_RIGHT_ACCESS_SYSTEM_SECURITY	0x1000000	The right to get or set the System ACL (SACL) in the object security descriptor (a specific security descriptor for system monitoring).
ADS_RIGHT_GENERIC_READ	0x80000000	The right to read permissions and properties, and to list its children if it is a container; if its parent container is listed, this object will also be listed.
ADS_RIGHT_GENERIC_WRITE	0x40000000	The right to read permissions on this object, write to all its properties, and perform all validated writes to this object.
ADS_RIGHT_GENERIC_EXECUTE	0x20000000	The right to read permissions on, and list the contents of, a container object.
ADS_RIGHT_GENERIC_ALL	0x10000000	The right to perform all other generic permissions.
ADS_RIGHT_DS_CREATE_CHILD	0x1	The right to create children of the object.
ADS_RIGHT_DS_DELETE_CHILD	0x2	The right to delete children of the object.
ADS_RIGHT_ACTRL_DS_LIST	0x4	The right to list children of this object
ADS_RIGHT_DS_SELF	0x8	The right to perform an operation controlled by a validated write access right.

Enumeration	Hex Value	Description
ADS_RIGHT_DS_READ_PROP	0x10	The right to read properties of the object.
ADS_RIGHT_DS_WRITE_PROP	0x20	The right to write to properties of the object.
ADS_RIGHT_DS_DELETE_TREE	0x40	The right to delete all children of this object, regardless of the permissions of the children.
ADS_RIGHT_DS_LIST_OBJECT	0x80	The right to list a particular object.
ADS_RIGHT_DS_CONTROL_ACCESS	0x100	The right to perform an operation controlled by an extended access right.

You can also use a combination of these values to allow different actions to be used in one single ACE object. If an access mask has *all* these values, then the trustee would have either full control or none, depending on the AceType.

AceType

The AceType is the property that determines whether the action defined in the AccessMask will be allowed or denied. The possible values are defined in the ADS_ACETYPE_ENUM:

Enumeration	Hex Value	Description
ADS_ACETYPE_ACCESS_ALLOWED	0	Allows access to the object for the trustee.
ADS_ACETYPE_ACCESS_DENIED	0x1	Denies access to the object for the trustee.
ADS_ACETYPE_SYSTEM_AUDIT	0x2	The ACE is a system audit ACE; this determines what types of access will cause system-level notifications.
ADS_ACETYPE_ACCESS_ALLOWED_OBJECT	0x5	The ACE grants access to a specific child object, property set, or property of the object. The ObjectType and/or InheritedObjectType properties of the ACE contain a globally unique identifier (GUID) that identifies the property set, property, extended right, or type of child object to which access is granted. (Windows 2000 only.)

Table Continues Overleaf

145

Enumeration	Hex Value	Description
ADS_ACETYPE_ACCESS_DENIED_OBJECT	0x6	The ACE denies access to a specific child object, property set, or property of the object. The ObjectType and/or InheritedObjectType properties of the ACE contain a GUID that identifies the property set, property, extended right, or type of child object to which access is granted. (Windows 2000 only.)
ADS_ACETYPE_SYSTEM_AUDIT_OBJECT	0x7	The ACE determines what types of access to a specific child object, property set, or property of the object will cause system notifications. The ObjectType and/or InheritedObjectType properties of the ACE contain a GUID that identifies the property set, property, extended right, or type of child object to which access is granted.
ADS_ACETYPE_SYSTEM_ALARM_OBJECT	0x8	Windows 2000/XP: Not used at this time.

Target Object

The target object can be the object to which the ACE belongs—a user, for example—or it can be one of its properties, such as a phone number. The target object can be detected if the Flags property of the ACE object has one of the ADS_FLAGTYPE_ENUM bit flags set. These values indicate whether the ACE object contains GUIDs in its ObjectType and InheritedObjectType properties:

Name	Hex Value	Description
ADS_FLAG_OBJECT_TYPE_PRESENT	0x1	The objectType is present in the ObjectType property.
ADS_FLAG_INHERITED_OBJECT_TYPE_PRESENT	0x2	The inheritedTypeObject is present in the InheritedTypeObject.

If the ADS_FLAG_OBJECT_TYPE_PRESENT is set, a GUID is present in the ObjectType property of the ACE representing the schemaIDGUID of the object in a string format. You can search for this value in the Active Directory schema to discover what child object, property, or property set is going to be targeted (phone number, URL, address, or whatever).

If the ADS_FLAG_INHERITED_OBJECT_TYPE_PRESENT is set, the InheritedTypeObject property of the ACE specifies the type of child object that can inherit from the current ACE. Like the ObjectType property, the InheritedObjectType also carries a string GUID representing the schemaIDGUID of the object that can inherit the ACE.

The following screenshot shows two ACE objects representing permissions for the **Administrators** group. Here, the ADS_FLAG_OBJECT_TYPE_PRESENT value is set for the Flags property for both of these ACEs, and in both cases points to the object **CN=User-Password** in the schema. The AccessMask and AceType of the first ACE are set to grant permissions for the password to be changed, and on the second they are set to allow the password to be reset.

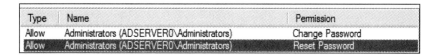

Type	Name	Permission
Allow	Administrators (ADSERVER0\Administrators)	Change Password
Allow	Administrators (ADSERVER0\Administrators)	Reset Password

At least one ACE must be defined in the ACL; otherwise, no one will be able to access that particular object.

If the Flags property of an ACE doesn't contain any value, then the ACE will apply to the current object.

AceFlags

You can control inheritance by using the AceFlags property of the ACE. Depending on the value you set, this property will behave differently. These values are defined in the ADS_ACEFLAG_ENUM in ADSI, as follows:

Enumeration	Hex Value	Description
ADS_ACEFLAG_INHERIT_ACE	0x2	Child objects will inherit this ACE. The inherited ACE is itself inheritable unless the ADS_ACEFLAG_NO_PROPAGATE_INHERIT_ACE flag is set.
ADS_ACEFLAG_NO_PROPAGATE_INHERIT_ACE	0x4	The system will clear the ADS_ACEFLAG_INHERIT_ACE flag for the inherited ACEs of child objects.
ADS_ACEFLAG_INHERIT_ONLY_ACE	0x8	This indicates an inherit-only ACE that does not exercise access control on the object to which it is attached. If this flag is not set, this ACE is an effective ACE that exerts access control on the object to which it is attached.
ADS_ACEFLAG_INHERITED_ACE	0x10	Indicates whether or not the ACE was inherited. The system sets this bit.

Table Continues Overleaf

Enumeration	Hex Value	Description
ADS_ACEFLAG_VALID_INHERIT_FLAGS	0x1f	Indicates whether the inherited flags are valid. The system sets this bit.
ADS_ACEFLAG_SUCCESSFUL_ACCESS	0x40	Generates audit messages for successful access attempts; this flag is used with ACEs that audit the system in a SACL.
ADS_ACEFLAG_FAILED_ACCESS	0x80	Generates audit messages for failed access attempts; this flag is used with ACEs that audit the system in a SACL.

When the AceType is set to one of the audit values in the enumeration, AceFlags can be set to make the system log the outcome of successful or failed authorizations by setting the AceFlags to ADS_ACEFLAG_SUCCESSFUL_ACCESS or ADS_ACEFLAG_FAILED_ACCESS. If you set both values for AceFlags, it will make the system log events for both behaviors.

The Discretionary ACL

The ACL is the container for all ACE objects. A discretionary ACL (DACL) is an ACL that is controlled by the owner of an object and determines what access specific users or groups can have to the object. (This is opposed to a system ACL, or SACL, which is used to generate system audit messages when an attempt is made to access the object.)

As you saw earlier, you can retrieve the ACL of a directory object through its ntSecurityDescriptor property, which is an ADSI property. You can do this in one of two ways. First, you could call the Get() method via the Invoke() method of the DirectoryEntry object, and pass the property name (ntSecurityDescriptor).

```
descriptor = user.Invoke("Get", new Object[]
                { "ntSecurityDescriptor" }) as IADsSecurityDescriptor;
```

Second, you could use the Properties indexer of the DirectoryEntry.

```
securityDescriptor = user.Properties["ntSecurityDescriptor"].Value
                                    as IADsSecurityDescriptor;
```

ADSI Security Interfaces

As you saw in the previous chapter, you can use ADSI directly in order to access Active Directory functionality. Here, we are going to show you some interfaces that provide ways to change permissions on an Active Directory object. At the time of this writing, using these interfaces is the only way to perform this task programmatically.

The `ActiveDs` imported type defines various security classes, including the ones that are NTFS specific. These control the ACEs within files and folders. Here we are going to explore the implementation and functionality of the ACEs that are used in Active Directory.

There are three ADSI interfaces we'll be using for this:

> **IADsSecurityDescriptor:** Provides access to the security descriptor of an ADSI object.
>
> **IADsAccessControlList:** Provides access to the ACL of an ADSI object.
>
> **IADsAccessControlEntry:** Represents an ACE within an ACL.

We introduced the `enum` types earlier in the chapter.

In order to help you better understand these classes, we'll begin by putting together some small examples to expose some of the functionality.

Retrieving ACEs

If you want to be able to retrieve ACEs from an Active Directory object, you must ensure that this object already exists in Active Directory. For these examples, we are going to have you create a new user. First you'll use ADSI Edit to create a user called trustee. Once you have done this, you can use ADSI Edit to examine its default ACEs:

Depending on the security policy applied to your server, you may have a different number of permission entries; on our server we can view up to 31, but this can vary if you insert more entries.

In the first example, you will use the `IADsSecurityDescriptor` and `IADsAccessControlList` interfaces. Respectively, these represent the security descriptor and the ACL of the trustee user you just created. The `IADsAccessControlList` object consists of a number of `IADsAccessControlEntry` objects, which you loop through, displaying some of their properties.

149

You should begin with the usual using directives for working with ADSI and System.DirectoryServices—don't forget that you need to add a reference to the ActiveDs library as you saw in Chapter 4.

```
using System;
using System.DirectoryServices;

using ActiveDs;
```

Now, start with the class definition and follow it with the Main() method.

```
class RetrieveACEs
{
  public static void Main()
  {
```

Then start using the ADSI interfaces—the first variable represents the SecurityDescriptor and the next is the reference to the ACL.

```
IADsSecurityDescriptor secDescriptor;
IADsAccessControlList controlList;
```

Now create a DirectoryEntry object that you'll use to view the permission entries (ACEs) for your new **trustee** user.

```
DirectoryEntry user = new DirectoryEntry(
        "LDAP://CN=trustee,CN=Users,DC=ADSERVER,DC=com");
```

Once you have the reference to the entry in the directory, you can call the Get() method on the underlying ADSI object using the Invoke() method, passing in the string "ntSecurityDescriptor" to retrieve the SecurityDescriptor of the entry. You can cast the object returned from the Invoke() method to an IADsSecurityDescriptor and use the as operator to ensure that no exception is thrown.

```
secDescriptor = user.Invoke("Get", new Object[]
        { "ntSecurityDescriptor" }) as IADsSecurityDescriptor;
```

Once you have the reference to the SecurityDescriptor, you can call the DiscretionaryAcl property of the SecurityDescriptor to retrieve a reference to the ACL of that same object, which will be cast to an IADsAccessControlList instance.

```
controlList = secDescriptor.DiscretionaryAcl as IADsAccessControlList;
```

With the ACL reference in place, you can iterate through the ACL to get the ACEs and output their values:

```
foreach(IADsAccessControlEntry ace  in controlList)
{

  Console.WriteLine("*********************************");
  Console.WriteLine("******Access Control Entry *****");
  Console.WriteLine("Trustee: {0}", ace.Trustee);
  Console.WriteLine("Access Mask: {0}", ace.AccessMask);
```

```
            Console.WriteLine("Ace Flag: {0}", ace.AceFlags);
            Console.WriteLine("Ace Type: {0}", ace.AceType);
            Console.WriteLine("********************************\n\n");
        }
        Console.WriteLine("********************************");
        Console.WriteLine("Total Access Control Entries: {0}",
                        controlList.AceCount);
    }
}
```

When you run the example, the output should look like the following:

Adding an ACE

Now we are going to show you how to add an ACE into an Active Directory object's ACL. In addition to the previous code, you must create an object that is instantiated from the `ActiveDs.AccessControlEntryClass` class. This object will be an empty ACE object; you are required to set at least the `Trustee` property, since this is a mandatory property and you cannot have an ACE without a trustee.

In the next code snippet, you are only adding a new definition of the `AccessControlEntryClass`, which will be the object representing the ACE.

```
using System;
using System.DirectoryServices;
using ActiveDs;

public class AddingAnAce
{
    public static void Main()
    {
        IADsSecurityDescriptor secDescriptor;
        IADsAccessControlList controlList;
        AccessControlEntryClass ace = new AccessControlEntryClass();
```

After performing the process of getting the ACL, you need to print the number of ACEs in the ACL so that you know how many you have at this stage:

```
DirectoryEntry user = new DirectoryEntry(
            "LDAP://CN=trustee,CN=Users,DC=ADSERVER,DC=com");
secDescriptor = user.Invoke("Get", new Object[]
        { "ntSecurityDescriptor" }) as IADsSecurityDescriptor;

Console.WriteLine("Total Access Control Entries: {0}",
                    controlList.AceCount);
```

Next, assign values for the new ACE object.

```
ace.Trustee    = "ADSERVER0\\Cert Publishers";
ace.AceType    = (int)ADS_ACETYPE_ENUM.
                                ADS_ACETYPE_ACCESS_ALLOWED;
ace.AccessMask = (int)ADS_RIGHTS_ENUM.ADS_RIGHT_GENERIC_READ;
ace.AceFlags   = (int)ADS_ACEFLAG_ENUM.ADS_ACEFLAG_INHERIT_ACE;
```

Then add the ACE object into the ACL:

```
Console.WriteLine("Adding new ACE...");
controlList.AddAce(ace);
```

You haven't finished yet; you still have some critical steps to perform. You must assign the secDescriptor, which is still holding the reference to the ACL controlList, back to the SecurityDescriptor of the object.

```
try
{
    user.Properties["ntSecurityDescriptor"].Value = secDescriptor;

    Console.WriteLine("Added...");
}
catch(Exception e)
{
    Console.WriteLine(e);
}
```

Finally, you need to call CommitChanges() on the DirectoryEntry object and print the new ACE count.

```
user.CommitChanges();
Console.WriteLine("Total Access Control Entries: {0}",
                    controlList.AceCount);
Console.Read();
    }
}
```

The output from this will be as follows, showing the increased number of ACEs:

The important part of adding an ACE is creating the ACE object and adding it to the security descriptor through the ACL.

Deleting an ACE

You can delete an ACE by iterating through the ACL and removing the ACE with the `RemoveAce()` method of the ACL object.

This example begins as the two previous examples did, and then you will see it loop through all the ACEs in the ACL:

```
using System;
using System.DirectoryServices;
using ActiveDs;

public class DeletingAnAce
{
    public static void Main()
    {
        IADsSecurityDescriptor secDescriptor;
        IADsAccessControlList controlList;
        AccessControlEntryClass ace = new AccessControlEntryClass();

        DirectoryEntry user = new DirectoryEntry(
                "LDAP://CN=trustee,CN=Users,DC=ADSERVER,DC=com");

        secDescriptor = user.Invoke("Get", new Object[]
                { "ntSecurityDescriptor" }) as IADsSecurityDescriptor;

        foreach (IADsAccessControlEntry ace in controlList)
        {
```

When you find an ACE whose `Trustee` property has the value `"Cert Publishers"`, you need to remove it from the ACL:

```
            if (ace.Trustee.Equals("ADSERVER0\\Cert Publishers"))
            {
                controlList.RemoveAce(ace);
```

After modifying the `SecurityDescriptor`, you must perform two more steps. First insert the modified `SecurityDescriptor` back into the properties cache, using the `Invoke()` method to call `Put()` on the underlying object.

```
try
{
    secDescriptor = user.Invoke("Put", new object[]
                    { "ntSecurityDescriptor", secDescriptor })
                                    as IADsSecurityDescriptor;
```

Then commit the changes and exit from the loop:

```
        user.CommitChanges();
        Console.WriteLine("Security descriptor updated ...");
    }
    catch(Exception e)
    {
        Console.WriteLine(e);
    }
    break;
            }
        }
    }
}
```

Creating the Managed Security Classes

You have just seen that it is not very difficult to perform security-based operations on the Active Directory, but they must be done via COM interop. Although .NET eases the Active Directory programmer's life by wrapping ADSI inside the `System.DirectoryServices` namespace, if you want to handle permissions, you still cannot do this directly since no support for it exists inside this namespace. In the same way that the `DirectorySearcher` class wraps ADSI's search functionality, you will wrap ADSI's security functionality into a set of managed classes.

In this section, you are going to learn to create a namespace with classes that will wrap the security functionality you need to manipulate permissions within Active Directory.

Planning the Application Security Context

The following will be the requirements for the classes within our namespace—they are quite straightforward but will occupy much of the remainder of the chapter:

❑   View information from entries in the directory.

❑   Add permissions to entries.

❑   Delete permissions from entries.

To simplify the process, you are going to add permissions to the entry only and not to any of its properties.

In order to achieve this functionality, you need to define the following classes, each of which is defined in a namespace called Apress.DirectoryServices.Security.

❑   AccessControlList

❑   AccessControlEntry

❑   AccessControlEntries

The AccessControlList class will be handling the direct operations to the ActiveDs classes. This will be the only point of contact with ActiveDs, and it will wrap any of the functionality that you require from the library.

When you look at the relationship between the AccessControlList and AccessControlEntries, note that the AccessControlList works as a container for AccessControlEntries. Thus, instead of creating an ArrayList of AccessControlEntry objects in the list, you've created another collection called AccessControlEntries that takes an AccessControlEntry via an Add() method, which is used privately by the AccessControlList. This approach ensures the complete encapsulation of the AccessControlEntries in the AccessControlList.

You should also understand that the ADSI interfaces, IADsAccessControlList and IADsSecurityDescriptor, are called as dependencies by the AccessControlList class where the logic is wrapped.

You will also need to give the design some room for further extensions. Here is a hierarchical view of the namespace seen in the **Object Browser**.

You can see here that you are trying to mimic some of the aspects of the Windows Security model.

Defining the Enumerations

As we mentioned earlier, the standard values AccessMask, AceType, AceFlags, and Flags used in the ACE are defined in the ActiveDs library. Here, you are going to port these to .NET code to let client applications use them from .NET enumerations and not from the ActiveDs library.

You'll give each of your enumerations the same name as the corresponding `ActiveDs` one. However, they will not all be of type `int`: one will be of type `uint` since some of the values are way too big to fit into an `int`, and another will be of type `byte`. Note that you've used the `[Flags]` attribute, which ensures that you can combine the values using bitwise operators.

We won't show the namespace definition here, but each of the enumerations is defined in your `Apress.DirectoryServices.Security` *namespace.*

Here are the definitions for your four enumerations:

ADS_RIGHTS_ENUM: Used with the `AccessMask` property.

```
[Flags]
public enum ADS_RIGHTS_ENUM : uint
{
    ADS_RIGHT_DELETE = 0x10000,
    ADS_RIGHT_READ_CONTROL = 0x20000,
    ADS_RIGHT_WRITE_DAC = 0x40000,
    ADS_RIGHT_WRITE_OWNER = 0x80000,
    ADS_RIGHT_SYNCHRONIZE = 0x100000,
    ADS_RIGHT_ACCESS_SYSTEM_SECURITY = 0x1000000,
    ADS_RIGHT_GENERIC_READ = 0x80000000,
    ADS_RIGHT_GENERIC_WRITE = 0x40000000,
    ADS_RIGHT_GENERIC_EXECUTE = 0x20000000,
    ADS_RIGHT_GENERIC_ALL = 0x10000000,
    ADS_RIGHT_DS_CREATE_CHILD = 0x1,
    ADS_RIGHT_DS_DELETE_CHILD = 0x2,
    ADS_RIGHT_ACTRL_DS_LIST = 0x4,
    ADS_RIGHT_DS_SELF = 0x8,
    ADS_RIGHT_DS_READ_PROP = 0x10,
    ADS_RIGHT_DS_WRITE_PROP = 0x20,
    ADS_RIGHT_DS_DELETE_TREE = 0x40,
    ADS_RIGHT_DS_LIST_OBJECT = 0x80,
    ADS_RIGHT_DS_CONTROL_ACCESS = 0x100
}
```

ADS_ACEFLAG_ENUM: Used with the `AceFlag` property.

```
[Flags]
public enum ADS_ACEFLAG_ENUM : byte
{
    ADS_ACEFLAG_INHERIT_ACE = 0x2,
    ADS_ACEFLAG_NO_PROPAGATE_INHERIT_ACE = 0x4,
    ADS_ACEFLAG_INHERIT_ONLY_ACE = 0x8,
    ADS_ACEFLAG_INHERITED_ACE = 0x10,
    ADS_ACEFLAG_VALID_INHERIT_FLAGS = 0x1f,
    ADS_ACEFLAG_SUCCESSFUL_ACCESS = 0x40,
    ADS_ACEFLAG_FAILED_ACCESS = 0x80
}
```

ADS_ACETYPE_ENUM: Used with the `AceType` property.

```
[Flags]
public enum ADS_ACETYPE_ENUM
{
    ADS_ACETYPE_ACCESS_ALLOWED = 0,
    ADS_ACETYPE_ACCESS_DENIED = 0x1,
    ADS_ACETYPE_SYSTEM_AUDIT = 0x2,
    ADS_ACETYPE_ACCESS_ALLOWED_OBJECT = 0x5,
    ADS_ACETYPE_ACCESS_DENIED_OBJECT = 0x6,
    ADS_ACETYPE_SYSTEM_AUDIT_OBJECT = 0x7,
    ADS_ACETYPE_SYSTEM_ALARM_OBJECT = 0x8
}
```

ADS_FLAGTYPE_ENUM: Used for the `Flag` property.

```
[Flags]
public enum ADS_FLAGTYPE_ENUM
{
    ADS_FLAG_OBJECT_TYPE_PRESENT = 0x1,
    ADS_FLAG_INHERITED_OBJECT_TYPE_PRESENT = 0x2
}
```

Sometimes you will have to take a value from one of these enumerations and pass it back to an ADSI object—in other words, you'll map it back to its original value. We will look at this later, in the section entitled "The AccessControlList Class."

The AccessControlEntry Class

Now you are going to define your version of an ACE in the `Apress.DirectoryServices.Security` namespace. This class is a very simple data structure that maintains direct dependencies to the `System.DirectoryServices.DirectoryEntry` object and the custom enumeration types. The class will have two constructors: one will accept `AccessControlEntry` details; the other has fewer parameters, and is more amenable for client code. Start by looking at the `using` directives and private fields of the class:

```
using System;

namespace Apress.DirectoryServices.Security
{
    public class AccessControlEntry
    {
        private string trustee;
        private string[] aceType;
        private string[] accessMask;
        private string[] aceFlags;
        private string[] flags;
        private string objectType = null;
        private string inheritedObject = null;
        private object nativeAce = null;
        ...
```

As you can see, this class will represent an ACE by storing the required values on these private members.

The first constructor will accept an ACE from the ACL. The code in the constructor just assigns the values of the parameters to the private fields, with some checking for null values:

```
...
public AccessControlEntry(string trustee,
          string[] aceType,
          string[] accessMask,
          string[] aceFlags,
          string[] flags,
          string objectType,
          string inheritedObject,
          object nativeAce)
{
   this.flags = flags;
   this.aceType = aceType;
   this.accessMask = accessMask;
   if (!(aceFlags.Length == 1))
      this.aceFlags = aceFlags;

   this.trustee = trustee;

   if (inheritedObject != null)
   {
      this.inheritedObject = inheritedObject;
   }

   if (objectType != null)
   {
      this.objectType = objectType;
   }
   this.nativeAce = nativeAce;
}
...
```

Note that you are also keeping the reference to the native ACE object, because the native ACL does not contain an indexer that you can use to reference a specific ACE. You will use this reference to the native ACE later, when you need to delete the object.

The second constructor is friendlier for client code. It takes two parameters: a string for the name of the trustee, and a bool value that will allow or forbid permissions.

```
public AccessControlEntry(string trustee, bool allow)
{
   this.trustee = trustee;

   if (allow)
   {
      this.aceType = new string[]
         { Enum.GetName(typeof(ADS_ACETYPE_ENUM),
            ADS_ACETYPE_ENUM.ADS_ACETYPE_ACCESS_ALLOWED) };
   }
   else
```

```
        {
            this.aceType = new string[]
                { Enum.GetName(typeof(ADS_ACETYPE_ENUM),
                    ADS_ACETYPE_ENUM.ADS_ACETYPE_ACCESS_DENIED) };
        }
    }
```

In the preceding code, the value of ADS_ACETYPE_ACCESS_ALLOWED or the ADS_ACETYPE_ACCESS_DENIED is added for that specific trustee, depending on the permissions selected in the Boolean parameter.

Now you need to define a method for creating new ACEs from client code. To do this, assign permissions to the ACE using the AddRights() method. This method takes a value from the ADS_RIGHTS_ENUM enumeration as a parameter, and adds it to the private accessMask array.

```
        public void AddRights(ADS_RIGHTS_ENUM enumValue)
        {
            ArrayList tempList = new ArrayList();
            if (this.accessMask != null)
            {
                foreach(string existingValue in this.accessMask)
                    tempList.Add(existingValue);
            }
            tempList.Add(Enum.GetName(typeof(ADS_RIGHTS_ENUM),
                                        enumValue));
            this.accessMask = (string[])
                                    tempList.ToArray(typeof(string));
        }
```

Next, you have the public properties to expose your private fields:

```
        ...

        public object NativeAce
        {
            get
            {
                return nativeAce;
            }
        }

        public string[] AceFlags
        {
            get
            {
                return aceFlags;
            }
        }

        public string ObjectType
        {
            get
            {
                return objectType;
            }
        }
```

```
        set
        {
            objectType = value;
        }
    }

    public string InheritedObject
    {
        get
        {
            return inheritedObject;
        }
        set
        {
            inheritedObject = value;
        }
    }

    public string Trustee
    {
        get
        {
            return trustee;
        }
        set
        {
            trustee = value;
        }
    }
```

Note that AceType and AccessMask will be read-only properties.

```
    public string[] AceType
    {
        get
        {
            return aceType;
        }
    }

    public string[] AccessMask
    {
        get
        {
            return accessMask;
        }
    }
    ...
```

The rest of the AccessControlEntry definition is for utility purposes. The next method you look at is used to translate the enumeration values into a more friendly string name for display purposes.

This code defines how callers can get this friendly name:

```
...
public static string GetFriendlyName(string enumName)
{
    string enumType = enumName.Split('_').GetValue(1).ToString();

    switch(enumType)
    {
        case "RIGHTS":
            return GetFriendlyAccessMask(enumName);

        case "ACEFLAG":
            return GetFriendlyAceFlag(enumName);

        case "FLAG":
            return GetFriendlyFlag(enumName);

        case "ACETYPE":
            return GetFriendlyAceType(enumName);
    }
    return string.Empty;
}
...
```

GetFriendlyName() takes a string with the name of one of your enumerations, splits the string at each _ character into a string array, and then checks the second entry in this array. Depending on what this second entry is, another method will be called to get the friendly name from the relevant enumeration.

For example, the code for getting the friendly name from the ADS_ACEFLAG_ENUM enumeration is as follows:

```
// Get Friendly name for the AceFlag Property
private static string GetFriendlyAceFlag(string enumName)
{
    switch(enumName)
    {
        case "ADS_ACEFLAG_INHERIT_ACE":
            return "This object and all child objects";

        case "ADS_ACEFLAG_NO_PROPAGATE_INHERIT_ACE":
            return "This object only";

        case "ADS_ACEFLAG_INHERIT_ONLY_ACE":
            return "Inherit only";

        case "ADS_ACEFLAG_INHERITED_ACE":
            return "Inherited";

        case "ADS_ACEFLAG_VALID_INHERIT_FLAGS":
            return "Valid";

        case "ADS_ACEFLAG_SUCCESSFUL_ACCESS":
            return "Audit Success";
        case "ADS_ACEFLAG_FAILED_ACCESS":
```

```
                          return "Audit Failed";
              }
              return string.Empty;
     }
```

We won't show any of the other friendly name methods—the code is similar for all of them, and you can find it in the code for this chapter, which you can access from the Downloads section of the Apress web site (http://www.apress.com). These methods will assist you when you use this class at the front-end of an application (we will cover this shortly).

You will find the AccessControlEntry to be very useful when you retrieve information about each ACE within an ACL, just as we did in the earlier examples, but now you will work within your own, custom .NET namespace, instead of using the unmanaged ActiveDs type library through COM interop.

The AccessControlEntries Class

Sometimes you'll have to use a collection of ACEs, especially when you are handling an entire ACL. This is the role of the AccessControlEntries class, which is a collection of AccessControlEntry objects. The AccessControlEntries class inherits from CollectionBase, so that much of the functionality for implementing a strongly-typed collection is already supplied. All you have to do is supply Add() and Remove() methods to add and remove items from the underlying collection, which is exposed by the List property. Finally, you'll need to add an indexer to return an AccessControlEntry based on a numerical index:

```
public class AccessControlEntries : CollectionBase
{
    public void Add(AccessControlEntry accessControlEntry)
    {
        List.Add(accessControlEntry);
    }

    public void Remove(AccessControlEntry accessControlEntry)
    {
        List.Remove(accessControlEntry);
    }

    public AccessControlEntry this[int index]
    {
        get
        {
            return (AccessControlEntry)List[index];
        }
    }
}
```

Even though this class uses simple techniques, you will find it helpful in the current model because the classes in the ActiveDs interop assembly do not support indexers.

The AccessControlList Class

This class was designed to follow the logic of the ACL, and it will work as an organized container for AccessControlEntries, encapsulating the functionality for loading and updating the security information in Active Directory objects.

Here is a list of the methods that you can implement in this class, in addition to a single constructor:

Fill(): This private method will fill the AccessControlEntries collection with AccessControlEntry objects.

NativeGUIDToOctetString(): This private method converts a native GUID of an Active Directory object to an octet string. You must have this to find the path of an object if you are given a GUID.

NativeGUIDToPath(): This private method takes the native GUID of an Active Directory object and returns the path of that object.

Remove(): This public method removes an ACE from the ACL.

CommitChanges(): This public method commits the changes back to the Active Directory from ACEs from an internal pending list.

The client code will use this class to retrieve individual ACEs from an Active Directory object. Let's start by looking at the using directives and noting that you are importing the ActiveDs ADSI library–this is the only class in your namespace that depends on COM interop.

```
...
using System;
using ActiveDs;
using System.Collections;
using System.DirectoryServices;
using System.IO;
using System.Text;

namespace Apress.DirectoryServices.Security
{
    public class AccessControlList : IEnumerable
    {
        ...
```

You can also see that this class implements the IEnumerable interface for collection support.

Next you have some key private fields, including two AccessControlEntries instances, a DirectoryEntry, an integer index, and IADsSecurityDescriptor and IADsAccessControlList ADSI interfaces. You can use one AccessControlEntries instance, aceList, to hold the collection of ACEs. The other, pendingAceList, will contain the ACEs that you are about to add to the aceList collection.

```
        private AccessControlEntries aceList =
                            new AccessControlEntries();
        private AccessControlEntries pendingAceList =
                            new AccessControlEntries();

        private DirectoryEntry user;
        private int index = -1;
```

163

```
private IADsSecurityDescriptor securityDescriptor;
private IADsAccessControlList accessControlList;
...
```

Constructor

Now we move on to the constructor definition. You only have one constructor, and it takes a `DirectoryEntry` object. Once you receive the object, get the `SecurityDescriptor` from the `ntSecurityDescription` property. Then get the native ACL by calling the `DiscretionaryAcl` property of the `SecurityDescriptor`. Note the call at the end of the code to a private `Fill()` method.

```
...
public AccessControlList(DirectoryEntry user)
{
    this.user = user;
    if (securityDescriptor == null)
    {
        try
        {
            securityDescriptor =
                    this.user.Properties["ntSecurityDescriptor"].Value
                                          as IADsSecurityDescriptor;
            accessControlList = securityDescriptor.DiscretionaryAcl
                                          as IADsAccessControlList;
        }
        catch(Exception e)
        {
            // Trace error
        }
    }
    Fill();
}
...
```

Filling with Existing ACEs

The `Fill()` method merely fills the `aclList` field with the existing ACEs contained within the ACL. This method is very important because most of the bridging between the native ACE and your managed ACE is done using this method.

We start by showing you how to declare a `foreach` loop to iterate through the native ACL and retrieve all the native ACEs. After that, you can create two string variables to hold the name of the `ObjectType` and `InheritedObjectType`; we will look at these shortly.

```
...
private void Fill()
{
    foreach (IADsAccessControlEntry ace in accessControlList)
    {
```

```
    string objectType = string.Empty;
        string inheritedObjectType = string.Empty;
        ...
```

Now you can start having fun—first, you can use the static Format() method of the System.Enum class to create a list of the values in the current native AccessMask property of the native ACE. It looks at the value of the native enumeration. Also, note that in order to get valid values for the unmanaged objects, you have to convert from integers to the real native ADSI types.

```
    try
    {
        // Set the AccessMask
        string accessMask  = Enum.Format(typeof(ADS_RIGHTS_ENUM),
                            Convert.ToUInt32(ace.AccessMask), "F");
        string[] arrayAccessMask = accessMask.Replace(" ", "").
                                            Split(',');

        // Set the AceType
        string aceType = Enum.Format(typeof(ADS_ACETYPE_ENUM),
                                    ace.AceType, "F");
        string[] arrayAceType = aceType.Replace(" ", "").Split(',');
        // Set the AceFlag
        string aceFlag = Enum.Format(typeof(ADS_ACEFLAG_ENUM),
                        Convert.ToByte(ace.AceFlags), "F");
        string[] arrayAceFlag = aceFlag.Replace(" ", "").Split(',');

        // Set the Flags
        string flag = Enum.Format(typeof(ADS_FLAGTYPE_ENUM),
                                ace.Flags, "F");
        string[] flagArray = flag.Replace(" ", "").Split(',');
```

Note that you need to break the strings into the separate enum values and create string arrays.

Now you need to check to see if the value of the Flags property is positive. This will tell you if you have an InheritedObjectType or ObjectType, and if so, you'll get a string that represents its common names cn. You can do this by passing the string GUID from these properties to the NativeGUIDToPath() method. We are going to look at this method shortly.

```
        if (ace.Flags > 0)
        {
            // Inherited object
            if (ace.InheritedObjectType != null)
            {
                inheritedObjectType =
                    NativeGUIDToPath(ace.InheritedObjectType);
            }

            // Object Type
            if (ace.ObjectType != null)
            {
                objectType = NativeGUIDToPath(ace.ObjectType);
            }
        }
```

Finally, you can add all this information to the list.

```
                aceList.Add(new AccessControlEntry(ace.Trustee,
                                        arrayAceType,
                                        arrayAccessMask,
                                        arrayAceFlag,
                                        flagArray,
                                        objectType,
                                        inheritedObjectType,
                                        ace));
        }
        catch (Exception e)
        {
            // Handle the error...
        }
    }
}
```

Converting GUIDs

You will now implement a couple of methods for "converting" GUIDs to different formats. One of these methods, `NativeGUIDToPath()` doesn't convert the GUID; it finds the object in the Active Directory corresponding to that GUID and returns its path as a string. In order to locate this object, you need the `NativeGUIDToOctetString()` method.

NativeGUIDToOctetString() Method

When you receive an `ObjectType` or an `InheritedObjectType`, this is a string representation of a GUID in a format such as the following:

```
{BF967ABA-0DE6-11D0-A285-00AA003049E2}
```

However, Active Directory defines the syntax for each attribute it contains, and in the case of GUIDs, the syntax is an octet string. Of particular interest is the `schemaGUIDID` attribute, which identifies different classes and attributes of a schema entry. By converting a string representing a GUID to an octet string, the format becomes something like this:

```
\BA\7A\96\BF\E6\0D\D0\11\A2\85\00\AA\00\30\49\E2
```

You can use this representation as a filter to search for the object.

The following code shows you how to define the `NativeGUIDToOctetString()` method to take a byte array and return the representation of it in an octet string format:

```
private static string NativeGUIDToOctetString(byte[] byteArray)
{
    StringBuilder builder = null;
    builder = new StringBuilder(byteArray.Length * 2);
    for (int count = 0; count < byteArray.Length; count++)
    {
        builder.Append(@"\");
        builder.Append(byteArray[iCount].ToString("X2"));
    }
    return builder.ToString();
}
```

NativeGUIDToPath() Method

Now let's go back to the `NativeGUIDToPath()`. This method simply takes a GUID, searches the Active Directory for the object with that GUID, and returns its path. The first thing you do is get the schema-naming context–this will be the scope for your search.

```
private static string NativeGUIDToPath(string GUID)
{
    // Create GUID
    Guid guid = new Guid(GUID);

    // Get the schema path
    string schemaPath = "LDAP://";
    schemaPath += new DirectoryEntry("LDAP://RootDSE").
                Properties["schemaNamingContext"].Value.ToString();
```

You can then use the schema path to create the search root:

```
    // Create a Schema path object
    DirectoryEntry schemaEntry = new DirectoryEntry(schemaPath);
```

Now pass the string GUID to the `NativeGUIDToOctetString()` method to get the octet string format. You will use this string as the filter for your search.

```
    // Translate the GUID object to an octet string
    string schemaIDGuid = NativeGUIDToOctetString(guid.ToByteArray());
```

Next, build the filter to find the object. You can define the filter with the octet string, and search the directory for the `schemaIDGUID` that matches this string.

```
    // Build a filter
    string filter = "(schemaIDGUID=" + schemaIDGuid + ")";

    // Create a Searcher object
    DirectorySearcher searcher = new DirectorySearcher(schemaEntry);
    searcher.Filter = filter;
```

You now search for the object in the schema. Since you're only after one object, you can use the `FindOne()` method to return just that. From the returned object, you can extract the common name property and return this as the value of your method:

```
    // Get result from search
    SearchResult result = searcher.FindOne();

    // Return common name
    string cn = (string)result.Properties["cn"][0];
    return cn;
}
```

Removing ACEs

Next, you have the method that removes the ACE from the ACL. As you saw when we defined the managed wrapper for the ACE, we've had you keep a reference for the native ACE in each managed ACE. Now it's just a matter of casting that object back to a native ACE and passing it to the Remove() method of the IADsAccessControlList, which will remove it from the native ACL. Note the call to CommitChanges() here—this is our own version of this method, which we'll discuss in a moment.

```
. . .
public void Remove(object nativeAce)
{
    this.accessControlList.RemoveAce(
                    nativeAce as ActiveDs.IADsAccessControlEntry);
    securityDescriptor.DiscretionaryAcl = this.accessControlList;
    CommitChanges();
}
. . .
```

Committing Internal Changes

When the client code adds an ACE in the ACL, it is kept in the pendingAceList collection. This list coverts any pending ACEs and creates a new native ACE to be placed in the current native ACL.

```
private void CommitPendingList()
{
    if (this.pendingAceList.Count > 0)
    {
        foreach (AccessControlEntry ace in this.pendingAceList)
        {
            ActiveDs.AccessControlEntryClass nativeAce = new
                                        AccessControlEntryClass();
            // Work out AccessMask
            ADS_RIGHTS_ENUM accessMask = (ADS_RIGHTS_ENUM)Enum.Parse(
                typeof(ADS_RIGHTS_ENUM), GetEnumString(ace.AccessMask));
            nativeAce.AccessMask =(int)accessMask;

            // Work out the AceType
            ADS_ACETYPE_ENUM aceType = (ADS_ACETYPE_ENUM)Enum.Parse(
                                typeof(ADS_ACETYPE_ENUM),
                                ace.AceType.GetValue(0).ToString());
            nativeAce.AceType = (int)aceType;
            nativeAce.Trustee = ace.Trustee;

            // Add new ACE to current ACL
            this.accessControlList.AddAce(nativeAce);
            securityDescriptor.DiscretionaryAcl = this.accessControlList;
        }
    }
}
```

Note that to get values from the managed ACE, you need to convert some of the values, including the enumeration types. For this, you can use a private method, GetEnumString(), which gets all values from a string array from the enumerations and returns a comma-delimited string.

```
private string GetEnumString(string[] enumArray)
{
   System.Text.StringBuilder builder =
                            new System.Text.StringBuilder();
   int index = 0;
   do
   {
      builder.Append(enumArray.GetValue(index));
      index++;
      if (enumArray.Length == index)
         break;
      builder.Append(',');
   } while(enumArray.Length != index)

   return builder.ToString();
}
```

Committing Changes

The AccessControlList class has a public CommitChanges() method that we mentioned
earlier. First of all, this method checks for any pending ACEs in pendingAceList, and if it finds
any, they are added to the accessControlList list of ACEs with the CommitPendingList()
method you just saw. You can use the Put() method to perform the update on the user
DirectoryEntry object, which sends the SecurityDescriptor back to the object; you can then
commit all these changes with the real CommitChanges() method (of the DirectoryEntry
class).

```
public void CommitChanges()
{
   try
   {
      // Commit for all
      if (this.pendingAceList.Count > 0)
         this.CommitPendingList();
      user.Invoke("Put", new Object[]
                 { "ntSecurityDescriptor",  securityDescriptor} );
      user.CommitChanges();
   }
   catch (Exception e)
   {
      // ....
   }
}
```

That completes the definition of our managed Active Directory security classes.

Implementation

We are now going to step you through the implementation of the
Apress.DirectoryServices.Security namespace classes in the Directory Browser
application you created in Chapter 2. The first thing that is you need to do is add a new entry to the
context menu for loading the security information:

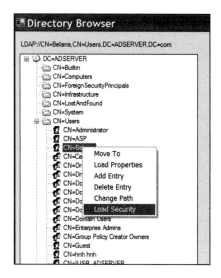

You will also need to add a new tab page called Security to the form. The main control of interest on this tab page is a ListView that displays the various security permissions. When complete, this part of the application should look like the following:

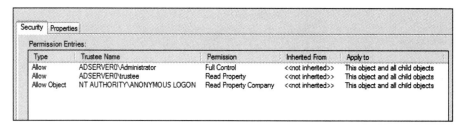

The columns in the ListView hold the following information:

Type: A value from ADS_ACETYPE_ENUM.

Trustee Name: The value of the Trustee property.

Permission: This column contains two pieces of information. The first is the AccessMask, and then there is the ObjectType. In the preceding screenshot, **Read Property** is the AccessMask, and **Company** is the ObjectType.

Inherited From: The value of InheritedObject.

Apply to: The value from ADS_ACEFLAG_ENUM.

Note that all the values from the enumerations are displayed with their friendly name. In the code for populating the `ListView`, you can get all details from the ACEs by iterating through with a `foreach` loop. As you go, you can obtain the type of `AceFlags` each ACEs is carrying. You can then use the `GetFriendlyName()` method to ensure that you produce a readable output for this value rather than just a number:

```
this.lvwPermEntries.Items.Clear();
AccessControlList acl = new AccessControlList(util.SharedEntry);

string accessMask = null;
string inheritedObject = null;
string aceFlags = null;

foreach (AccessControlEntry ace in acl)
{
    aceFlags = AccessControlEntry.GetFriendlyName(
                             "ADS_ACEFLAG_INHERIT_ACE");

    if (ace.AceFlags != null)
    {
        foreach (string flag in ace.AceFlags)
        {
            if (flag == "ADS_ACEFLAG_NO_PROPAGATE_INHERIT_ACE")
            {
                aceFlags = AccessControlEntry.GetFriendlyName(flag);
                break;
            }
        }
    }
}
```

As you continue to get details from the ACEs, you develop the logic for getting the `AccessMask`. This method checks to see if the `AccessMask` contains 13 items. If it does, the application shows Full Control as the permission for this value; otherwise it displays the value itself.

```
switch (ace.AccessMask.Length)
{
    case 1:
        accessMask = AccessControlEntry.GetFriendlyName(
                         ace.AccessMask.GetValue(0).ToString());
        break;
    case 13:
        accessMask = "Full Control";
        break;

    default:
        accessMask = "Special";
        break;
}
```

Now you can check to see if the ACE has an `ObjectType`; if so, print it beside the permission being applied to that object.

```
if (ace.ObjectType.Length > 1)
    accessMask += " " + ace.ObjectType;

if (ace.InheritedObject.Length == 0)
    inheritedObject = "<<not inherited>>";
else
    inheritedObject = ace.InheritedObject + " Objects";
```

Lastly, build a string array and add it to the `ListView`. Make sure to hold on to the `ListViewItem` that is added to the `ListView` here, and be sure to add an object array to its `Tag` property. This object array allows you to retrieve the native ACE (it can be deleted later).

```
string[] items = new string[] {
            AccessControlEntry.GetFriendlyName(
                ace.AceType.GetValue(0).ToString()),
            ace.Trustee,
            accessMask,
            inheritedObject,
            aceFlags };
ListViewItem item = this.lvwPermEntries.Items.Add(
                            new ListViewItem(items));
item.Tag = new object[] { ace.AccessMask, ace };
```

Now, when you load the permissions, here is the outcome:

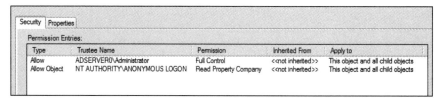

To add or delete permissions, you can add another context menu:

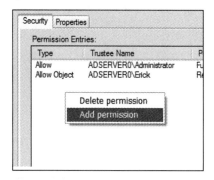

The dialog for adding permissions looks similar to the following:

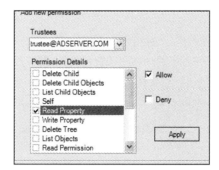

The application loads all the friendly names, as well as the values for the ADS_RIGHTS_ENUM behind the permission list. You can also load the user principal names of the users in the directory into the combo box. Now the user can check **Allow** or **Deny** and the permissions defined in the list box will be applied to that object.

Now take a quick look at the code for deleting permissions. First, you can get the object stored in the Tag property of the ListViewItem (remember this is an object array) and get the second object from that array (the managed ACE). Once you have the ACE, you can pass it to the Remove() method and commit the changes, as shown here:

```
object[] hiddenObject = (object[])this.lvwPermEntries.
                                        SelectedItems[0].Tag;

AccessControlEntry ace = (AccessControlEntry)hiddenObject.GetValue(1);

AccessControlList acl = new AccessControlList(util.SharedEntry);
acl.Remove(ace);

acl.CommitChanges();
```

Furthermore, if the InheritedObject is present, you can add it to the **Inherited From** column. The following screenshot shows two ACEs with permissions inherited from the User and Group objects in the schema.

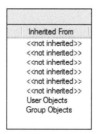

This has only been a quick walk-through of the implementation, and we would recommend that you download the code from the Downloads section of the Apress web site (http://www.apress.com) to work through this at your leisure.

Summary

In this chapter, you've looked in depth at how you can manage security for Active Directory objects. You began this chapter by revising some basic security concepts that are important for using Directory Services: *authentication* and *permissions*. Then you looked at such things as ACEs, which specify access rights, and the ACL, which is a container for ACEs.

You then moved on to explore the ADSI security interfaces, and you learned how to create a managed wrapper for these classes–the `Apress.DirectoryServices.Security` namespace.

Finally, you took a quick walk through the wrapper implementation in the Directory Browser application that you created in Chapter 2.

In this chapter you've seen

- ❏ How Windows security relates to .NET security

- ❏ How to perform authentication using the `System.DirectoryServices` namespace

- ❏ That Windows security uses ACEs and ACLs to manage permissions

- ❏ How to access the ACEs and ACLs of `DirectoryEntry` objects using the native ADSI interfaces

- ❏ That you can create a managed wrapper for these interfaces to simplify managing Active Directory security from .NET code

This chapter ends the first part of the book, which looked at all the concepts you need to know to use Directory Services from .NET code. The remaining chapters of the book look at a few practical scenarios where you can use Directory Services. In the next chapter, you'll see how you can use Directory Services to manage the users and groups in an Active Directory domain.

Part II

Directory Services in Action

6

User Management

Up to this point in this book, we've been looking at the basic techniques for working with Directory Services in .NET. You've seen how you can use the classes in the System.DirectoryServices namespace to search for and retrieve entries in a directory, and to add, update, and delete directory objects, and you've learned how to work with the Active Directory Service Interfaces (ADSI) through Component Object Model (COM) interop to access additional functionality, particularly security. We're going to spend the rest of the book looking in more detail at some real uses of .NET Directory Services.

We debated whether or not to call this chapter "Object Management" because users are really nothing more than objects in a directory service. However, users are quite possibly the most complex objects and are arguably the most important. Also, if we cover everything that you can do with a user, we will have covered the vast majority of things that you would want to do with any other type of object in a directory. So, in this chapter, the User object will be the object of choice in all our examples. In what follows, we will investigate the following topics:

- ❑ Creating a user

- ❑ Viewing and modifying a user's properties

- ❑ Creating groups

- ❑ Adding users to a group

- ❑ Listing user memberships and group members

- ❑ Deleting, disabling, and moving users

We'll begin with a brief overview of objects in a directory service, looking at the User object in particular.

Objects in Directory Services

There are many objects in a directory that you might need to manipulate. Virtually everything in a network environment can be represented as an object in Directory Services.

As discussed in Chapter 1, directory objects are exposed through ADSI as either *container objects* or *leaf objects*. Container objects can house other objects (both other container objects and leaf objects). In contrast, leaf objects cannot contain other objects and thus represent an end point of a particular "branch" of a directory tree. The User object is a leaf object whereas an *organizational unit (OU)* is a container object. An OU can contain other OU and User objects (actually an OU object can contain pretty much any directory object), but a User object cannot contain any other object. One might reasonably suspect that a group is a container object, but in fact, it is a leaf object. A group can have members, but it does not contain users as far as the *Directory Information Tree (DIT)* is concerned. You'll better understand the difference between membership and containment when we look at how you can assign group membership to a user later in this chapter.

There are a number of container objects. The following is a list of these as they are exposed by ADSI:

- ❑ Namespace
- ❑ Country
- ❑ Locality
- ❑ Organization
- ❑ Organizational unit
- ❑ Domain
- ❑ Computer

The following is a list of leaf objects exposed by ADSI:

- ❑ User
- ❑ Group
- ❑ Alias
- ❑ Service
- ❑ Print queue
- ❑ Print device
- ❑ Print job
- ❑ File service
- ❑ File share
- ❑ Session
- ❑ Resource

How these objects are organized in a directory depends almost entirely on how the directory has been designed. When you design a directory tree structure, you have a great deal of freedom: the only real limitation imposed by today's Lightweight Directory Access Protocol (LDAP)–compliant directories is that leaf objects cannot contain other objects.

The following diagram shows a directory with an OU (OU1) immediately below the root of the tree (in this case, the root is a domain). Because an OU object is a container object, it can contain any other container objects and any other leaf objects. So, in this sample DIT, OU1 contains a user, a group, a print queue, and another OU (OU2). Once again, because OU2 is a container object, it can contain other container objects and other leaf objects. OU2 contains a user, a group, and a computer object.

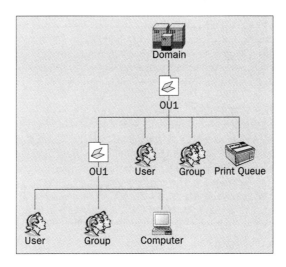

The User Object

The User object, which in many ways is just another object, is a special sort of object, and it will almost certainly be the focus of the vast majority of your Directory Services administration. User objects are useful because they can contain attributes that are used by network administrators, other users, applications, and services. Perhaps most importantly, a User object is a representation of an actual user–a real person–and these users are the reason why your directory service exists in the first place. (Of course, there may be exceptions to this; it is very likely that you will create user accounts that an application or a service uses exclusively.) The User object is the object that all your other objects revolve around; it is used for both security purposes and information distribution (as you will see in detail when you look at Microsoft Exchange Server in Chapter 8).

A directory service is an excellent place to maintain all the information about a user that you might need to track. Both Active Directory and Novell Directory Services (NDS) allow you to extend schemas in appropriate ways. This means that if you need to add your own custom properties to User objects (or any object, for that matter), you can. The directory service is an ideal place to track additional user information for three reasons:

1. A directory (or parts of a directory) is usually replicated on multiple servers at multiple sites, and it provides fault tolerance and speedy access to users and applications. You can, of course, accomplish this with a standard relational database that employs replication, but doing so would mean investing in additional hardware, software, and database administrators, not to mention development time and costs.

2. A directory service is secure—it is, after all, your main tool for controlling security on a network.

3. A directory service enables you to exploit existing technologies, hardware, and processes.

Precisely how you go about extending a schema depends on the directory service you are using and the way in which you needed to extend it; it is beyond the scope of this book. However, it is worth mentioning that extending a schema is not an operation you should take lightly. It can have far-reaching repercussions—on security, for instance—so make sure that you understand what you're doing when you extend it.

The User object has a vast number of properties, as you can see when you look at the property sheet of a user. Some of the more common properties of the User object, and the properties we tend to focus on in this chapter, are First Name, Initials, Last Name, Display Name, Office, Telephone number, E-mail, Web page, Address, UPN, sAMAccountName, Title, Department, and Manager. These are all informational properties, but the User object also stores functional properties such as the path to the user's roaming profile, logon hours, remote control information, terminal services profile, logon scripts, and information about the users Exchange account, if they have one.

The Sample Application and Your Development Environment

In this chapter, you will develop a fairly extensive sample application. So initially, you should make sure that you set up your development environment in the appropriate way. First, you should create a typical Directory Services environment into which you can put your user. In order to isolate the example from other things you might have created on your development server, you need to create an OU in the directory tree. It is in this OU that all your user manipulation will take place.

Some functionality in the sample code will not work against Directory Services other than Microsoft's Active Directory. For example, some code creates a group in the underlying directory service; it specifies a group scope and group type. Group scope and group type are Active Directory–specific and would therefore not be supported in an NDS directory. Having said this, all the sample code and examples in this chapter use LDAP, which is not Active Directory–specific. So, despite a few incompatibilities, you should still be able to utilize this code, which reveals one of ADSI's main advantages: it provides a set of interfaces for manipulating your network resources that are independent of particular Directory Services providers.

When we tested the following, we used a client machine that was a member of our domain. However, it is not necessary for it to be a member of a domain, as you will see later in the chapter. This code should run on any machine or operating system that has the .NET Framework installed.

We strongly discourage you from experimenting with .NET and ADSI code in a production environment. You don't want to spend hours trying to restore your Directory Information Base (DIB) from a backup and then have to try to force it to replicate out to other directory servers!

The Sample Application

First let's run through what your sample application is supposed to do. To do this, you'll need to take a brief look at the six forms of which it consists.

Complete code for this application may be downloaded from the Downloads section of the Apress web site (http://www.apress.com).

The initial form is called frmMain, which is essentially a menu that enables you to open the other five forms, which in turn enable you to perform various different Directory Services operations. frmMain looks like this:

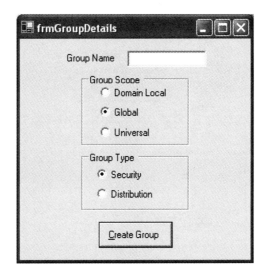

Because you will use the LDAP path in each of your directory operations, we have set up the following public constants in the initial form (frmMain) that you can use throughout the rest of the sample code. You will need to populate them with information specific to your development environment.

```
// The name of the server you wish to bind to
public const string strServerName = "ServerName";

// The name of the organizational unit that will be in your LDAP string
public const string strOU = "Dev";

// The third-level domain in your LDAP string
public const string strThirdLevelDomain = "internal";

// The second-level domain in your form
public const string strSecondLevelDomain = "apress";
```

```
// The top-level domain in your form
public const string strTopLevelDomain = "com";
```

Also, note that you must add a reference to the name System.DirectoryServices namespace to the top of each form:

```
using System.DirectoryServices;
```

The next form, the user form (frmUserDetails), does quite a lot. You can use this form to create new users, modify existing users, delete users, and disable or enable users. frmUserDetails also contains a list box that displays the Distinguished Name (DN) of any groups to which the user may belong.

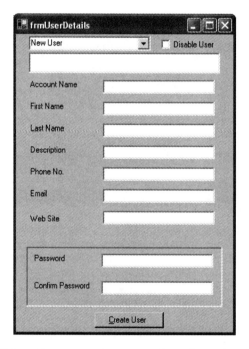

The buttons that are visible on the frmUserDetails form depend on whether you are creating a new user or modifying or deleting an existing user. Also, frmUserDetails contains a panel on which two text boxes (txtPassword and txtConfirmPassword) reside; these are enabled or disabled depending on whether or not you are creating a new user or modifying an existing user. If you are modifying an existing user, a check box displays that allows you to specify whether or not you will be modifying the password. If the box is checked, the password text boxes are enabled, the code behind the form checks to make sure the passwords exist, and the directory is updated.

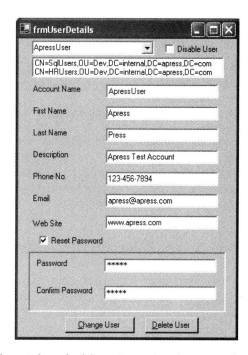

The `frmGroupDetails` form is launched from `frmMain` when you select the **Create Group** radio button and click **OK**. From there, you can create a group in the Dev OU, specifying its name, *group scope*, and *group type*. We will explain group scope and group type later in the chapter in the "Creating Groups" section:

The third form launched from `frmMain` is called `frmUserToGroup`.

This form lets you select a `User` object from the left list box (`cboUser`) and a `Group` object from the right list (`cboGroup`) box; it then lets you add that user to that group by clicking the **Add User to Group** button.

When you select **View Group Members**, the `frmGroupMembership` form is launched. This form lists the DNs of all the members of the selected group on form load in the combo box (`cboGroups`). In the following screen shot, you can see that we have selected the group **HRUsers** from the combo box. The application then enumerates the group's members and writes them out to the list box (`lstMembers`). In this example, `HRUsers` has two members, `TestUser` and `ApressUser`.

The final form is `frmMoveUser`:

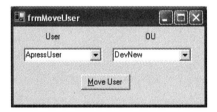

This form contains two combo boxes (`cboUser` and `cboOU`). `cboUser` is populated with a list of all users in your development OU (`OU=Dev`) at form load. `cboOU` is populated with a list of all OUs that are directly below the tree root. If you click the **Move User** button, the user `ApressUser` will move out of `OU=Dev` and into `OU=DevNew`.

Tools

No matter which directory service you are working with, we strongly recommend that you get hold of a tool that allows you to view the underlying objects and their properties. These tools provide an easy way to view the hierarchy of the whole directory service tree and to view all the properties of individual objects within the tree.

If you are working with Active Directory, an excellent tool to use is ADSI Edit. This tool lets you view the LDAP path and all of the properties of all the objects in Active Directory. ADSI Edit is one of the support tools available on the Windows Server CD.

Creating a User

Let's begin by investigating the creation of a user. In the sample code, this done in `frmUserDetails`, which is composed of a combo box (for listing existing users in your development OU), a check box (used to disable or enable the user), a list box (used to list the groups a user is a member of) and some text boxes (used for entering or changing user details).

Of course, the first thing you will need to do is determine the LDAP path to the object in which you want to create your user. You may want to configure this statically or use the path returned from a `DirectorySearcher` query. Since you spent some time investigating the `DirectorySearcher` in Chapter 3, we will simply set the LDAP path of your development OU to a variable so that you can set it to a `DirectoryEntry` object.

```
string ldapPath = "LDAP://" + frmMain.serverName + "/OU=" +
                  frmMain.ou + ",DC=" + frmMain.thirdLevelDomain +
                  ",DC=" + frmMain.secondLevelDomain + ",DC=" +
                  frmMain.topLevelDomain;
```

The contents of `ldapPath` will look like this:

```
LDAP://serverName/OU=Dev,DC=internal,DC=apress,DC=com
```

If you are writing code to work against Active Directory, you can use something called *serverless binding*. Serverless binding lets you specify an LDAP binding string that does not contain a server name. Windows 2000 Server and Windows Server 2003 have a locator service that finds the best domain controller for you.

The one proviso with using serverless binding is that the domain controller you use will always be in the default domain. This means that if you attempt to connect to Active Directory with serverless binding, your application will only be able to connect to domain controllers in the home domain of the user that is running the application (or the user that the application is running under). This might cause a problem if your application is running on a site where only domain controllers for Domain A reside under the security context of an account that resides in Domain B. In this scenario, the locator service will not find a domain controller from that security context's home domain and will therefore not refer your application to a domain controller on that site. A site is essentially equivalent to a local area network (LAN), so if you have a network with multiple LANs (or sites) connected via wide area network (WAN) links, the Windows locator service will ensure that your traffic stays within the LAN in which the user of your application is physically located.

Serverless binding is beneficial for two reasons. The first is that it prevents you as the programmer from having to determine what domain controllers exist, and which is the best one for each user of the application. In short, it eliminates the need for messy configuration files or Registry entries. The other reason is that it can significantly improve performance. The reason serverless binding can improve performance is that the Windows locator service will keep traffic within sites by finding a domain controller in the user's site if at all possible.

If you want to take advantage of serverless binding, simply drop the server name from your LDAP connection string, like this:

```
"LDAP://OU=Dev,DC=internal,DC=apress,DC=com"
```

The `DirectoryEntry` object (a component class of `System.DirectoryServices`) accepts the path of the object to which you wish to bind. Optionally, it also accepts a username, password, and authentication type. We will look at specifying a username, password, and authentication type later in this chapter (in the section on "Authentication and Authorization"). The `DirectoryEntry` object will serve as a representation of the object (whether it is a leaf or container object) that you bind to, and this will enable you to add or delete children and view or modify its properties.

You need to declare a `DirectoryEntry` object and pass it `ldapPath`. In addition, if you haven't already done so, you will need to add a reference to the `System.DirectoryServices` namespace.

```
DirectoryEntry ouEntry = new DirectoryEntry(ldapPath);
```

You can also set the path after calling the default constructor, like this:

```
DirectoryEntry ouEntry = new DirectoryEntry();
ouEntry.Path = ldapPath;
```

Next, create another `DirectoryEntry` object (we'll call it `newUser`) and set it to the result of the `Children.Add()` method, which is called on the `ouEntry` object. The `Add()` method accepts the required name of the object and the name of the schema class of the object that you want to create.

The following line of code creates a user object that is a child of `ouEntry` (or `OU=Dev`, as it is known in your directory). Its name is taken from the contents of the `txtAccountName` text box:

```
DirectoryEntry newUser = ouEntry.Children.Add("cn=" + txtAccountName.Text,
                                              "User");
```

At this point, the user only exists as an object in your code. You will need to set at least one property and then call the `CommitChanges()` method. The reason you need to set at least one property is that an object represented by the `DirectoryEntry` instance has one mandatory property: `sAMAccountName`. In Active Directory, the `sAMAccountName` is the username used by Microsoft clients prior to Windows 2000. Note that this property is only mandatory in Active Directory. Each directory service will have its own mandatory properties. In NDS, the object's `cn` is a mandatory property.

Some properties are multivalued while others are not. In order to reference a specific value in a multivalued property, you would need to use a zero-based subscript, much like you would with an array. We will look at how to address multivalued properties a bit later in the chapter.

So, to add the `sAMAccountName` property, you would execute the following line of code:

```
newUser.Properties["sAMAccountName"].Add(txtAccountName.Text);
```

Once the `sAMAccountName` is set,

```
newUser.CommitChanges();
```

will create the user in your directory.

However, at this point, your user will not be of much use to you: creating a user without setting the `userPassword` and the `userAccountControl` results in a disabled user.

Take a look at the property pages on your user management console; this should reveal the abundance of properties that you can set for a user:

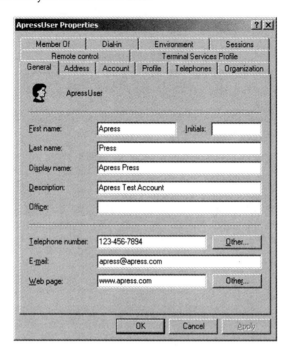

As we mentioned earlier, you can add custom attributes to a directory object. Applications that use your directory often do this. Microsoft Exchange Server 2000 is one such application. We will investigate some of the schema extensions Exchange makes to Active Directory in Chapter 8.

We have chosen some of the most common built-in properties to set here: first name, last name, display name, description, telephone number, e-mail address, home page, account name, and user principal name. The following code sets these properties, accepting the values from the text boxes. The property values are set to the text in the text boxes on the frmUserDetails form.

```
newUser.Properties["givenName"].Add(txtFirstName.Text);
newUser.Properties["SN"].Add(txtLastName.Text);
newUser.Properties["displayName"].Add(txtFirstName.Text + " " +
➥ txtLastName.Text);
newUser.Properties["description"].Add(txtDescription.Text);
newUser.Properties["telephoneNumber"].Add(txtPhoneNumber.Text);
newUser.Properties["mail"].Add(txtEmail.Text);
newUser.Properties["wWWhomePage"].Add(txtWebSite.Text);
newUser.Properties["userPrincipalName"].Add(txtAccountName.Text);
```

The final step before you call CommitChanges() is to set the user property flags and the user password.

For now you will set the user account bit to ADS_UF_NORMAL_ACCOUNT (which is 0X0200–the integer value &H200 or 512). This establishes the user as a normal type of account. Other types of accounts include accounts that don't require passwords, or accounts that have permissions to delegate.

ADS_UF_NORMAL_ACCOUNT comes from an enumeration in `frmUserDetails`. The enumeration originally came from `http://msdn.microsoft.com/library/en-us/netdir/adsi/ads_user_flag_enum.asp`. You will use a couple of the other user flags, from the same enumeration a little later in the chapter, in the section on "Modifying a User's Properties."

The user flag (`userAccountControl`) is just another property like `displayName` or `mail`, so you can set it in the same way that you would set any other flag:

```
newUser.Properties["userAccountControl"].Add(

ADS_USER_FLAG_ENUM.ADS_UF_NORMAL_ACCOUNT);
```

Once you have set all the properties you want your user to have, you can call `CommitChanges()` to take all the property values set on your user object in code, and then you can actually write them to your DIT.

```
newUser.CommitChanges();
```

The final step in the process of creating a new user is to set a password for the new account. The reason you did not call it before you called `CommitChanges()` is because you must use the `Invoke()` method to set the password; also, if you are using the LDAP provider, you cannot call `Invoke()` on an object that does not actually exist in your directory. This creates a problem if you have a minimum length password policy in your directory service. If you do, you may need to use a provider specific to your directory service. For example, if you are accessing Active Directory, you may need to use the WinNT provider, and if you are using NDS, you may need to use the NDS provider. In Active Directory, if you do not have a minimum password requirement (or if your minimum password length is zero), you do not have to set a password on your user account. If you do not , the user will be prompted to set one when they first log in.

Here is how you set the password:

```
newUser.Invoke("SetPassword", txtPassword.Text);
```

You do not need to call `CommitChanges()` after calling `Invoke()` to set the password. The methods executed by `Invoke()` are executed on the directory at the point at which they are called.

In the download code, another function checks to make sure the passwords entered in the `txtPassword` and `txtConfirmPassword` text boxes match, but you needn't concern yourself with that detail here, as it has nothing to do with Directory Services. (You can access the code from the Downloads page of the Apress website at `http://www.apress.com`.)

Error Handling

You probably need to include some error handling when you use `CommitChanges()`. There are a lot of reasons why you may not be able to create a particular user, and you need to accommodate this in your code. For example, you may need to conform to a specific password length and/or password complexity policy. Another common reason `CommitChanges()` may fail is that an object with the same distinguished name already exists. This, of course, is not allowed because each object's DN must be unique in the directory.

In any event, the point at which you invoke SetPassword() and call CommitChanges() is an obvious possible point of application failure, so you will want to take steps to prevent it from breaking.

As you can see in the sample code, we have placed CommitChanges() and SetPassword inside a try block:

```
try
{
    newUser.CommitChanges();
    newUser.Invoke("SetPassword", txtPassword.Text);
}
```

We also implement catch blocks for two more common exceptions. The first occurs if the user's DN already exists in the directory; the second occurs if a password requirement is violated.

```
catch (System.Runtime.InteropServices.COMException ex)
{
    MessageBox.Show(ex.Message, "Error",
                    MessageBoxButtons.OK, MessageBoxIcon.Error);
}

catch (System.Reflection.TargetInvocationException ex)
{
    MessageBox.Show("An error has occurred. It is possible that " +
                    "your password does not satisfy the password " +
                    "policy: " + ex.Message, "Error",
                    MessageBoxButtons.OK, MessageBoxIcon.Error);
}
```

And of course, you would always want to close your objects and set them to null. You will put this clean-up code inside your finally block, as shown here:

```
finally
{
    ouEntry.Close();
    ouEntry = null;
    newUser.Close();
    newUser = null;
}
```

Authentication and Authorization

ADSI enables authentication and authorization. This allows you to pass these tasks over to your directory service (since authentication and authorization are things that Directory Services does very well). Doing this provides for good security and single sign-on functionality. For Active Directory users, an application can authenticate users with Kerberos or NTLM.

The DirectoryEntry object allows you to specify a user ID and password as one of the parameters you pass when you create the object, or separately, after you have created the object.

For example, in your *Create User* example, you could have specified a username and password like this:

```
DirectoryEntry ouEntry = new DirectoryEntry(ldapPath, "username", "password");
```

or like this:

```
DirectoryEntry ouEntry = new(ldapPath);
ouEntry.Username = "username";
ouEntry.Password = "password";
```

You can also set one (or more) of 11 authentication types.

```
ouEntry.AuthenticationType = AuthenticationType;
```

If you do not specify a username and password, `System.DirectoryServices` will attempt to connect using the Windows credentials the user of the application has used to log in. If you are writing a web application, this user is the user that your web application runs under. You can configure this in the `machine.config` file.

You would be best off using Windows Integrated Authentication if possible. This reduces administrative overhead and gives the user the benefit of single sign on.

The 11 authentication types are defined in the `AuthenticationTypes` enumeration in `System.DirectoryServices`. The possible values are listed in the previous chapter.

You can specify the authentication type when you instantiate the `DirectoryEntry` object, like this:

```
DirectoryEntry user = new DirectoryEntry(ldapPath,
                                         userName,
                                         password,
                                         AuthenticationTypes.FastBind);
```

Sometimes you may need to set more than one authentication type—for example, when you use the `Sealing` authentication type, you also need to choose the `Secure` authentication type. In this case, you need to set the authentication types after you call the constructor. You would do this in the following way:

```
DirectoryEntry user = new DirectoryEntry(ldapPath);
user.Username = userName;
user.Password = password;
user.AuthenticationType = AuthenticationTypes.Sealing;
user.AuthenticationType = AuthenticationTypes.Secure;
```

Viewing a User's Properties

Viewing a user's properties is definitely the easy part of interacting with Directory Services. All that is required is that you bind to the user object and write out its properties.

When you created your user, you perform a bind to the OU and called the `Children.Add()` method. In this instance, you bind directly to the user object. Recall that you created the user in OU=Dev, DC=internal, DC=Apress, DC=com. If you add the name of the user object to the path to your OU, your LDAP string will give you this:

```
LDAP://serverName/CN=userName,OU=Dev,DC=internal,DC=apress,DC=com
```

Your sample application creates the LDAP path based on the selection the user has made in `frmUserDetails` in the combo box `cboUsers`:

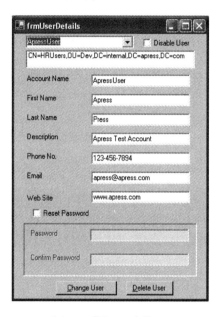

Thus, the string to bind to your `User` object will be as follows:

```
string ldapPath = "LDAP://" + frmMain.strServerName +
                  "/CN=" + cboUsers.Text +
                  ",OU=" + frmMain.ou +
                  ",DC=" + frmMain.thirdLevelDomain +
                  ",DC=" + frmMain.secondLevelDomain +
                  ",DC=" + frmMain.topLevelDomain;
```

In this example, `cboUsers.Text = "ApressUser"`.

You set your LDAP path to a `DirectoryEntry` in the same way that you did when you bound to OU=Dev.

```
DirectoryEntry user = new DirectoryEntry(ldapPath);
```

At this point, you can reference all the properties of the user object (with the exception of the `userPassword`). For security reasons, the `userPassword` is a property that you cannot read.

The sample application writes some of the values of the User object out to the text boxes on the frmUserDetails form.

```
txtFirstName.Text = user.Properties["givenName"].Value.ToString();
txtLastName.Text = user.Properties["SN"].Value.ToString();
txtDescription.Text = user.Properties["description"].Value.ToString();
txtPhoneNumber.Text = user.Properties["telephoneNumber"].Value.ToString();
txtEmail.Text = user.Properties["mail"].Value.ToString();
txtWebSite.Text = user.Properties["wWWhomePage"].Value.ToString();
txtAccountName.Text = user.Properties["sAMAccountName"].Value.ToString();
```

When you have done this, you can simply close user and set it to null.

```
user.Close();
user = null;
```

Modifying a User's Properties

Modifying a user's properties is really no different from programmatically changing the text in a text box. The only difference is that you must create an instance of a DirectoryEntry and bind it to the User object whose properties you wish to modify.

As you will see in the sample code, the previous section ("Viewing a User's Properties") was a bit of a setup for this section. In the previous section, you retrieved some properties of a User object and wrote them out to some text boxes on a form. In this section, you will take the values in those text boxes (whether or not they have been modified) and update the User object in the directory.

Once again, you will bind to your User object by creating a DirectoryEntry object and passing it the LDAP path to your User object. In this case, the username in the LDAP path comes from the Text property of the cboUsers combo box:

```
string ldapPath = "LDAP://" + frmMain.strServerName +
                  "/CN=" + cboUsers.Text +
                  ",OU=" + frmMain.ou +
                  ",DC=" + frmMain.thirdLevelDomain +
                  ",DC=" + frmMain.secondLevelDomain +
                  ",DC=" + frmMain.topLevelDomain;

DirectoryEntry user = new DirectoryEntry(ldapPath);
```

The next step simply reverses what you did when you viewed the user properties. Here you set the properties of your object to the values contained in the text boxes.

```
user.Properties["givenName"].Value = txtFirstName.Text;
user.Properties["SN"].Value = txtLastName.Text;
user.Properties["displayName"].Value = txtFirstName.Text + " " +
                                       txtLastName.Text;
user.Properties["description"].Value = txtDescription.Text;
user.Properties["telephoneNumber"].Value = txtPhoneNumber.Text;
user.Properties["mail"].Value = txtEmail.Text;
user.Properties["wWWhomePage"].Value = txtWebSite.Text;
user.Properties["sAMAccountName"].Value = txtAccountName.Text;
user.Properties["userPrincipalName"].Value = txtAccountName.Text;
```

It is probably rather unnecessary to change all of your properties at once, but for simplicity's sake, you will just set them all. The following code checks to see whether the `chkDisableUser` check box is checked and disables or enables the user depending on the check box's status.

```
if (chkDisableUser.Checked == true)
{
    // Disable the user
    user.Properties["userAccountControl"].Value =
                            ADS_USER_FLAG_ENUM.ADS_UF_ACCOUNTDISABLE;
}
else
{
    // Normal account
    user.Properties["userAccountControl"].Value =
                            ADS_USER_FLAG_ENUM.ADS_UF_NORMAL_ACCOUNT;
}
```

The preceding code uses an enumeration that contains the possible user account flags. The following code is the enumeration that we introduced earlier, in `frmUserDetails`.

```
public enum ADS_USER_FLAG_ENUM
{
    ADS_UF_SCRIPT = 0x0001,
    ADS_UF_ACCOUNTDISABLE = 0x0002,
    ADS_UF_HOMEDIR_REQUIRED = 0x0008,
    ADS_UF_LOCKOUT = 0x0010,
    ADS_UF_PASSWD_NOTREQD = 0x0020,
    ADS_UF_PASSWD_CANT_CHANGE = 0x0040,
    ADS_UF_ENCRYPTED_TEXT_PASSWORD_ALLOWED = 0x0080,
    ADS_UF_TEMP_DUPLICATE_ACCOUNT = 0x0100,
    ADS_UF_NORMAL_ACCOUNT = 0x0200,
    ADS_UF_INTERDOMAIN_TRUST_ACCOUNT = 0x0800,
    ADS_UF_WORKSTATION_TRUST_ACCOUNT = 0x1000,
    ADS_UF_SERVER_TRUST_ACCOUNT = 0x2000,
    ADS_UF_DONT_EXPIRE_PASSWD = 0x10000,
    ADS_UF_MNS_LOGON_ACCOUNT = 0x20000,
    ADS_UF_SMARTCARD_REQUIRED = 0x40000,
    ADS_UF_TRUSTED_FOR_DELEGATION = 0x80000,
    ADS_UF_NOT_DELEGATED = 0x100000,
    ADS_UF_USE_DES_KEY_ONLY = 0x200000,
    ADS_UF_DONT_REQUIRE_PREAUTH = 0x400000,
    ADS_UF_PASSWORD_EXPIRED = 0x800000,
    ADS_UF_TRUSTED_TO_AUTHENTICATE_FOR_DELEGATION = 0x1000000
}
```

The following code verifies whether the `chkResetPassword` box has been checked. If it has, it sees whether the passwords in `txtPassword` and `txtConfirmPassword` match and then resets the password.

```
if (chkResetPassword.Checked == true)
{
    //Set the password from the form
    user.Invoke("SetPassword", txtPassword.Text);
}
```

When you are finished setting all your properties, you need to call CommitChanges(). In the following code, we have implemented the same type of error handling that we did in the "Creating a User" section.

```
try
{
    user.CommitChanges(); //Commit the changes to the directory service

    // Check to see if the user has elected to reset the password
    if (chkResetPassword.Checked == true)
    {
        // Set the password from the form
        user.Invoke("SetPassword", txtPassword.Text);
    }
    // Inform the user that the change has been made
    MessageBox.Show("User " + txtAccountName.Text + " has been changed!",
                    "User modified",
                    MessageBoxButtons.OK, MessageBoxIcon.Information);
}
catch (System.Runtime.InteropServices.COMException ex)
{
    MessageBox.Show("An error has occurred: " + ex.Message, "Error",
                    MessageBoxButtons.OK, MessageBoxIcon.Error);
}
catch (System.Reflection.TargetInvocationException ex)
{
    // The invoke method failed for some reason.
    // For example, the password may violate a password policy
    MessageBox.Show("An error has occurred. It is possible that your " +
                    "password does not satisfy the password policy: " +
                    ex.Message,
                    "Error", MessageBoxButtons.OK, MessageBoxIcon.Error);
}
finally
{
    //Free resources
    user.Close();
    user = null;
}
```

Creating Groups

Because this chapter is all about user management, we considered leaving this section out. However, groups are an integral part of user management. Also, we decided to leave this information in so that you could see the similarities between creating a group and creating a user object. This comparison really reveals the way in which *everything* in your directory service is just an object with properties.

The code in this section is contained in the frmGroupDetails form. It allows you to select a group type of either Security or Distribution, and set the scope of the group to Domain Local, Global, or Universal, as shown in the following graphic:

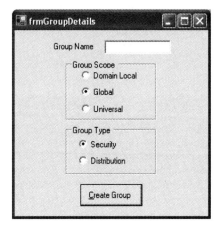

So, if a group is an object in the same way that a user is an object—that is, they differ only in the properties they are associated with—then it follows that you should be able to create the group in exactly the same way that you created the user.

To recap, the steps involved in creating an object are as follows:

1. Bind to the node in the DIT under which you want to create your object by passing the LDAP path to an instance of the `DirectoryEntry` object:

```
string ldapPath = "LDAP://" + frmMain.serverName +
                  "/OU=" + frmMain.ou +
                  ",DC=" + frmMain.thirdLevelDomain +
                  ",DC=" + frmMain.secondLevelDomain +
                  ",DC=" + frmMain.topLevelDomain;

DirectoryEntry ouEntry = new DirectoryEntry(ldapPath);
```

2. Create the object under that node by calling the `Children.Add()` method and setting it to another instance of the `DirectoryEntry` object. Note that here you are using the schema class `"Group"` instead of `"user"`:

```
DirectoryEntry newGroup = ouEntry.Children.Add("cn=" + txtGroupName.Text,
                                               "Group");
```

3. Set the various properties of that object as follows:

```
newGroup.Properties["sAMAccountName"].Value = txtGroupName.Text;
```

4. Call `CommitChanges()`:

```
newGroup.CommitChanges();
```

Again, a likely point of failure is when you call CommitChanges(), so we have included some rudimentary error-handling code that will catch all exceptions:

```
try
{
   newGroup.CommitChanges(); // Update the DIT

   // Inform the user that the update was successful
   MessageBox.Show("The group " + txtGroupName.Text + " has been created.",
                   "Group Created", MessageBoxButtons.OK,
                   MessageBoxIcon.Information);
}
catch (Exception ex)
{
   MessageBox.Show(ex.Message, "Error", MessageBoxButtons.OK,
                   MessageBoxIcon.Error);
}
finally
{
   // Free resources
   ouEntry.Close();
   newGroup.Close();
}
```

As mentioned earlier, Active Directory has groups with three different types of scope–Domain Local, Global, and Universal–and two types of groups–Security and Distribution.

The scope and type of an Active Directory group is a bit beyond the extent of this book, so we will only briefly describe them:

❑   A group with **Domain Local** scope can accept members from any domain but can only be granted access to resources in its home domain.

❑   A group with **Universal** scope can have members from any domain and can be assigned to resources in any domain.

❑   A group with **Global** scope can only have members from the domain that the group was created in, but it can be assigned access to resources in any domain.

❑   A **Distribution** group is used exclusively to distribute information to its members. You cannot use a Distribution group to grant or deny access to resources.

❑   A **Security** group type, on the other hand, is a group you can use to grant or deny access to resources. You can also use a Security group for distribution. Groups with any scope can be either a distribution group or a security group.

NDS only has one group type and makes no distinction between Security and Distribution group types.

In the following code, we use an enumeration to specify the group type in the sample code. In the sample code, you can find this enumeration in frmGroupDetails. Again, the enumeration originally came from MSDN at http://msdn.microsoft.com/library/en-us/netdir/adsi/ads_group_type_enum.asp.

```
public enum ADS_GROUP_TYPE_ENUM
{
    ADS_GROUP_TYPE_GLOBAL_GROUP = 0x00000002,
    ADS_GROUP_TYPE_DOMAIN_LOCAL_GROUP = 0x00000004,
    ADS_GROUP_TYPE_LOCAL_GROUP = 0x00000004,
    ADS_GROUP_TYPE_UNIVERSAL_GROUP = 0x00000008,
    ADS_GROUP_TYPE_SECURITY_ENABLED = -2147483648
}
```

The group types and scopes are fairly self-explanatory.

The default group type is Security and the default group scope is Domain Local. At least this is true, if you don't specify your group type and scope. To specify a group of a specific type and scope, you need to set the groupType property as shown in the following code.

This sample code assigns values from the enumeration to some integer variables based on the user's selections on the form. The values are then used to set the groupType property a little later in the code. (This code is still from the frmGroupDetails form.)

```
    // Set the Group Scope
if (optDomainLocal.Checked)
{
    groupScope = (int)ADS_GROUP_TYPE_ENUM.ADS_GROUP_TYPE_DOMAIN_LOCAL_GROUP;
}
else if (optGlobal.Checked)
{
    groupScope = (int)ADS_GROUP_TYPE_ENUM.ADS_GROUP_TYPE_GLOBAL_GROUP;
}
else
{
    groupScope = (int)ADS_GROUP_TYPE_ENUM.ADS_GROUP_TYPE_UNIVERSAL_GROUP;
}

// Set the group type
if (optSecurity.Checked)
{
    groupType = (int)ADS_GROUP_TYPE_ENUM.ADS_GROUP_TYPE_SECURITY_ENABLED;
}
else
{
    groupType = 0;
}
```

Once the integer variables have been populated, the code tests to see whether the group type is security or distribution and then assigns a value to the new group's groupType property.

```
    // Set the group type and scope
if (groupType == 0)
{
    // The group is a distribution group
    newGroup.Properties["groupType"].Add(groupScope);
}
else
{
    // The group is a security group
    newGroup.Properties["groupType"].Add(groupScope ^ groupType);
}
```

Note that if the group type is Security, you need to perform a bitwise XOR on the groupScope and groupType integer values. Once you have this value, you can use it to set the group's groupType property.

Of course, the final step is to call CommitChanges() and free up your resources.

Adding a User to a Group

To add a user to a group, you will need to bind to the Group object and call the Invoke() method, passing it the method name, Add, and the LDAP path of the User object. The sample code (frmUserToGroup) has two combo boxes: one that is populated with all the groups in OU=Dev (cboGroup), and one that is populated with all the users in OU=Dev (cboUser).

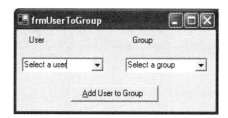

You can create two paths based on the user's selections in the two combo boxes: groupPath is the path to the Group object that the user will be added to, and strUserPath is the path of the User object you will assign to a group.

```
// The fully qualified path to our group object
string groupPath = "LDAP://" + frmMain.serverName +
                   "/CN=" + cboGroup.Text +
                   ",OU=" + frmMain.ou +
                   ",DC=" + frmMain.thirdLevelDomain +
                   ",DC=" + frmMain.secondLevelDomain +
                   ",DC=" + frmMain.topLevelDomain;

// The fully qualified path to our user object
string userPath = "LDAP://" + frmMain.serverName +
                  "/CN=" + cboUser.Text +
                  ",OU=" + frmMain.ou +
                  ",DC=" + frmMain.thirdLevelDomain +
                  ",DC=" + frmMain.secondLevelDomain +
                  ",DC=" + frmMain.topLevelDomain;
```

The next step is to bind to the group to which you want to add the user.

```
DirectoryEntry group = new DirectoryEntry(groupPath);
```

Once you are bound to your User object, you can add the user to your group by calling the Invoke() method and passing it the path to the User object.

```
group.Invoke("Add", userPath);
```

Your user is now added to the group, and all you have left to do is free up resources by closing group and setting it to null.

Listing a User's Group Membership

The sample code for this section (frmUserDetails) populates a combo box and, depending on the item selected in that combo box, populates a list box with a user's group. This is the same form you used to create and modify a user.

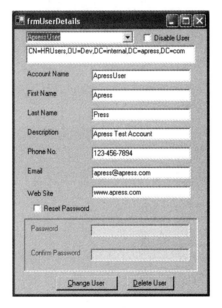

Recall that we mentioned multivalued properties earlier in the chapter. In order to list the groups to which a user object belongs, you will use the multivalued property memberOf.

Because this is a multivalued property, you will want to loop through it in much the same way you would with an array. As usual, you will bind to the object in which you have an interest. The sample code gets the username from a combo box called cboUsers.

```
string ldapPath = "LDAP://" + frmMain.strServerName +
                  "/CN=" + cboUsers.Text +
                  ",OU=" + frmMain.strOU +
                  ",DC=" + frmMain.strThirdLevelDomain +
                  ",DC=" + frmMain.strSecondLevelDomain +
                  ",DC=" + frmMain.strTopLevelDomain;

DirectoryEntry user = new DirectoryEntry(ldapPath);
```

Next, enumerate the list of groups and display them. Then write them out to a list box called lstGroups.

```
foreach (string strGroupName in user.Properties["memberOf"])
    lstGroups.Items.Add(strGroupName);
```

If you want to access one particular group name, you can do this using the zero-based index of the memberOf property, like this:

```
user.Properties["memberOf"][0];
```

A word of warning here—this method only lists the groups that a user is a member of in the user's domain. If your user is a member of groups in another domain, you will need to query the Global Catalog. Also, this method does not identify the user's primary group. For this, you need to read the primaryGroupID property of the User object.

Note that a Group object can be a member of another Group object. If you want to see what groups a Group object is a member of, you must simply query the memberOf property, just as you did for the User object.

Listing a Group's Members

The Group object has a multivalued property called member. This property stores the distinguished names of all the objects that are members of that Group object.

As always, you can start out by binding to the Group object. You can do this by passing its LDAP path to a DirectoryEntry object, as shown here:

```
string groupPath = "LDAP://" + frmMain.serverName +
                   "/CN=" + cboGroups.Text +
                   ",OU=" + frmMain.ou +
                   ",DC=" + frmMain.thirdLevelDomain +
                   ",DC=" + frmMain.secondLevelDomain +
                   ",DC=" + frmMain.topLevelDomain;

DirectoryEntry group = new DirectoryEntry(groupPath);
```

Once you have bound to the Group object, you can enumerate its member property in the same way that you did for your User object. The following lines of code retrieve the distinguished names of the Group object's members and write them out to a list box.

```
foreach (string memberName in group.Properties["member"])
    lstMembers.Items.Add(memberName);
```

Removing a User

Now that you know how to add a user to a group, view a user's group membership, and view a group's members, you need to learn how to remove a user from a group and how to delete that user entirely, or simply disable it. First, we'll show you how to remove a user from a group.

Removing a User from a Group

Removing a user from a group is pretty much the same as adding a user to a group, but you pass to Invoke() the method name of Remove instead of Add.

```
group.Invoke("Remove", userPath);
```

If the user is not a member of a group at the moment that you call Remove, a System.Reflection.TargetInvocationException will be thrown. Therefore, it is a good idea to make sure that this user is, in fact, a member of the group just before you call Remove. However, even doing this may not be sufficient. It is possible that someone (or some other application) will remove that user from that group between the time you check that it exists at the time you call Remove. This means that we should employ some error handling:

```
try
{
    // Removes a group member from the group object
    group.Invoke("Remove", userPath);

    // Inform the user that the member has been removed
    MessageBox.Show("Group member has been removed from " + cboGroups.Text +
        ".",
                "Group Membership",MessageBoxButtons.OK,
                MessageBoxIcon.Asterisk);

    // Remove the user from the list box
    lstMembers.Items.RemoveAt(selectedItem);
}
catch (System.Reflection.TargetInvocationException ex)
{
    MessageBox.Show("An error has occurred. It is possible that the " +
                "user you are attempting to remove is no longer " +
                "a member of that group: " + ex.Message, "Error",
                MessageBoxButtons.OK, MessageBoxIcon.Error);
}
finally
{
    // Free resources
    group.Close();
    group = null;
}
```

Deleting a User

In order to remove an object, you need to bind to the container object of the object you want to remove and call the `Children.Remove()` method. This operation executes immediately, and therefore, you do not need to call `CommitChanges()`. For the same reason, be careful when you are deleting objects.

You might wonder whether it is possible to remove a `User` object while the user is logged in to the directory and actively using resources. Somewhat surprisingly, you can. However, if you delete a user while they are logged in, that user will be able to stay logged in to their workstation but will immediately be unable to do anything that requires them to be authenticated against the directory.

In the following code, you will pass the `Children.Remove()` method a `DirectoryEntry` object that is bound to the object that you wish to remove. Once again, you will use the form `frmUserDetails`.

You can build the path to the user with the username in the `Text` property of `cboUsers`.

```
string userPath = "LDAP://" + frmMain.serverName +
                  "/CN=" + cboUsers.Text +
                  ",OU=" + frmMain.ou +
                  ",DC=" + frmMain.thirdLevelDomain +
                  ",DC=" + frmMain.secondLevelDomain +
                  ",DC=" + frmMain.topLevelDomain;

DirectoryEntry ouEntry = new DirectoryEntry(ouPath);
DirectoryEntry user = new DirectoryEntry(userPath);
```

To remove the object, simply call the `Remove()` method, and it's gone.

```
ouEntry.Children.Remove(user);
```

Calling the `Remove()` method is another place in your code where a failure is likely to occur, so make sure you use some form of error handling. Such a failure is apt to occur if the user has already been removed from the directory service; here is some error handling that tests for the exception that is thrown if this occurs:

```
try
{
    // Remove the user object
    ouEntry.Children.Remove(user);

    // Inform the user of the object deletion
    MessageBox.Show(cboUsers.Text + " has been removed.",
                "User Deleted", MessageBoxButtons.OK,
                MessageBoxIcon.Information);
}
catch(System.Runtime.InteropServices.COMException ex)
{
    if (ex.ErrorCode == -2147016656)
    {
        // The user object does not exist.
        MessageBox.Show("The user " + cboUsers.Text +
```

```
                            " does not exist in the Directory.",
                            "User does not exist",
                            MessageBoxButtons.OK, MessageBoxIcon.Error);
        }
        else
        {
            MessageBox.Show("An error was encountered deleting " + cboUsers.Text +
                            " " + ex.ErrorCode + " " + ex.Message, "Error",
                            MessageBoxButtons.OK, MessageBoxIcon.Error);
        }
    }
    finally
    {
        // Free resources
        user.Close();
        user = null;
        ouEntry.Close();
        ouEntry = null;
    }
}
```

You can use another method of the `DirectoryEntry` object, called `DeleteTree()`, to delete an object. As the name would imply, the `DeleteTree()` method deletes the object you are bound to and all objects below it in the DIT. If you are bound to a leaf object (such as a `User` object), there will be no objects underneath it, so the `DeleteTree()` method will remove only the leaf object.

> *Be careful when you use `DeleteTree()`. When you call this method, the object and the entire tree below it will be deleted! If you are bound to the wrong object, you may end up with serious problems on your hands.*

You do not have a safety net with `DeleteTree()`. If you do accidentally delete objects with this method, your only recourse is to restore the tree from backup. This can be a very messy job indeed, and it could itself have some serious repercussions. So, if you are going to use `DeleteTree()`, you may want to create your own undo method. For example, you could write a routine that enumerates an object and all objects below it in a tree, and records all the objects properties and the precise tree structure. This would allow you to create another routine that parses that file and re-creates the object in the directory.

Disabling a User

To disable a user, you must modify the `userAccountControl` property of a `User` object. As you have already seen, the `userAccountControl` is an integer property type that might have various settings that control many aspects of the user account other than disabling it.

The following is a list of some of the more common user control flags. These are from the enumeration that you have been using throughout the examples in this chapter.

ADS_UF_SCRIPT: Set this flag to execute the logon script. This flag cannot be read from or written to with the LDAP provider. For those of you with Active Directory or WinNT domains, use the WinNT provider.

ADS_UF_ACCOUNTDISABLE: Set this flag to disable the user.

ADS_UF_HOMEDIR_REQUIRED: Set this flag to require a home directory.

ADS_UF_LOCKOUT: Use this flag to check to see whether an account has been locked out; then reset it.

ADS_UF_PASSWD_NOTREQD: Set this flag to prevent a password from being required.

ADS_UF_PASSWD_CANT_CHANGE: Check this flag to see whether the user has the ability to change their password. This flag is read-only.

ADS_UF_ENCRYPTED_TEXT_PASSWORD_ALLOWED: Set this flag to allow the user to send an encrypted password.

ADS_UF_TEMP_DUPLICATE_ACCOUNT: Set this flag to make this account a local user account. When this flag is set, the user can log in to his own domain but not any domains that trust his domain.

ADS_UF_NORMAL_ACCOUNT: Set this flag on the User object to create a normal account. This would be a default-enabled user.

ADS_UF_DONT_EXPIRE_PASSWD: Set this flag to prevent the user's password from expiring.

ADS_UF_SMARTCARD_REQUIRED: Set this flag to require the user to log in with a smart card.

ADS_UF_TRUSTED_FOR_DELEGATION: Set this flag if you want the user account (or computer account) to be trusted for Kerberos delegation.

ADS_UF_USE_DES_KEY_ONLY: Set this flag to require the user to use the Data Encryption Standard (DES) algorithm to encrypt keys.

ADS_UF_PASSWORD_EXPIRED: This read-only flag indicates that the user's password has expired. You can use USER_INFO_3 to mark the user's password as expired for Windows NT and Windows 2000 users and you can use USER_INFO_4 to do this for Windows XP users.

Each of the flags has a hexadecimal value. The hex value of the ADS_UF_ACCOUNTDISABLE is 0x0202–514 in decimal. As mentioned earlier in the chapter, the ADS_USER_FLAG_ENUM, can be found in frmUserDetails.

To disable the user account, set the userAccountControl property to 0x0202, like this:

```
user.Properties["userAccountControl"].Value =
                              ADS_USER_FLAG_ENUM.ADS_UF_ACCOUNTDISABLE;
```

Then call the CommitChanges() method of your DirectoryEntry() object (in this case, user):

```
user.CommitChanges();
```

Moving a User to a Different Container

Sometimes you may need to move user objects to other containers. For example, if your OU structure is organized around departments, you will need to move a user to a different OU if she switches departments. For this example, we have created another development OU (OU=DevNew) into which you can move users. We put this at the same level as OU=Dev, but the new container could be anywhere in the directory hierarchy. In order to move your user object, you will need to create two DirectoryEntry objects. One will be bound to the user object you wish to move, and one will be bound to the object to which you wish to move the user.

In the following example, we have created a form (frmMoveUser) with two combo boxes (cboUser and cboOU). The form load event populates cboUser with all the users in OU=Dev, and cboOU with all OUs in DC=Internal.

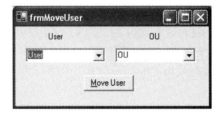

In the button click event, two LDAP strings are built. One is the LDAP path to the user you wish to move, as shown here:

```
string userPath = "LDAP://" + frmMain.serverName +
                  "/CN=" + cboUser.Text +
                  ",OU=" + frmMain.ou +
                  ",DC=" + frmMain.thirdLevelDomain +
                  ",DC=" + frmMain.secondLevelDomain +
                  ",DC=" + frmMain.topLevelDomain;
```

The other is the LDAP path of the destination object (which will only be an OU because the sample code filters on objectClass=organizationalUnit):

```
string destinationPath = "LDAP://" + frmMain.serverName +
                  "/OU=" + cboOU.Text +
                  ",DC=" + frmMain.thirdLevelDomain +
                  ",DC=" + frmMain.secondLevelDomain +
                  ",DC=" + frmMain.topLevelDomain;
```

Now that your two LDAP strings are built, you need to bind to the two locations in your DIT by instantiating two DirectoryEntry objects and passing them your LDAP paths:

```
DirectoryEntry user = new DirectoryEntry(userPath);
DirectoryEntry destination = new DirectoryEntry(destinationPath);
```

Finally, call the MoveTo() method of user, passing it the destination object (objDestination):

```
user.MoveTo(destination, name);
```

Note that the second argument of the MoveTo() method is the name of the object. This appears in the destination container, thus enabling you to rename it when it is moved. However, at the time of this writing, this does not work properly. If you specify a new name for the object, it does get moved and renamed, but an exception is thrown with the message Value cannot be null. We did find a post in microsoft.public.adsi.general from Microsoft Developer Support stating the following:

> I have been able to reproduce the problem. I will make sure the appropriate people are aware of this (if it hasn't already been fixed in later builds).

Summary

In this chapter, we looked at one of the most common tasks you will need to work with Directory Services—creating and managing users. We showed you how to

- ❏ Create a user
- ❏ Create a group
- ❏ Add a user to a group
- ❏ View a group's membership
- ❏ View a user's group memberships
- ❏ Disable and delete a user

Despite the fact that the sample code was written against Active Directory, ADSI (and hence .NET System.DirectoryServices) code is directory service–independent and can be executed against any LDAP-aware directory. Furthermore, the methods we discussed for manipulating a User object can be directly applied to all other objects exposed by ADSI.

7

Server and Resource Management

Active Directory provides you with powerful and flexible methods for managing servers and resources in a single information store that is globally accessible throughout an enterprise. Knowing how and when to use the directory effectively lets you develop applications that safely and conveniently store infrastructure information without the need for Registry entries, configuration files, or database tables, all of which can be difficult to manage and deploy.

In this chapter, we will investigate various tasks that can be accomplished using the .NET `System.DirectoryServices` namespace. Using various examples, we will show you how to discover directory objects and how to publish important information in Active Directory.

In brief, we will discuss the following topics:

- ❑ Creating computer accounts
- ❑ Discovering Flexible Single Master Operations (FSMO) servers
- ❑ Discovering domain controllers
- ❑ Discovering group policy objects
- ❑ Publishing Service Connection Points
- ❑ Creating custom resource classes and attributes
- ❑ Managing replication latency

❑ Discovering printers

❑ Discovering sites and servers

❑ Reporting

We will demonstrate each task using the Active Directory management tools–mainly the Microsoft Management Console (MMC)–to explain how to execute the task manually before we investigate how to do the same programmatically.

> *Note that for all the MMC examples, you must have the Windows 2000 Administration Tools Package (Adminpak) installed on your machine. When a server is promoted to a domain controller, most of the required tools will be installed. Alternatively, you can install the Adminpak from the I386 directory on the Windows 2000 Server CD.*

We will begin by showing you some of the basics of working with servers and resources in the directory. This will prepare you for what you'll be doing for the rest of the chapter.

> *The code examples we provided are for demonstration only. In production, you should include proper error handling in the code. The samples that are examined here may provide basic functionality, which you may expand as required.*

Creating Computer Accounts

In the Active Directory, each computer has an associated `Computer` object. A `Computer` object is a *security principal* that enables machine authentication. This means that if a `Computer` object is a security principal, a user cannot authenticate to a server, but a server can authenticate itself back to the user so that the user can be sure that she's dealing with the expected server. Also, the object allows servers to authenticate between themselves, which ensures secure communication.

A `Computer` object can also act as a container for other objects, including Service Connection Points. We will investigate the use of Service Connection Points in "Publishing Service Connection Points."

Using the MMC

The Active Directory Users and Computers MMC snap-in lets you create and manage computer accounts. Open the management console by clicking **Start | Programs | Administrative Tools | Active Directory Users and Computers**. Once this dialog box is open, right-click in the detail pane of the appropriate organizational unit (OU). This allows you to create a new `Computer` object.

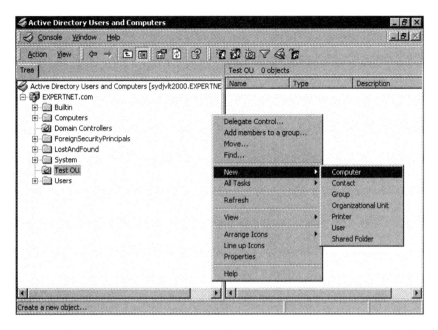

When you create the computer account, you need to specify a computer name and, for pre-Windows 2000 machines, a Windows Internet Naming Service (WINS)–compatible name.

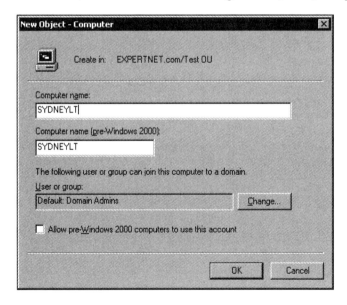

After you create the account, right-click the new Computer object in the object listing summary to specify additional properties (as shown in the following screenshot).

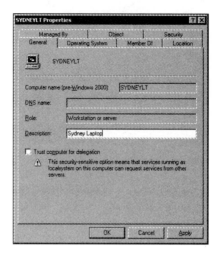

Creating Computer Objects Programmatically

Creating a Computer object via the System.DirectoryServices namespace is a very straightforward process. In the sample application, your form is designed to load up a list of OUs in which you can create the new computer account. Here is how this is done:

```
// Get the rootDSE object to determine the default naming context
DirectoryEntry rootDSE = new DirectoryEntry(" LDAP://rootDSE");

// Connect to the Global Catalog
DirectoryEntry root = new DirectoryEntry("GC://" +
    rootDSE.Properties["defaultNamingContext"].Value.ToString());
```

Here you can see the defaultNamingContext that you met in Chapter 2. Active Directory provides this value to accommodate connections to the root domain of the forest. In this example, the defaultNamingContext would be "DC=EXPERTNET,DC=com".

```
DirectorySearcher mySearcher = new DirectorySearcher(root);

// Search for all Organizational Units
mySearcher.Filter = "(objectClass=organizationalUnit)";

foreach (SearchResult ou in mySearcher.FindAll());
{
    // For each OU found, add it to the listbox for selection
    lbOUs.Items.Add(ou.GetDirectoryEntry().Properties
                        ["distinguishedName"].Value.ToString());
}
```

It is important that you note that in all the examples in this chapter that use the
`DirectorySearcher` object, whether you're using a Global Catalog query or a domain level
query, the searching root is determined using the `rootDSE` object and its
`defaultNamingContext` property. This allows the code to be environment agnostic and portable,
because it avoids having to hard code values.

You can change the filter–`objectClass=organizationalUnit`, in this example– if you need to
create the computer account under a different object, such as a container, rather than an OU.
Although we don't recommended doing this (a container is not a security principal and can't have
delegated administration nor can it have group policy applied to it), you can accomplish this with
minimal effort.

In the sample application from which the code has been taken, we can select the appropriate OU
and enter the required properties. The application will then create the computer account. The
required properties are `cn` and `sAMAccountName`.

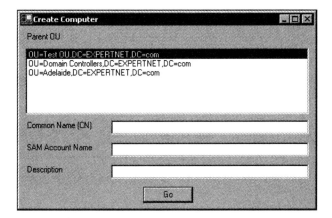

By default, when computer accounts are created, they are disabled. To enable them, set the
`userAccountControl` property, as you saw in Chapter 6. In this example, you are using a
number constant, whereas in Chapter 6, you used an enumeration.

Finally, call `CommitChanges()` to flush the cache and commit the operation to the directory.

```
// Get a reference to the selected OU
DirectoryEntry ou = new DirectoryEntry("LDAP://" + lbOUs.
    SelectedItem.ToString());
// Get a reference to the objects the selected OU contains
DirectoryEntries children = ou.Children;

// Create your new computer object
DirectoryEntry computer = new DirectoryEntry();

// Add the computer object to the OU's children collection
computer = children.Add("CN=" + txtCN.Text, "computer");
computer.Properties["sAMAccountName"].Add(txtSAM.Text);
computer.Properties["description"].Add(txtDescription.Text);
```

```
// Enable the new account
computer.Properties["userAccountControl"].Value = 544;

// Flush the property cache
computer.CommitChanges();
```

Discovering FSMO Servers

Within the Active Directory, many tasks lend themselves to a mutilmaster replicated model, where each server in a particular role is able to perform required tasks by itself but shares information with the all the other servers in that role. Adding additional domain controllers, for example, will eliminate the single point of failure that exists when there is only one domain controller on the network. When a server is promoted to a domain controller, it automatically receives a full replicated copy of the directory in order to service client requests.

Additionally, servers like print servers, file servers, and Global Catalog servers all lend themselves to redundancy. By having two servers run as Global Catalog servers, for example, not only will client response time be improved, but it will also ensure that if one server fails, another can still perform the required tasks.

There are server roles, however, that are best suited to reside on a single server. Operations like updating the Active Directory schema are best performed on an individual server, especially where replication collision could cause major system difficulties (have a look at the "Managing Replication Latency" section, later in this chapter, for a brief description of collisions). Any updates you make on these single servers will then replicate a read-only copy of the changes out to the other domain controllers in the forest.

Thus, you need a single server to take responsibility for the management of certain operations. Such a server takes on a **Flexible Single Master of Operations** (**FSMO**) role. There are five FSMO server roles within the directory, of which three are domain wide and two are forest wide:

> **Relative ID (RID) Master:** The RID Master ensures that each object within the directory (users, computers, etc.) has a unique identifier that becomes available when the object is created. The RID Master also works with RID Masters in other domains to ensure object uniqueness across multiple domains.

> **Domain Naming Master:** The Domain Naming Master controls all domain creations and deletions and makes sure that the domain structure information in the directory is kept consistent and up to date. The Domain Naming Master is a forest-wide FSMO.

> **Infrastructure Master:** Adding and deleting users from groups has serious security implications, and it is absolutely vital that user group membership is accurate at all times. The role of the Infrastructure Master is to maintain group membership additions, deletions, and changes. It also resolves conflicts when group membership changes are made at different locations within the replication window.

If there is more than one domain controller within the domain, do not *assign the Infrastructure Master role to a server that is also a Global Catalog server. This would prevent other domain controllers in the domain from seeing group membership changes.*

Schema Master: The Active Directory schema contains all the class and attribute objects that make up the directory. Each class or attribute object consists of various properties that are taken into account when objects are created and modified. Extending the schema for custom classes and attributes is a very serious operation and the directory needs to ensure that any modifications to the schema are controlled and consistent. A single server within the forest is responsible for handling schema extensions and modifications, and all changes can only be made on this server.

Primary Domain Controller (PDC) emulator: It is sometimes vital for Active Directory to interact with legacy clients, most importantly, Windows NT clients and servers. The PDC emulator services any requests from machines that expect a PDC to be present–this is something that doesn't exist natively in Active Directory.

It is essential to monitoring and health watch applications that they are able to identify these FSMO roles programmatically when you are using them to identify and analyze individual servers for availability of load. We will first show you how to identify these using the MMC before we show you how to access them programmatically.

Finding the RID Master with the MMC

You may locate the RID Master, PDC Emulator, and the Infrastructure Master with the MMC through the Active Directory Users and Computers snap-in. Open the MMC, and then right-click the Active Directory Users and Computers node. Select Operations Masters.

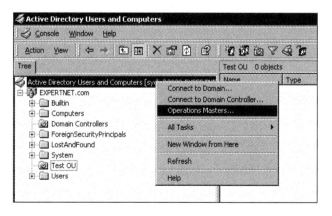

Each tab on the dialog box allows you to investigate and modify the server assigned to each role:

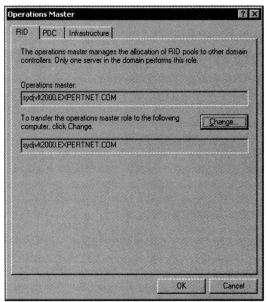

Programmatically Finding the RID Master

You can find the RID Master from code by executing a standard `DirectorySearcher` query, specifying an object class of `rIDManager` as the filter.

Note that the query is executed against the Global Catalog to find the RID Master for each domain in the forest. An individual domain can be specified for the RID, PDC, and Infrastructure Masters to discover the FSMO for that particular domain by changing the search root from GC:// to LDAP://.

```
// Get the rootDSE to determine the default naming context
DirectoryEntry rootDSE = new DirectoryEntry("LDAP://rootDSE");

// Connect to the Global Catalog
DirectoryEntry root = new DirectoryEntry("GC://" +
    rootDSE.Properties["defaultNamingContext"].Value.ToString());
DirectorySearcher mySearcher = new DirectorySearcher(root);

// Set the filter to the chosen role
mySearcher.Filter = "(objectClass=rIDManager)";

foreach (SearchResult res in mySearcher.FindAll())
{
```

Note that the search will return the actual FSMO role, which is a child of the actual server performing the role. So you need to get the role and then get the role's parent, which will be the server you are looking for:

```
    // If we are searching for a FSMO and not a domain controller,
    // we need to return the path of the parent and not the item
    // returned from the search

DirectoryEntry fSMOEntry = new DirectoryEntry("LDAP://" +
    res.GetDirectoryEntry().Properties["distinguishedName"].
                                        Value.ToString());

DirectoryEntry fSMOOwner = new DirectoryEntry("LDAP://" +
    fSMOEntry.Properties["fSMORoleOwner"].Value.ToString());

DirectoryEntry fSMOParent = new DirectoryEntry(fSMOOwner.Parent.Path);

lbResults.Items.Add(fSMOParent.Path);

}
```

When running, your application will present a dialog box. When you select a particular type of FSMO role, the application will specify the server that fulfills that role.

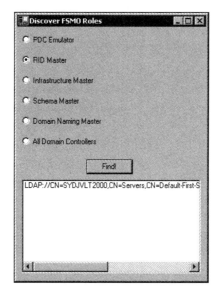

Programmatically Finding the PDC Master

The code you would use to locate the PDC Master is identical to the code you'd use to discover the RID Master, except the object class has been changed to domainDNS:

```
// Set the filter to the chosen role
mySearcher.Filter = "(objectClass=domainDNS)";
```

217

Programmatically Finding the Infrastructure Master

Again, the Infrastructure Master location code is identical to the previous code, except that the object class has been changed to `infrastructureUpdate`:

```
// Set the filter to the chosen role
mySearcher.Filter = "(objectClass=infrastructureUpdate)";
```

Finding the Domain Naming Master with the MMC

To find the Domain Naming Master in the directory, open the Active Directory Domains and Trusts snap-in. Right click the **Active Directory Domains and Trusts** node and select **Operations Master**.

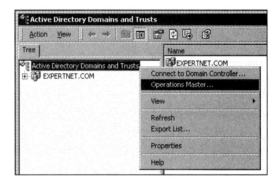

As with the other FSMOs, selecting the **Operations Master** menu choice opens a dialog box that will enable you to investigate and modify the server assigned to the role:

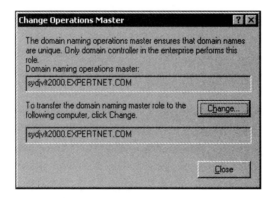

Programmatically Finding the Domain Naming Master

To find the Domain Naming Master, simply repeat the code you have been using for the other FSMO roles, except now specify an object class of `crossRefContainer`. Note that for the Domain Naming and Schema Masters, you have to specify the Global Catalog as the search root to discover the role owner (whereas for the other FSMO roles, searching on the Global Catalog is optional).

This is because these are forest-wide roles and searching on a domain will not return the server you're searching for.

```
// Set the filter to the chosen role
mySearcher.Filter = "(objectClass=crossRefContainer)";
```

Finding the Schema Master with the MMC

The Active Directory Schema snap-in is not available by default on standard Windows 2000 and 2003 Server installations. You must install the Adminpak as described in the beginning of this chapter and then open a generic MMC console (by clicking Start, Run, and typing mmc /a). From the generic console, click Add/Remove Snap-in and then click Add. Choose the Active Directory Schema snap-in and then Close.

To locate the Schema Master, open the Active Directory Schema snap-in. Right click the Active Directory Schema node and choose Operations Master.

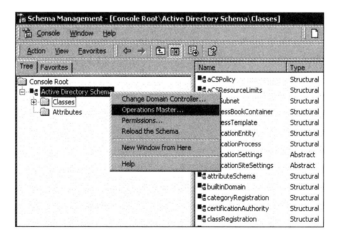

By now, you are familiar with the dialog box to view and modify the role owner. Note that to extend the schema (as you will see how to do later) you must check the box for The Schema May Be Modified On This Domain Controller because the schema is read-only by default.

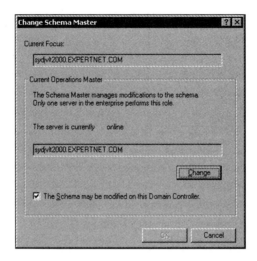

Programmatically Finding the Schema Master

As with the Domain Naming Master discovery code, to find the Schema Master, you have to specify the Global Catalog as the search root because it is a forest-wide role. The code is the same as it is for the other examples, except that you specify dMD as the object class for the search filter.

```
// Set the filter to the chosen role
mySearcher.Filter = "(objectClass=dMD)";
```

Discovering Domain Controllers

Domain controllers contain a complete replicated copy of the directory. They are responsible for network authentication, directory searches, account management, and so on. Querying for domain controllers allows you to do various administration tasks, including monitoring their health, executing directory operations with server affinity (see "Managing Replication Latency" for an explanation of server affinity), and making direct authentication requests.

Finding Domain Controllers with the MMC

When a server is promoted to a domain controller, its corresponding Computer object is moved to the domain controller's OU for that domain. After opening the Active Directory Users and Computers snap-in for the desired domain, click the Domain Controller OU to list all the available domain controllers.

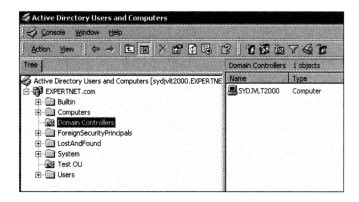

Programmatically Finding Domain Controllers

To locate domain controllers in the directory, you should conduct a standard DirectorySearcher query, as you have done previously, by specifying nTDSDSA as the object class for the searching filter. In the following example, note that the search is executed at the Global Catalog level to list all domain controllers in the forest. As with the other discovery operations you have looked at, you can change this query to specify a search domain, which will limit the scope of the domain controllers returned to the specified domain.

```
// Get the rootDSE to determine the default naming context
DirectoryEntry rootDSE = new DirectoryEntry("LDAP://rootDSE");

// Connect to the Global Catalog
DirectoryEntry root = new DirectoryEntry("GC://" + rootDSE.
               Properties["defaultNamingContext"].Value.ToString());
DirectorySearcher mySearcher = new DirectorySearcher(root);

// Set the filter to the chosen role;
mySearcher.Filter = "(objectClass=nTDSDSA)";

foreach (SearchResult res in mySearcher.FindAll())
{
// If you are searching for a DC (as opposed to an FSMO role),
// return its path

  DirectoryEntry fSMOEntry = new DirectoryEntry("LDAP://" +
          res.GetDirectoryEntry().Properties["distinguishedName"].
                                            Value.ToString());

  lbResults.Items.Add(fSMOEntry.Path);
}
```

Note that you do not have to return the object's parent in this example because you are searching for the domain controller object, and not a role that is owned by another object.

Discovering Group Policy Objects

Although this chapter is not meant to be an introduction to Active Directory administration, a small introduction to Group Policy is warranted.

As an organization and its network grow, one of the largest difficulties becomes managing individual desktop machines. Whole support departments are dedicated to helping users who have problems with their computers ranging from insufficient disk space to crashing applications and operating systems. Compounding the problem is the fact that most users want to have complete control over their own machine; this can be a particular problem because most end users do not have the proper training to modify most system and resource settings. Even if the user is properly trained, they might make changes that conflict with company policy, or—even worse—expose a security risk.

To help system administrators manage individual computers, Windows 2000 provides Group Policy objects (GPOs) that enable generic security and configuration policy to be applied to users and computers automatically based on account, group, or OU.

> Note that Group Policy cannot be applied to containers (as opposed to OUs) because they are not security principals. This is the main reason for not creating computer or user objects in the default user or computer containers.

GPOs can also be used to automatically deploy software on demand, thus eliminating another tedious and costly system administration task.

As you will see, when GPOs are created, they are stored in the file system (on the shared system volume, SYSVOL, which is replicated to all the other domain controllers in the domain), with basic discovery and description information stored in Active Directory. This provides you with the necessary information to connect to the GPO and explanatory properties. Using the MMC, you can examine the policy as a whole, but searching the directory will only provide summary information, which will allow for programmatic access to the appropriate file system.

Finding GPOs with the MMC

To view the GPOs in the directory, you must first open the Group Policy snap-in. After you click Start, Run, and type 'mmc', click Console and choose Add/Remove Snap-in.

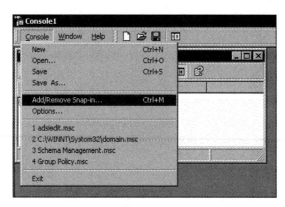

Then choose to add the Group Policy snap-in.

If you manage Group Policy objects for a domain, change the default GPO from Local Computer to the domain GPO by clicking Browse on the Select Group Policy Object dialog box.

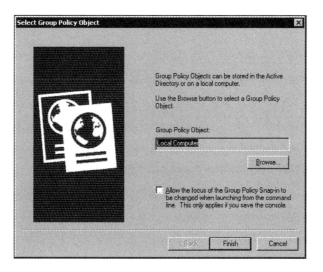

Select a policy to manage. In this case, this means you should choose the Default Domain Policy.

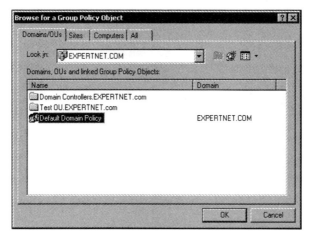

Now that the Group Policy snap-in is open, expand the chosen policy and browse through the available policy options.

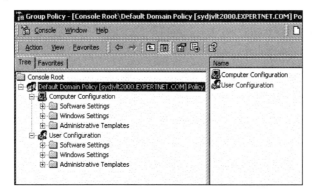

Programmatically Finding GPOs

As mentioned before, GPOs in Active Directory contain connection information for the actual policy in the file system. To search for the GPOs, execute the standard `DirectorySearcher` query you have used for other resource objects in the directory. Specify an object class of `groupPolicyContainer` for the query filter.

```
// Get the rootDSE to obtain the default naming context
DirectoryEntry rootDSE = new DirectoryEntry("LDAP://rootDSE");

// Connect to the Global Catalog
DirectoryEntry root = new DirectoryEntry("GC://" + rootDSE.
        Properties["defaultNamingContext"].Value.ToString());

DirectorySearcher mySearcher = new DirectorySearcher(root);

// Set the filter to the Group Policy class
```

```
mySearcher.Filter = "(objectClass=groupPolicyContainer)";

foreach (SearchResult groupPolicyObject in mySearcher.FindAll())
{
    // Add each found item to the listbox
    lbGPO.Items.Add(groupPolicyObject.GetDirectoryEntry().
                Properties["distinguishedName"].Value.ToString());
}
```

Once the GPOs are returned from the query, you can inspect them for description and discovery information. The optional Group Policy Container object attributes are as follows:

❑   PC File System Path (gPCFileSysPath)

❑   Display Name (displayName)

❑   Version Number (versionNumber)

❑   PC User Extension Names (gPCUserExtensionNames)

❑   PC Machine Extension Names (gPCMachineExtensionNames)

❑   PC Functionality Version (gPCFunctionalityVersion)

The most useful of these values is the PC File System Path, because it will provide information to locate the GPO in the SYSVOL share on the file system. This value also allows you to manage the actual GPO, using file system tools and classes.

After listing the GPOs, you can then get the properties for the actual object you have chosen. Note that you are simply ignoring empty properties. When an attribute is defined as optional in the schema, you can create the object with that attribute set to null. An error will fire if there is an attempt to retrieve such a null property. If you use proper Try/Catch blocks, you can ignore these errors.

```
// Connect to the chosen Group Policy object
DirectoryEntry gPOObject = new DirectoryEntry("LDAP://" +
                                lbGPO.SelectedItem.ToString());

// Clear the value text boxes

txtDisplayName.Clear();
txtVersionNumber.Clear();
txtUserExtensionNames.Clear();
txtMachineExtensionNames.Clear();
txtPCFunctionality.Clear();

// Ignore errors in case a property is empty (not the preferred method
// in production)
try
{
    // Add each value to the appropriate text boxes
    txtPCFileSysPath.Text = gPOObject.Properties["gPCFileSysPath"].
                                        Value.ToString();
    txtDisplayName.Text = gPOObject.Properties["displayName"].Value.
```

```
                                                            ToString();
        txtVersionNumber.Text = gPOObject.Properties["versionNumber"].
                                                    Value.ToString();
        txtUserExtensionNames.Text = gPOObject.Properties
                            ["gPCUserExtensionNames"].Value.ToString();
        txtMachineExtensionNames.Text = gPOObject.Properties
                            ["gPCMachineExtensionNames"].Value.ToString();
        txtPCFunctionality.Text = gPOObject.Properties
                            ["gPCFunctionalityVersion"].Value.ToString();
        txtPCFileSysPath.Text = gPOObject.Properties["gPCFileSysPath"].
                                                    Value.ToString();
}
catch (Exception e)
{
    // Handle any exceptions here
}
```

In your application, the returned values are displayed in the following way:

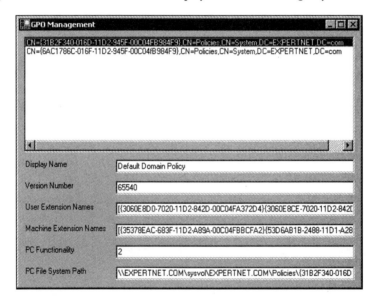

Publishing Service Connection Points

One of the most important functions of Active Directory is that it enables you to store resource location and connection information. Unfortunately, many developers do not understand the power and flexibility that the directory provides and continue to store resource information in flat files, Registry settings, XML configuration files, and database tables. This is not only insecure but may easily lead to errors. Such methods are also difficult to deploy and keep synchronized in a server farm scenario.

By publishing resource information in the directory, applications have a single location in which to find the necessary server resources that are available, including database servers, web servers, load balancers, message queues, and so on. Each resource entry can also access level security control applied so that application specific resources can only be discovered by the appropriate application. This also provides significant flexibility in a hosted environment, where one client application cannot be aware of another client's applications and resources.

Active Directory provides an abstract class named `connectionPoint`, which is the parent class for many structural classes. All objects that publish resource information should inherit from the `connectionPoint` class, as it provides the basic attributes needed for all resource information. The directory provides the following structural classes for publishing resource information:

Class	Purpose
Print Queue	For shared printers
Volume	For file shares
RPC Entry Points	For any service that is available via Remote Procedure Call (RPC)
Service Instances	For machine-level system services
Service Connection Points	A generic class for resource publication

These objects are very useful in enabling client applications to discover the resources they need.

As you will see later, you can create your own classes for publishing resource information. This is very useful if the classes that are included are not suitable for a specific purpose.

In this section, you are going to concentrate on creating Service Connection Point objects. You can create a Service Connection Point under a computer, container, or OU, but preferably, you should create them as children of the computer hosting the service.

The most useful properties of the Service Connection Point object are the multivalued properties: `keywords`, and `serviceBindingInformation`. Client applications need to search for required services using a keyword search, and then bind to the appropriate service using the binding information provided. You will see how to do this in the following example.

Publishing Service Connection Points with the MMC

To create Service Connection Points using the MMC, you must install the *Windows 2000 Support Tools* from the Support directory of the Windows 2000 Server CD. This package installs the ADSI Edit MMC console, which will allow you to create any type of structural class in the directory.

After you install and open the ADSI Edit MMC snap-in, navigate to the computer hosting the service that you wish to publish. Right-click the Computer object and choose **New**.

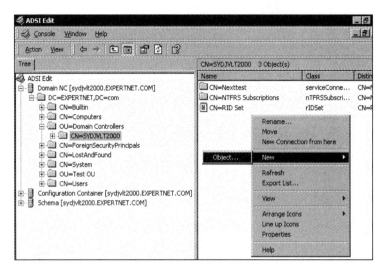

Next, choose the appropriate object class in the **Create Object** dialog box, which, in this instance, is serviceConnectionPoint:

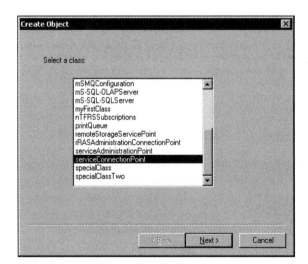

ADSI Edit will ask you to provide the mandatory properties of the desired class. In this example, cn is the only required attribute (here, your cn will be TestSCP, which stands for Test Service Connection Point).

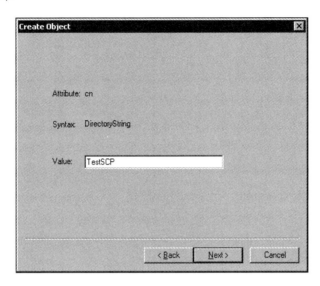

After entering the mandatory attribute values, you can set more attributes (keywords, serviceBindingInformation, etc.). In most instances, you will need to do this for the object you create to be of any value. Otherwise, applications could find your Service Connection Points, but the objects wouldn't provide any information for the application to use.

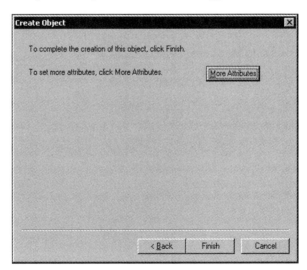

In the **More Attributes** dialog box, you can set optional properties.

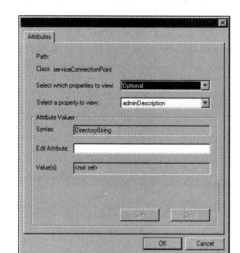

Now that you have created your Service Connection Point, applications can query it and use its properties to connect and consume the actual service.

Programmatically Publishing Service Connection Points

Being able to publish services in the directory gives you quite a bit of power and flexibility. Services can publish their information at runtime and can change their details on the fly. `Service Connection Point` objects are created in exactly the same way as other objects in the directory. As we mentioned in the last section, the most important attributes to set are keywords and `serviceBindingInformation`. In this example, you fill a listbox with all the values for those attributes and then add them to the value set of the object.

```
// Connect to the selected computer;
DirectoryEntry computer = new DirectoryEntry("LDAP://" +
                            lbComputers.SelectedItem.ToString());
```

Notice that you are initially connecting to a computer. As mentioned earlier, Service Connection Points should be created as children of the computer actually hosting the service. After connecting to the computer, you get the children collection and add your new Service Connection Points.

```
// Get the children of the computer to add the SCP
DirectoryEntries children = computer.Children;

// Add a new SCP to the children collection of the computer
DirectoryEntry serviceConnectionPoint = children.Add("CN=" +
                            txtCN.Text, cboSCPClass.Text);

// Flush the property cache
serviceConnectionPoint.CommitChanges();
```

Now that you have created the service connection point and committed the changes, you can set the optional properties of the object, which allow applications to find your service and connect to it.

```
// Set the optional properties
serviceConnectionPoint.Properties["serviceClassName"].Value =
                                          txtServiceClassName.Text;
serviceConnectionPoint.Properties["serviceDNSName"].Value =
                                          txtServiceDNSName.Text;
```

As you have seen, keywords allow applications to discover your service at runtime and service binding information allows you to connect to the service. For example, if you were to publish a load-balancing device, you would probably want to add the device name, manufacturer, model, and the words "load balancer" as keywords. For the service binding information, you would enter the machine name and the virtual IP of the balancer.

```
// Keywords and serviceBindingInformation are multivalued, so grab all
// entered values and add to the value collection of the property

for (int i = 1; i < lbKeywords.Items.Count; i++)
{
    serviceConnectionPoint.Properties["keywords"].Add(
                          lbKeywords[i - 1].ToString());
}

for (int i = 1; i < lbServiceBindingInformation.Items.Count; i++)
{
    serviceConnectionPoint.Properties["serviceBindingInformation"].
                Add(lbServiceBindingInformation[i - 1].ToString());
}

// Flush the property cache once more
serviceConnectionPoint.CommitChanges();
```

As with the service connection point you created manually, your service is now published and available for client applications to query and use.

Discovering Service Connection Points

To discover Service Connection Points, you search for serviceConnectionPoint objects with the appropriate keyword for the service required. Using your load balancing service example, you would search for "load balancer" by using appropriate keywords. This would find all Service Connection Points in the directory that point to load balancing devices.

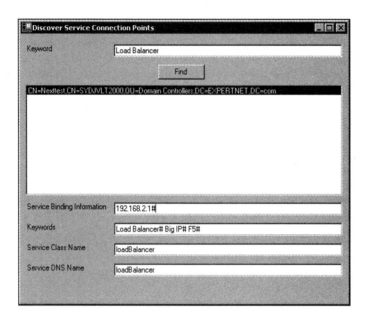

You can implement this in the following way:

```
// Get the rootDSE to determine the default naming context;
DirectoryEntry rootDSE = new DirectoryEntry("LDAP://rootDSE");

// Connect to the Global Catalog;
DirectoryEntry root = new DirectoryEntry("GC://" + rootDSE.
            Properties["defaultNamingContext"].Value.ToString());
DirectorySearcher mySearcher = new DirectorySearcher(root);

// If there is a keyword, use that as the search criteria, otherwise
// just return all SCPs
if (txtKeywords.Text != "")
{
    mySearcher.Filter = "(&(objectClass=serviceConnectionPoint)" +
                      "(keywords=" + txtKeywords.Text + "))";
}
else
{
    mySearcher.Filter = "(objectClass=serviceConnectionPoint)";
}

// Add the path for each found object to the listbox;
foreach (SearchResult groupPolicyObject in mySearcher.FindAll())
{
    lbSCPs.Items.Add(groupPolicyObject.GetDirectoryEntry().
            Properties["distinguishedName"].Value.ToString());
}
```

In this example, you simply search for Service Connection Points and then list their values. In a real application, after you find the Service Connection Points that meet the keyword criteria, you can query them to discover binding information that you can use to connect to and consume the service.

```
// Connect to the chosen service connection point;
DirectoryEntry gPOObject = new DirectoryEntry("LDAP://" +
                                lbSCPs.SelectedItem.ToString());

// Clear the text boxes
txtSBInfo.Clear();
txtKeywordList.Clear();
txtClassName.Clear();
txtDNSName.Clear();
```

Remember that when you get the optional attributes of an object, you need to make sure you handle the errors that are raised when the attributes are null.

```
// Ignore errors raised by empty values(not to be used in production)
try
{
  // Add all the keywords and delimit them with #
  for (int i = 1; i < gPOObject.Properties["keywords"].Count; i++)
  {
    txtKeywordList.Text = txtKeywordList.Text + "# " +
                        gPOObject.Properties["keywords"][i - 1];
  }

  // Add all the serviceBindingInformation and delimit them with #
  for (int i = 1; i < gPOObject.Properties
                    ["serviceBindingInformation"].Count; i++)
  {
    txtSBInfo.Text = txtSBInfo.Text + "# " +
          gPOObject.Properties["serviceBindingInformation"][i - 1];
  }

  txtClassName.Text = gPOObject.Properties["serviceClassName"].
                                          Value.ToString();
  txtDNSName.Text = gPOObject.Properties["serviceDNSName"].
                                          Value.ToString();
}
catch (Exception e)
{
  // Code to handle exceptions here
}
```

Note that because keywords and serviceBindingInformation are multivalued attributes, you can iterate through their values and populate the single text box with all appropriate information, delimiting the values with the pound sign (#).

As you can see, the output from the query gives you the information you need to consume the resource. Following your load balancer example, our application can now connect to the device using the IP address that is provided in the service binding information.

Creating Custom Resource Classes and Attributes

Upon installation, Active Directory provides a number of attributes and classes in the schema. Most of these attributes and classes will enable us to store and retrieve all the information of value to our applications, such as configuration information, start up values, user accounts, and so on.

There are, however, circumstances in which the attributes and classes that are provided do not provide all that is necessary for robust development. In these circumstances, we can extend the Active Directory schema with custom attributes and classes.

> *Extending the Active Directory schema is not an operation to be taken lightly; schema modifications are irreversible and permanent. As you saw when you looked at FSMO servers, the Schema Master is a forest-wide role, so any changes to the schema will be propagated throughout the enterprise. Creating custom extensions in a detached development environment is* highly *recommended.*

Here are some things that you need to become familiar with before you consider creating schema extensions:

Object Identifier (OID): The directory uses an OID to ensure that each and every class and attribute is unique. This number should be universally unique so that extensions can be migrated from one Active Directory forest to another without causing collisions. The Windows 2000 Resource Kit includes a utility called OIDGEN to provide an organization with a universally unique OID root for all classes and attributes. (In production, it is best to obtain an enterprise OID root from a naming authority, such as ANSI because maintaining the OID root yourself is the only way to ensure permanent uniqueness. OIDGEN uses Microsoft's root, which means that it is out of your control).

Abstract class: An abstract class in the schema is identical to an abstract class in many programming languages. It is a class that supplies a template for classes that inherit from it, providing them with required and optional attributes. An abstract class can't be instantiated.

Auxiliary class: An auxiliary class is a schema class that is attached to an existing structural class so that additional attributes can be stored on the existing class without modifying the class itself. For example, if you wanted to store birthdays for users, you could add an auxiliary class to the user class that has a birthday attribute.

Structural class: A structural class is created in the schema that inherits from another existing class. Objects can be created directly from a structural class.

Naming objects: These objects are classes and attributes added to the directory that have two name properties: Common Name and LDAP Display Name:

A **Common Name** should be unique and follow the following format: `Company-Product-Year-Object-Name`. For example, the previously mentioned auxiliary class for birthdays could be named `Acme-PhoneBook-2003-Birthday-Class`. You can add a version number to the end in your production environment.

An **LDAP Display Name** should follow this format: *companyProductYearObjectName*. In this case, your birthday class would be acmePhoneBook2003BirthdayClass. As with OIDs, all attribute and classes that are added to the schemas should have their Common Name and LDAP Display Name properly documented so that other developers and administrators can refer to them at a later time.

Creating Custom Resource Classes and Attributes with the MMC

Although we don't recommend using the Schema MMC snap-in to extend the Active Directory schema—because you have no way to control and duplicate the extension and, as a result, you do not have access to all the necessary properties—it can be done. You can do this only if you are in a development environment because the object global unique identifier (GUID) cannot be directly specified. The risk is that this could cause GUID collisions with other objects that already exist in the directory, which would render the schema useless when you migrated it to a production environment.

To extend the schema, right-click either the Classes or Attributes node and select Create Class or Create Attribute. For this example, first you will create a custom attribute called birthday, which is simply a string value.

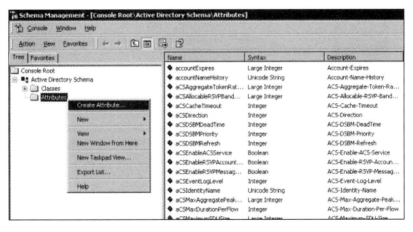

As mentioned before, you will be warned that such changes are permanent.

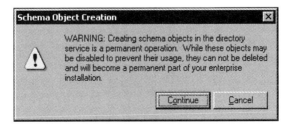

After you choose to create the new attribute, populate the necessary fields as we discussed earlier. The OID entered is provided by the OIDGEN utility. You can specify the syntax of a Unicode string because this is simply a free-form text attribute.

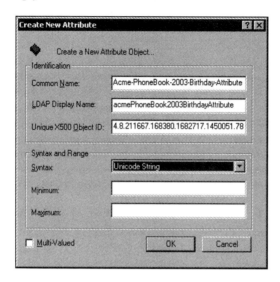

Now that your attribute has been created, you can create the auxiliary class that uses the new attribute.

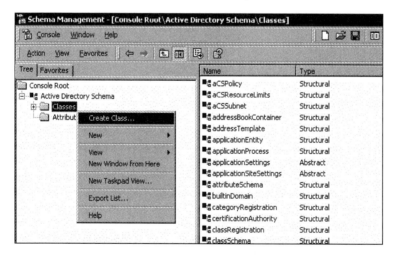

In the **Create New Schema Class** dialog box, you will find five available properties to set for the new class. However, you cannot export the values you supply at the time of entry. Instead, you can export them later using a tool called LDIFDE (LDIF stands for the Lightweight Directory Interchange Format), which we will discuss later in the section entitled "Schema Extensions with LDIF," but there is a good chance that you will forget to document the extension after it has been created. This makes it very difficult to migrate schema extensions from a development environment to a production environment and to maintain control when multiple developers are simultaneously making schema changes.

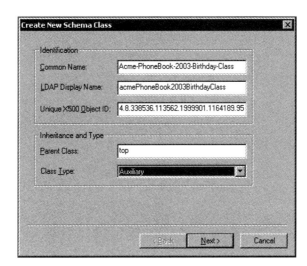

Now that your class has been created, you can add the birthday attribute to its Optional properties.

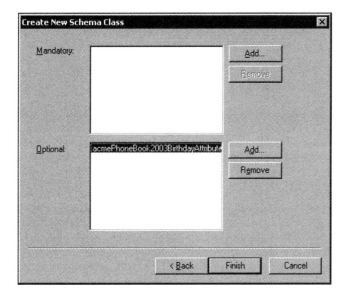

Programmatically Creating Custom Resource Classes and Attributes

As we mentioned earlier, you can use the MMC to create custom classes, but it is not recommended. In addition, it is unacceptable to use the MMC to deploy schema changes in staging and production environments.

A better option involves creating custom attributes and classes programmatically. This will allow you access to many more critical properties than the MMC, and your code can also be used repeatedly.

The code you will see momentarily creates a custom attribute in the schema. As discussed, you can create custom attributes to store values in the directory that aren't easily or properly stored using the attributes the directory provides by default.

Your application will allow you to control attributes via the following form:

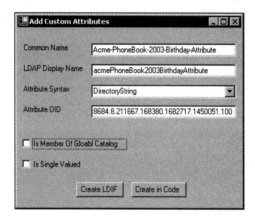

Note the following about this form:

❑ The attribute syntax has an associated oMSyntax. The sample allows you to choose the attribute syntax and it automatically chooses the associated oMSyntax. The oMSyntax is an integer that is the Extended Data Service (XDS) representation of the syntax. The combination of the attributeSyntax and oMSyntax properties determines the syntax of the attribute.

❑ The schemaIDGUID property is a binary GUID property. The System.GUID namespace allows you to create new GUIDs on the fly and convert them to the required binary format.

For a complete explanation of all properties and syntax, see "What You Must Know Before Extending the Schema" in the Active Directory Programmer's Guide, included in the ADSI SDK, available at http://www.microsoft.com/ADSI.

In this example, you create your birthday attribute in code. You have the option of either creating the attribute in code or producing an LDIF script for attribute creation. Here, you allow the creation to occur in code.

```
string attributeSyntax;
int oMSyntax;

// Get the needed values from the form;
string ldapDisplayName = txtLDAPDisplayName.Text;
string distinguishedName = txtCN.Text;
string attributeID = txtAttributeID.Text;
```

Note that if you want your attribute to be single valued or to be replicated to the Global Catalog, you can check those values on the form that set when the attribute is created.

```
bool isSingleValued = chkSingleValued.Checked;
bool isMemberOfGC = chkGC.Checked;
```

For clarity and brevity, the code that associates attributeSyntax with the relevant oMSyntax has been removed here. The associated code sample lists all the syntax associations.

```
// Declare a GUID array to set the schemaIDGUID property
byte[] guidArray();

// Create a new GUID
Guid guidID = Guid.NewGuid();

// Convert the GUID to a binary GUID
guidArray = guidID.ToByteArray();

// Get the rootDSE to determine the default naming context
DirectoryEntry rootDSE = new DirectoryEntry("LDAP://rootDSE");
```

Note that up until now you have been using the defaultNamingContext property of the rootDSE. Now you are going to use the schemaNamingContext, which allows you to dynamically connect to the schema.

```
// Connect to the schema root
DirectoryEntry root = new DirectoryEntry("LDAP://" +
    rootDSE.Properties["schemaNamingContext"].Value.ToString());

// Obtain the list of attributes
DirectoryEntries children = root.Children;

// Create an attribute object in the schema and
// set the appropriate properties
DirectoryEntry schemaAttribute = children.Add("cn=" +
                distinguishedName, "attributeSchema");
```

After adding the attribute to the children of the schema, you have to set the mandatory properties. Keep in mind that you are programmatically setting the oMSyntax. Refer to the complete code sample for the full picture. (You can download the code from the Downloads page of the Apress web site at http://www.apress.com.)

```
schemaAttribute.Properties["adminDisplayName"].Value = distinguishedName;
schemaAttribute.Properties["adminDescription"].Value = distinguishedName;
schemaAttribute.Properties["description"].Value = distinguishedName;
schemaAttribute.Properties["lDAPDisplayName"].Value = ldapDisplayName;
schemaAttribute.Properties["isSingleValued"].Value = isSingleValued.ToUpper();
schemaAttribute.Properties["instanceType"].Value = 4;
```

```
schemaAttribute.Properties["oMSyntax"].Value = oMSyntax;
schemaAttribute.Properties["attributeSyntax"].Value = attributeSyntax;
schemaAttribute.Properties["isMemberOfPartialAttributeSet"].Value =
                                        isMemberOfGC.ToUpper();
schemaAttribute.Properties["attributeID"].Value = attributeID;
schemaAttribute.Properties["schemaIDGUID"].Add(guidArray);

// Flush the property cache
schemaAttribute.CommitChanges();
```

Schema Extensions with LDIF

Finally, the best option for extending the directory is to create a LDIF file to import with the
LDIFDE utility. You will still encounter the same problems concerning the permanency of the
extension, but this LDIF file creates your extensions in a simple text file that can be versioned and
archived. It also makes migrating schema changes from a development environment to a
production environment fairly seamless. The LDIFDE tool is provided by default on all domain
controllers. You'll notice that the following code is very similar to the code you just used in
"Programmatically Creating Custom Resource Classes and Attributes" to create attributes and
classes, except for two important differences:

❑ The schemaIDGUID is converted to a Base64-encoded string, which is required for the
property in LDIF files.

❑ Instead of creating a new DirectoryEntry of class attributeSchema, the properties
are written out to a physical file that you can import later using the LDIFDE utility.

The difference from executing the extension in code is that here you create a text file in the file
system that you will import later. First create a new StreamWriter object, which will let you
create your file and output the values.

```
// Open a text LDIF file for output of the values
StreamWriter streamWriter = new StreamWriter(
        Application.StartupPath + "\" + distinguishedName + ".ldf");

// Send all values to the LDIF file;
streamWriter.WriteLine("dn: CN=" + distinguishedName + "," +
        schemaRoot.Properties["distinguishedName"].Value.ToString());
streamWriter.WriteLine("changetype: add");
streamWriter.WriteLine("adminDisplayName: " + distinguishedName);
streamWriter.WriteLine("cn: " + distinguishedName);
streamWriter.WriteLine("instanceType: 4");
streamWriter.WriteLine("isSingleValued: " + UCase(isSingleValued));
streamWriter.WriteLine("lDAPDisplayName: " + ldapDisplayName);
streamWriter.WriteLine("distinguishedName: CN=" + distinguishedName + "," +
        schemaRoot.Properties["distinguishedName"].Value.ToString());
streamWriter.WriteLine("objectCategory: CN=Attribute-Schema," +
        schemaRoot.Properties["distinguishedName"].Value.ToString());
streamWriter.WriteLine("objectClass: attributeSchema");
streamWriter.WriteLine("oMSyntax: " + oMSyntax);
streamWriter.WriteLine("name: " + distinguishedName);
streamWriter.WriteLine("showInAdvancedViewOnly: TRUE");
streamWriter.WriteLine("isMemberOfPartialAttributeSet: " +
                                        isMemberOfGC.ToUpper());
```

Note that you are working with the properties in much the same way you did to extend the schema in code, but for each property, you output the value to the file instead.

```
// In an LDIF file, the schemaIDGUID must be Base64 encoded
streamWriter.WriteLine("schemaIDGUID:: " +
                        Convert.ToBase64String(guidArray));
streamWriter.WriteLine("attributeID: " + attributeID);
streamWriter.WriteLine("attributeSyntax: " + attributeSyntax);
streamWriter.WriteLine("description: " + distinguishedName);
streamWriter.WriteLine("");
streamWriter.WriteLine("dn:");
streamWriter.WriteLine("changetype: modify");
streamWriter.WriteLine("add: schemaUpdateNow");
streamWriter.WriteLine("schemaUpdateNow: 1");
streamWriter.WriteLine("-");

// Close the file.
streamWriter.Close();
```

The resulting LDIF file resembles the one shown momentarily. Of course, yours will vary depending on your environment variables (domain name, configuration container location, etc.) and the name of the attribute you created. You can see how simple the LDIF format is and just how flexible the process of creating extensions in this manner can be.

```
dn: CN=Custom-Class,CN=Schema,CN=Configuration,DC=EXPERTNET,DC=com
changetype: add
adminDisplayName: Custom-Class
cn: Custom-Class
lDAPDisplayName: customClass
distinguishedName: CN=Custom-Class,CN=Schema,CN=Configuration,
➥ DC=EXPERTNET,DC=com
objectCategory: CN=Class-Schema,CN=Schema,CN=Configuration,DC=EXPERTNET,DC=com
objectClass: classSchema
name: Custom-Class
schemaIDGUID:: Wql4A7VgAUKKT75t2o2K/w==
description: Custom-Class
adminDescription: Custom-Class
governsID:
1.2.840.113556.1.5.7000.111.28688.28684.8.274447.471189.369869.1332068
subClassOf: serviceConnectionPoint
objectClassCategory: 1
possSuperiors: organizationalUnit
possSuperiors: computer
possSuperiors: serviceConnectionPoint

dn:
changetype: modify
add: schemaUpdateNow
schemaUpdateNow: 1
```

To import the file, use the LDIFDE utility. Click Start, Run, and type the following:

```
ldifde.exe -i  <filename.ldf> -s <SchemaFSMOServer> -v
```

241

The second modification block commits the addition immediately to the schema and causes a refresh. This is critical if you want to create a class immediately that references your newly created attribute. If you don't refresh immediately, the class will reference an object that doesn't exist in the schema until the next refresh, which might be a few minutes away.

Managing Replication Latency

Active Directory is a distributed directory service with a multimaster replication model. When a change is made on one domain controller, that change is replicated to all other domain controllers within the domain according to the site replication schedule. Although this design has many benefits that are immediately evident—such as high availability, increased performance, and reduced load—it does present a number of challenges for the application developer.

Three distinct problems arise when applications store information in the directory and that information is replicated to other servers.

Version skew: Version skew occurs when an object is modified in one location and has not replicated to all servers in the environment. This becomes a problem when a user connects to one server and then connects to a different server to read the changed information, but the change has not yet been replicated.

Partial update: Partial update occurs when an object has multiple attributes updated and is read while those attributes are being replicated. This causes some attributes to be current and others to be out of date. It is very uncommon for this to happen because object replication is fairly efficient, but if you keep the size of object updates to a minimum, you will reduce the risk even further.

Collision: A collision occurs when two updates are made to the same object in two different locations. Generally, this is not a problem for attribute updates, because the last update will win. Collision is more of a problem for object creation, where the object created first has its common name appended to its GUID.

These problems arise when you are using serverless binding, which is most commonly used when you are making LDAP calls. Using serverless binding allows you to make directory updates without specifying a server, and it lets Active Directory chose the operational server. Although serverless binding is very effective and efficient most of the time, for critical updates, we recommend that you use server affinity.

Specifying a particular server when making an LDAP call is known as server affinity. You can then use a specified server throughout the lifetime of the user's session, thereby ensuring that any updates are seen immediately.

There are many different ways of determining which server to use, the easiest of which is a random round-robin system. Other ways include using Windows Management Instrumentation (WMI) to determine load and discover the least utilized domain controller, and using a straight round-robin in which each domain controller is used consistently in turn. In the random round-robin scenario, you obtain the list of available domain controllers and choose a random server for use during the user session. The key is not to use the PDC Emulator for updates, as it is a high-load server and should be left to serve client authentication requests. Putting extra load on this server could have a detrimental effect on the performance of client logins and other authentication processes.

In this example, you are going to create a Computer object in a specified OU using server affinity. First, search for all OUs in which you can create the Computer object.

```
// Get the rootDSE to determine the default naming context
DirectoryEntry rootDSE = new DirectoryEntry("LDAP://rootDSE");

// Connect to the Global Catalog
DirectoryEntry root = new DirectoryEntry("GC://" +
        rootDSE.Properties["defaultNamingContext"].Value.ToString());
DirectorySearcher mySearcher = new DirectorySearcher(root);

// Filter for OUs to create the new computer object
mySearcher.Filter = "(objectClass=organizationalUnit)";

// Add all OUs to the listbox
foreach (SearchResult ou in mySearcher.FindAll())
{
    lbOUs.Items.Add(ou.GetDirectoryEntry().Properties
                        ["distinguishedName"].Value.ToString());
}
lbOUs.SelectedIndex = 0;
```

Now that you have a list of all the OUs, you can query all the domain controllers in the forest so that you can randomly choose one on which to create the new Computer object.

```
// Execute another search
DirectoryEntry domainRoot = new DirectoryEntry("LDAP://" +
        rootDSE.Properties["defaultNamingContext"].Value.ToString());
DirectorySearcher domainSearcher = new DirectorySearcher(root);

// Return all domain controllers
domainSearcher.Filter = "(objectClass=nTDSDSA)";
```

The key to the random round-robin method is to create a random number object you can use to pick a random domain controller in the list of domain controllers that you have just found. Remember that a DirectorySearcher call returns a number of objects that meet the search filter, and you can specify which item you want to obtain from that collection.

```
// Create a new random number to choose a DC
Random randomInt = new Random();

// Get the list of DCs
SearchResultCollection dcs = mySearcher.FindAll();

// Pick a random DC with the random number object
DirectoryEntry domain = dcs[randomInt.Next(dcs.Count)].
                                    GetDirectoryEntry();
```

Here, you simply set a label to the name of the discovered domain controller to show the user just which server you are going to use to create the Computer object.

```
lblDC.Text = domain.Parent.Properties["cn"].Value.ToString();
```

Create the Computer object in your chosen OU using server affinity. Note that instead of LDAP://DC=domain,DC=com, your example will use LDAP://servername/DC=domain,DC=com.

```
// Connect to the OU chosen on the single DC found by random;
DirectoryEntry ou = new DirectoryEntry("LDAP://" +
    lblDC.Text + "/" + lbOUs.SelectedItem.ToString());
```

Now that you have connected to the OU you need on a specific server, you can create the computer account as you have done before.

```
// Grab the children to add the new computer to
DirectoryEntries children = ou.Children;

// Create a new computer object in the OU
DirectoryEntry computer = children.Add("CN=" + txtCN.Text, "computer");
computer.Properties["sAMAccountName"].Add(txtSAM.Text);
computer.Properties["description"].Add(txtDescription.Text);
computer.Properties["userAccountControl"].Value = 544;
computer.CommitChanges();
```

Discovering Printers

When printers are shared from a computer, you may publish the printer in the directory. This allows users to search for printers within the organization, based on a number of search criteria. The most common criteria are name, location, and model.

Searching for printers in Windows is normally a straightforward matter. Clicking Start, Search, Printers presents you with a dialog box into which you can enter the necessary criteria for the printer that you want to find, or you can leave it empty in order to find all published printers.

Programmatically Searching for Printers

As with the search for the GPOs, the following code executes a standard DirectorySearcher query with a filter of the object class printQueue; it then populates the properties of each printer when it is chosen from the listbox on the form.

You can see that the initial query for all print queues is similar to other searching code you have seen. You can filter for objects of class printQueue and populate a listbox with the results.

```
// Get the rootDSE to determine the default naming context
DirectoryEntry rootDSE = new DirectoryEntry("LDAP://rootDSE");

// Connect to the Global Catalog;
DirectoryEntry root = new DirectoryEntry("GC://" +
```

```
        rootDSE.Properties["defaultNamingContext"].Value.ToString());
    DirectorySearcher mySearcher = new DirectorySearcher(root);

    // Set the filter to all printers
    mySearcher.Filter = "(objectClass=printQueue)";

    // Add each printer found to the listbox;
    foreach (SearchResult groupPolicyObject in mySearcher.FindAll())
    {
        lbPrinters.Items.Add(groupPolicyObject.GetDirectoryEntry().
                    Properties["distinguishedName"].Value.ToString());
    }
```

As with GPOs, when you choose a print queue from the listbox, the code connects to the printQueue object and then retrieves the necessary information.

```
    // Connect to the chosen printer
    DirectoryEntry gPOObject = new DirectoryEntry("LDAP://" +
                                    lbPrinters.SelectedItem.ToString());

    // Clear all text boxes
    txtPrinterName.Clear();
    txtServerName.Clear();
    txtShortServerName.Clear();
    txtUNCName.Clear();
    txtVersionNumber.Clear();

    // Ignore empty property errors (not to be used in production)
    try
    {
      // Fill each text box with the properties
      txtPrinterName.Text = gPOObject.Properties["printerName"].
                                                Value.ToString();
      txtVersionNumber.Text = gPOObject.Properties["versionNumber"].
                                                Value.ToString();
      txtServerName.Text = gPOObject.Properties["serverName"].
                                                Value.ToString();
      txtShortServerName.Text = gPOObject.Properties["shortServerName"].
                                                Value.ToString();
      txtUNCName.Text = gPOObject.Properties["uNCName"].Value.ToString();
    }
    catch (Exception e)
    {
      // Code to handle exceptions here
    }
```

Discovering Sites and Servers

In Active Directory, a site is a collection of machines that have fast connections between them. Sites allow machines to query for the closest domain controller, Domain Name System (DNS) server, file server, and so on. Sites also serve as the foundation of the replication infrastructure in the directory. *Intrasite replication* (replication within a site) is controlled automatically by Active Directory because the connectivity between machines is reliable and bandwidth is not a major concern. *Intersite replication*, on the other hand, requires administrators to set up site links and replication schedules to control replication. This is because connections between sites would be less reliable and slower.

Sites are published in DNS and also in the directory. The topology of a site is held in the directory, and details of the site links are stored in DNS. The following example queries for site link objects in the directory and then returns the list of computers in the site.

Finding Sites and Servers with the MMC

To view the sites and servers inside the directory, open the Active Directory Sites and Services MMC snap-in from the **Administrative Tools** menu.

Once the MMC is open, open the Sites node, followed by the site you want to investigate. Beneath each site is a Servers node that lists all computers within that particular site.

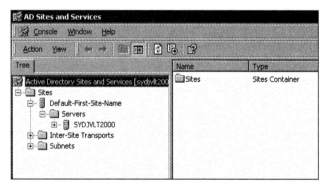

Programmatically Finding Sites and Servers

Locating sites and servers in the directory is simple. You can execute a standard DirectorySearcher query with a filter value of site.

```
// Get the rootDSE to obtain the default naming context
DirectoryEntry rootDSE = new DirectoryEntry("LDAP://rootDSE");

// Connect to the Global Catalog;
DirectoryEntry root = new DirectoryEntry("GC://" + rootDSE.
    Properties["defaultNamingContext"].Value.ToString());
DirectorySearcher mySearcher = new DirectorySearcher(root);

// Set the filter to the site class
mySearcher.Filter = "(objectClass=site)";
```

```
foreach (SearchResult siteObject in mySearcher.FindAll())
{
    // Add each found item to the listbox
    lbSites.Items.Add(siteObject.GetDirectoryEntry().
                    Properties["distinguishedName"].Value.ToString());
}

// Set a default selection;
lbSites.SelectedIndex = 0;
```

Once you have located all the sites and chosen one, you can open the Servers container under the site in the directory. The Servers container lists all computers within the site.

```
// Connect to the chosen Group Policy object;
DirectoryEntry siteObject = new DirectoryEntry("LDAP://CN=Servers," +
    lbSites.SelectedItem.ToString());

// Clear the list box
lbServers.Items.Clear();

// Add each server in the site to the list box
foreach (DirectoryEntry server in siteObject.Children)
    lbServers.Items.Add(server.Path);
```

Putting It All Together (Reporting)

One of the most powerful things that programming against the directory provides is the ability to compile reports of servers and resources and to deliver the reports in whatever format is most useful to us. The following sample code puts together all of the tasks that we have shown so far. It also adds some additional functionality. Here are the functions we have investigated so far:

❑   Searching for sites

❑   Searching for FSMOs

❑   Searching for Service Connection Points

❑   Searching for domain controllers

❑   Searching for GPOs

❑   Searching for printers

❑   Searching for OUs

The application that we've constructed to bring together all this functionality also includes the following functions:

❑ Searching for users

❑ Searching for computers

❑ Searching for groups

> *Be aware that running intensive reporting and querying functions against the directory can add significant load to the server being queried. If you frequently need to perform such tasks, consider installing a standalone domain controller/Global Catalog server that can act as a single point of contact for reporting functions.*

The following sample application allows the user to choose a number of Active Directory resources and servers. It returns the results of each search in the details box. The code can also be modified to output information in XML, flat file, HTML, database tables, or any other type of format.

> *You may download the code for the full application from the Downloads page of the Apress web site at* http://www.apress.com.

The main form of your application is constructed in the following way.

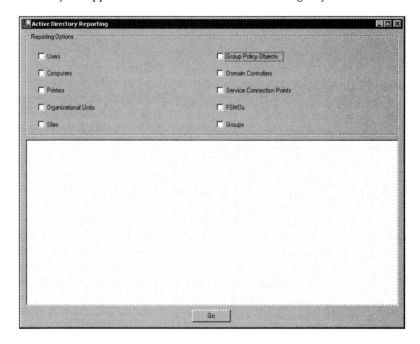

When the user clicks the Go button, the code checks the status of the check boxes provided and calls the appropriate procedures to report on the requested object types. For example, if the Users check box is chosen, the code evaluates the check box and then calls a FindUsers() method in the following way:

```
if (chkUsers.Checked)
    txtResults.Text = txtResults.Text + "\r\n\r\n" + FindUsers();
```

As you can see in the following section, the FindUsers method searches for all users by executing a DirectorySearcher query and specifying a filter for the User object class.

```
public string FindUsers()
{
  // -----------------------------------------------------------------
  // Method: FindUsers
  // Purpose: Searches for all users
  // Written by: Jamie M Vachon
  // Date 10/02/03
  // -----------------------------------------------------------------

  string userList = "User List" + "\r\n" +
      "-----------------------------------------------" +
      "-----------------------------------------------" + "\r\n";
  // Get the rootDSE to determine the defaultNamingContext
  DirectoryEntry rootDSE = new DirectoryEntry("LDAP://rootDSE");

  // Connect to the default domain;
  DirectoryEntry root = new DirectoryEntry("LDAP://" + rootDSE.
      Properties["defaultNamingContext"].Value.ToString());
  DirectorySearcher mySearcher = new DirectorySearcher(root);

  // Set the filter to users
  mySearcher.Filter = "(objectClass=user)";

  foreach (SearchResult res in mySearcher.FindAll())
  {
    userList += res.Path + "\r\n";
  }

  return userList;
}
```

This method returns all users in the forest and adds the results to the output text box.

By using the techniques shown in this section, you can easily report many different types of objects in the directory.

Summary

In this chapter, we have investigated various ways to manage server and resource information in Active Directory. Active Directory provides a very powerful mechanism for storing and retrieving data vital for application operation and network administration.

All servers and computers are stored in the directory, along with their associated roles. You can publish resource information in the directory using the built-in resource classes or extend the directory to create custom resource classes for your applications. You have seen just how simple it is to discover resources and printers in the directory using the `System.DirectoryServices` namespace.

In this chapter we showed you

- ❑ How to create computer accounts

- ❑ How to discover FSMO servers

- ❑ How to discover domain controllers

- ❑ How to publish resource information using Service Connection Points

- ❑ How to extend the schema to store custom resources

- ❑ How to discover resources

- ❑ How to discover printers

- ❑ How to discover sites and servers

- ❑ How to report on Active Directory resources

8

Exchange Administration

A common misconception among nonprogramming staff is that we have to live and work with the common tools that Microsoft provides. You can, however, accomplish all the everyday tasks in Exchange administration using either the Exchange System Administrator or the Active Directory Users and Computers MMC snap-in. But be aware that certain configuration settings, and more importantly, automation routines, are not available for the standard user interfaces. As a consequence, you must realize that class libraries can tune and tweak a server to its maximum performance and provide nice interfaces for automating common administrative tasks. You can also create custom tools to expose only particular functionalities to nonadministrative users, and thus let them access areas they need, but at the same time, keep the rest of the system secure.

In this chapter, we will explain how to

☐ Find your way around the Exchange Directory.

☐ Analyze the Active Directory schema and identify attributes and objects you need for Exchange Server programming.

☐ Create a filtered address similar to the Global Address List found in Microsoft Outlook.

☐ Create and map mailboxes to Active Directory objects.

☐ Delete mailboxes.

☐ Know when to use `System.DirectoryServices` and other Exchange Server programming APIs.

Directory Services programming changed fundamentally between Exchange 5.5 and Exchange 2000. Exchange 2000 is fully integrated into the Active Directory and shares a common object directory with Windows 2000. This means that you no longer have to make changes to connect to the right Lightweight Directory Access Protocol (LDAP) port, nor do you have to create separate accounts for Windows 2000 and Exchange.

On the other hand, certain simple Active Directory Services Interface (ADSI) programming tasks do not translate straightforwardly into `System.DirectoryServices`. By the end of this chapter, you will know which class library to turn to when `System.DirectoryServices` does not provide the functionality for what you need to do. In addition you will be introduced to the complementary class libraries CDO, CDOEX, and CDOEXM.

Navigating and applying filtered searches to the directory has never been easier. You will learn how to use the `DirectorySearcher` object to build both simple and complex queries against Active Directory and, in particular, against Exchange Server.

Introduction to the Exchange Directory

Quite a lot has changed with each new implementation of different versions of the Exchange Server and how they relate to Active Directory integration and the underlying management layers. Instead of having its own directory and synchronizing with Windows 2000 as Exchange 5.5 did, Exchange 2000 integrates with Active Directory.

Exchange Server has been split into two administrative parts: one part is concerned with configuration and the other is concerned with storage. Everything relating to configuration has been merged into Active Directory. This means that you can modify any settings available in Exchange using `System.DirectoryServices`. Entries related to Exchange Server can be found in the three naming contexts: Domain, Configuration, and Schema. The Schema holds the new Exchange-specific object types that are added to Active Directory when Exchange is installed. In addition, in Exchange 2000, Exchange 5.5 recipients have been transformed into Active Directory objects and can be found in the Domain naming context as Users, Distribution Groups, and Contacts, whereas server-related configuration resides in the Configuration Naming context.

The Exchange system focuses on message transport and storage. Mailboxes are kept in the Mailbox Store, but these are nothing more than storage areas. Each Mailbox is connected to an Active Directory object where any information such as e-mail addresses, names, direct reports, and custom attributes are stored.

You can compare the basic architectures of Active Directory and Exchange Server using the following diagram:

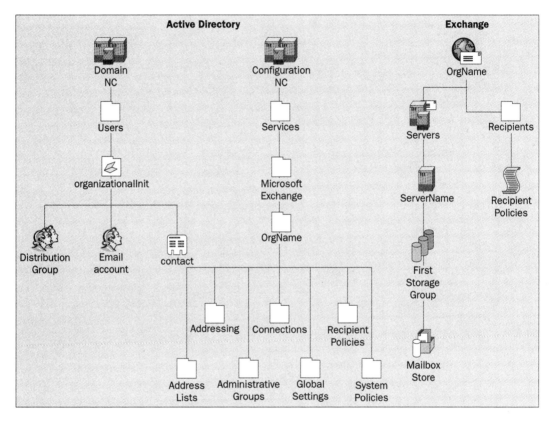

One of the most useful items in the Exchange developer's toolkit is ADSI Edit, a Microsoft Management Console (MMC) snap-in that enables us to browse and edit Active Directory objects.

Since Exchange 2000 now integrates into the Active Directory instead of running a directory of its own, there are no more LDAP port conflicts like those associated with Exchange 5.5. On the other hand, Exchange 5.5 was much easier to browse, because all the objects that were available in its directory were actually related to the Exchange Server; this is not the case with the Active Directory–integrated Exchange 2000 Server.

When you are browsing the directory, it is more important than ever that you know where to start looking. The following screenshot is from ADSI Edit. It shows the entry point for the Exchange 2000 configuration in the Active Directory. It provides you with a graphical representation that corresponds to the following LDAP path:

```
LDAP://servername.domain.com/CN=OrgName,CN=Microsoft Exchange,CN=Services,
CN=Configuration,DC=domain,DC=com
```

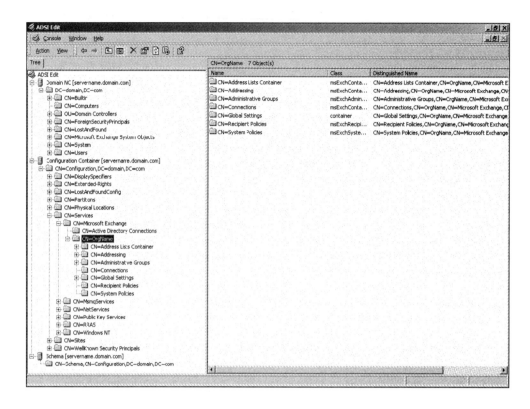

You will find most of the Exchange-related objects in one of four containers:

❑   Microsoft Exchange System Objects

    CN=Microsoft Exchange System Objects,DC=domain,DC=com

❑   Default Users container

    CN=Users,DC=domain,DC=com

❑   Microsoft Exchange Service

    CN=Microsoft Exchange,CN=Services, CN=Configuration,DC=domain,DC=com

❑   Schema

    CN=Schema,CN=Configuration,DC=domain,DC=com

You should remember that ADSI Edit is not only a simple tool for browsing the Active Directory, but it is also a powerful instrument for editing any of the properties of the objects contained within the directory. However, this easy use comes with a cost—if you change a property you find while traversing the directory, you might have disastrous consequences, depending on what property it is. In the Properties dialog box, shown here, find distinguishedName. This is one of the properties you should not meddle with unless you are absolutely certain that it will not ruin your system setup.

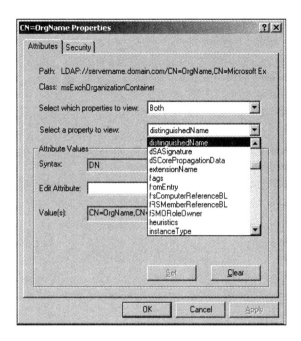

Mailboxes and Distribution Lists

Active Directory Users and Distribution Groups in Exchange 2000 are identical to what was known as Mailboxes and Distribution Lists in Exchange 5.5. This means that you no longer use the Exchange administrator to manage Mailboxes; instead, you use the Active Directory Users and Computers MMC snap-in, which should be familiar to you from Windows 2000. The only difference is that the `CustomRecipient` object is replaced by the equivalent Active Directory `Contact` object.

The following table illustrates Exchange 5.5 objects and their Active Directory equivalents.

Exchange 5.5 Object	Active Directory Equivalent
Mailbox	User
CustomRecipient	Contact
DistributionList	DistributionGroup

As we saw in the Chapter 6, an Active Directory group is either a security group or a distribution group. The main difference between these is that distribution groups are not security enabled, whereas security groups are. By being security enabled, a security group can be used to grant or deny permissions on objects in Active Directory. Although a security group can also receive e-mail, it is primarily used to apply access rights and results in a certain overhead when you are creating and calling upon the user security token. A distribution group is merely used to group users, and it will not affect the system performance at logon—or any other time. Therefore, it is recommended that you use distribution groups if your purpose is only to send e-mail to a collection of users.

Building an Exchange Management Application

In this chapter, we will show you how to develop code that will build the parts of a basic Exchange management application. The application is very simple: we focused on making it easier to understand and interpret rather than on its design. Therefore, it is intended for demonstration purposes only, and you should not use it in a live environment, although you may certainly use it as a starting point from which you can build such an application.

The project setup is simple; it has a main form from which you initiate all calls. We have used an extra form to help with data input and have devised two classes: DSTools.cs, which holds all functionality related to System.DirectoryServices programming, and OtherTechnologies.cs, which accommodates sample code for other class libraries related to Exchange programming.

Most of the functionality of this project resides within these two classes, and we have kept the logic in the form to a minimum. It is a good strategy to keep as much of your code as possible in classes; this makes it a lot easier to reuse.

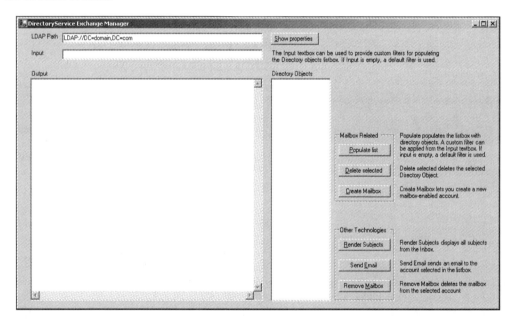

This sample application provides some of the functionality that you usually need a number of tools for. For instance, it allows you to create and destroy Active Directory objects as well as disconnect Mailboxes from Active Directory objects. You can use it to list all recipients in an organization or, if you prefer, to create your own filter to decide what objects should appear. Using this list of objects—or, if you prefer, using an LDAP path to an object—you can view the raw properties for any object. Finally, this application functions as a test bed for other examples in which we utilize functionality from other class libraries.

Retrieving a Mailbox

As stated earlier, a mailbox is nothing but an Exchange-enabled Active Directory object. Of course, some elements of the Exchange Store are still used, but these are related more to the actual storage of the mailbox, and they are not accessible via `System.DirectoryServices`. In the following section, you will see how to connect to a specific `User` object. A simple way for you to implement functionality to do this would be to bind to the object's LDAP path. However, this is not particularly friendly for the user and is not really how a production application like Microsoft Outlook would work. When you are searching for a recipient in the Global Address List, normally you want to use a name or e-mail address.

We will be using the same filter rule in this example as we will use later in the All Users address list example. In our code example, the filter will be hardcoded, but you might as well have connected to

```
LDAP://servername.domain.com/CN=All Users,CN=All Address Lists,CN=Address
Lists Container,CN=OrgName,CN=Microsoft
Exchange,CN=Services,CN=Configuration,DC=domain,DC=com
```

and pulled the `purportedSearch` attribute. This would be overdoing things since you are simply concerned with proving the concept of LDAP filters rather than trying to mimic the functionality of a messaging client.

Viewing the Attributes of a Directory Object

From here on, we will investigate code that you can use for a custom administrative application that you build with the `System.DirectoryServices` classes. One of the prerequisites of any administrative tool is its ability to view information about the objects that should be managed, so that is where we will start. You will build most of the functionality of this application into classes for easier transition between web-based and Windows-based applications. This way, you only have to reference the class for the core functionality and take care of user interaction in your Windows form or web page.

The following code places the properties of an object into a `String`, preparing the text to be displayed in a text box. This is a basic method and, for brevity, we have not tried very hard to address objects that you cannot convert to a `String` with the `ToString()` method. To make this more complete, you would have to call the `GetType()` method on each attribute object and treat it according to its object type. Based on the result from `GetType()`, you would then need to interpret the property value–from an octet string, for instance–and translate it into a proper string representation.

Another important feature of this code is that it demonstrates the difference between the properties of the `DirectoryEntry` object and the underlying properties available from the `Properties` collection attribute. Confusingly, the `DirectoryEntry.Name` property corresponds to an Active Directory Relative Distinguished Name (RDN) instead of the Active Directory attribute `Name`, which would have been more appropriate. The `DirectoryEntry.SchemaClassName` would let you know that the object is of the type `user`, whereas the `objectClass` for the returned object states that it belongs to the four categories `top`, `person`, `organizationalPerson`, and `user`.

```
public string DisplayDEProperties(string ldapPath)
{
  DirectoryEntry dirEnt;
  string tempOut;

  try
  {
    dirEnt = new DirectoryEntry(ldapPath);
  }
  catch(Exception ex)
  {
    ExceptionOutput += ex.Message;
    return null;
  }
```

`DisplayDEProperties()` takes an LDAP path as input and uses it to create a reference to the corresponding Active Directory object. The `try...catch` statement takes care of any errors in case of a mistyped LDAP path. If an exception occurs, its message is stored for later retrieval via a property on the class, and the method aborts and returns `null`.

```
tempOut=("Name\t\t= " + dirEnt.Name + "\r\n");
tempOut+=("Path\t\t= " + dirEnt.Path + "\r\n");
tempOut+=("SchemaClassName\t= " + dirEnt.SchemaClassName + "\r\n");
tempOut+=("\r\n");
tempOut+=("Properties:" + "\r\n");
```

When the Active Directory object is instantiated into a `DirectoryEntry` object, the `Name`, `Path`, and `SchemaClassName` properties of the `DirectoryEntry` object are dumped in order to compare them to the corresponding Active Directory object's properties that are enumerated here:

```
foreach(string key in dirEnt.Properties.PropertyNames)
{
  tempOut+=(key + "\t= ");
  foreach(object val in dirEnt.Properties[key])
  {
    tempOut+=("\t" + val.ToString() + "\r\n");
  }
}
return tempOut;
}
```

The two nested loops in the preceding code handle the property objects. The outer loop iterates through all the properties, whereas the inner loop makes sure that all items of a multivalued property are accounted for.

If you call `DisplayDEProperties()`, you should get results in an output similar to the following screenshot. This shows the properties of a `DirectoryEntry` object together with the corresponding raw Active Directory properties.

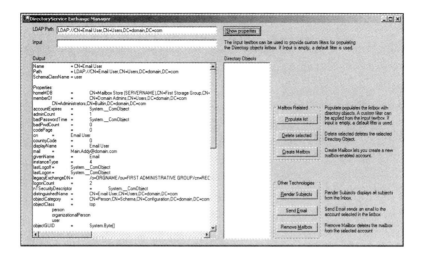

Searching for Mailbox-Enabled Objects

Designing tools that search and filter directories or databases is one of the most complex and critical tasks in application development. Fortunately, Microsoft has released the `DirectorySearcher` object to help you build applications that allow you to re-sort and parse filtered container objects.

One of the most commonly used tools for searching for Mailbox-enabled accounts, or if you prefer, e-mail recipients, is Outlook's Select Names dialog box, which pops up from the To... button in the message window. From here, you can choose from which address list you want to search for a recipient.

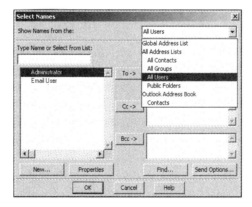

A `DirectorySearcher` object provides the simplest access to directory searching and, despite its simplicity, is extremely powerful.

As you saw in Chapter 3, the constructor of `DirectorySearcher` accepts a number of initial property values and one of these allows you to simply give the LDAP path of the search root. Once you have a valid `DirectorySearcher` object, you must specify a search filter. In the following snippet, we bind to the domain's root and search it for an object where `cn=Administrator`. The default search scope is to iterate throughout the entire directory to find objects that match the search criteria.

```
rootDSE = new DirectoryEntry("LDAP://RootDSE");
searcher = new DirectorySearcher(new DirectoryEntry("LDAP://" +
                   rootDSE.Properties["defaultNamingContext"].Value));
searcher.Filter = ("cn=Administrator");
```

Once the filter is applied, you need to call one of two methods to activate the search; FindAll() returns a SearchResultCollection of all matches in the directory, while FindOne() halts the search once the first item is found and returns a single SearchResult.

```
searchResults = searcher.FindAll();
```

The following filter string mimics the All Users address list of Outlook. After some dissecting, we are confident that you will have a lot of fun building filter strings optimized for specific corporate use. You can save a lot of time in searches by using the proper base filter!

```
(&(mailnickname=*)(|(&(objectCategory=person)(objectClass=user)
(&(objectCategory=person)(objectClass=user)
(|(homeMDB=*)(msExchHomeServerName=*))))))
```

Filter strings are covered in more detail in Chapter 3.

Our FindDirectoryObjects() method returns a SearchResultCollection object and depends on the receiving method to parse the returned object and extract useful information. A SearchResultCollection is, as its name suggests, a collection of SearchResult objects. The SearchResult object, in turn, is very similar to a DirectoryEntry object or, if you prefer, an Active Directory node. The main difference between DirectoryEntry objects and SearchResult objects is that each instantiation of a DirectoryEntry object yields a request to Active Directory, whereas SearchResult objects are stored in the SearchResultCollection cache. To make the method a little dynamic, you need to take the search root and search filter as input parameters. You can then use these to instantiate the DirectorySearcher object that provides the SearchResultCollection, as shown here:

```
public SearchResultCollection FindDirectoryObjects(string ldapPath,
                                                string searchCriteria)
{
  DirectoryEntry dirEnt;
  DirectorySearcher searcher;
  SearchResultCollection searchResults;

  try
  {
    dirEnt = new DirectoryEntry(ldapPath);
  }
  catch(Exception ex)
  {
    ExceptionOutput += ex.Message;
    return null;
  }

  searcher = new DirectorySearcher(dirEnt);
  searcher.Filter = (searchCriteria);
```

```
try

  {
    searchResults = searcher.FindAll();
  }
  catch (Exception ex)
  {
    ExceptionOutput += "\n";
    ExceptionOutput += ex.Message;
    return null;
  }

  return searchResults;
}
```

In the following code, we have chosen to trigger `FindDirectoryObjects()` from a button. This will use either a predefined search filter (the default), as defined earlier, or it will take the filter as input from the Input text box.

```
private void btnPopulate_Click(object sender, System.EventArgs e)
{
  int resultCounter = 0;
  DSTools propertyTool = new DSTools();
  String filterString = "";

  if (Input.Text == "")
    filterString = "(&(mailnickname=*)" +
                   "(|(&(objectCategory=person)(objectClass=user))" +
                   "(&(objectCategory=person)(objectClass=user)" +
                   "(|(homeMDB=*)(msExchHomeServerName=*)))))";
  else
    filterString = Input.Text;

  SearchResultCollection searchResults =
                propertyTool.FindDirectoryObjects(ldapPath.Text,
  filterString);
```

In the following code section, a `string` array—m_LdapPaths—keeps track of the LDAP paths of the objects (which, incidentally, are the same as an Active Directory DN, a `distinguishedName`) and adds its `DirectoryEntry` property name to a listbox. The array is synchronized with the listbox so that the listindex of an item matches the proper array index. In the case of retrieving the name property in the following code section, we know that there is only one entry, and thus we reference item 0 in the collection. Also, note the difference in the result between when we called the name property earlier and calling the name property on the `DirectoryEntry` object.

> *Objects are regularly identified by LDAP paths. An LDAP path is the same as an Active Directory DN, which is also known as a `distinguishedName`. In addition to DN, the LDAP path is also sometimes referred to as ADsPath. For a `DirectoryEntry` object, the property `Path` is the same as the LDAP path.*

```
m_LdapPaths = new String[searchResults.Count];
  try
  {
    foreach(SearchResult result in searchResults)
    {
      ResultPropertyCollection coll = result.Properties;
      DirectoryObjects.Items.Add(result.Properties["name"][0].
                                                    ToString());

      m_LdapPaths[resultCounter] = result.GetDirectoryEntry().Path;
      resultCounter++;
    }
  }
  catch (Exception ex)
  {
    Output.Text = ex.Message;
  }

}
```

Since the `DisplayDEProperties()` method takes care of all text formatting and prepares the directory object for display, you only have to call it and display the results in a textbox, `Output`.

```
private void DirectoryObjects_SelectedIndexChanged(object sender,
                                                 System.EventArgs e)
{
  DSTools propertyTool = new DSTools();

  Output.Text = propertyTool.DisplayDEProperties(
                  m_LdapPaths[DirectoryObjects.SelectedIndex]);
}
```

In this section, we have created the functionality to populate a list with Active Directory objects. Since the `SelectedIndexChanged()` method calls `DisplayDEProperties()`, properties for each object are displayed in the **Output** textbox as you move between the entries. This is illustrated in the following screenshot:

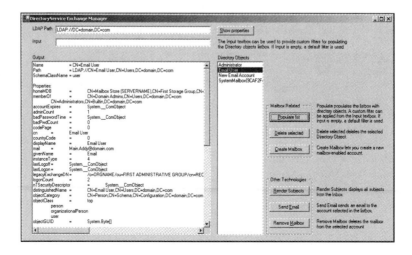

Creating a Mailbox

As a result of the consolidation of the Exchange directory and Active Directory, the process of creating a Mailbox object has changed and become much easier. You no longer have to synchronize separate objects by obscure, nonmatching IDs. We would not even talk about creating Mailbox objects, but rather mail- or mailbox-enabling a User or Group object in the Active Directory.

An Active Directory User object is normally not mailbox-enabled when it is created; you have to manipulate it a bit before you can use it to send or receive Exchange messages.

This example requires a reference to a COM component called *CDOEXM*, which we describe in more detail at the end of this chapter. For now, just know that it is a set of management interfaces for Exchange Server that combines the functionality of CDO and System.DirectoryServices into one administrative class library.

> *When you use CDOEXM in code, you might encounter a complication because it is only installed with Exchange 2000 Server. This means that you must run any code that references the CDOEXM library on the same computer as an Exchange server.*

You need CDOEXM in order to create a reference to an IMailboxStore interface; this is crucial when you go to map the User object to an information store. CDOEXM is a versatile tool, and much of what you can do with System.DirectoryServices and Exchange 2000 you can also do with CDOEXM. Apart from the regular parameters for creating a User object, you also need to know what homeMDB you want to map the mailbox to. The homeMDB property defines in what mailbox store and on which server the mailbox will reside. This corresponds to a physical location where the account's messages will be stored.

In a smaller organization, you often need to use the same syntax we used in the earlier example when we were searching for objects, but in a larger organization, you are apt to have a number of Exchange servers, and the mailboxes are apt to be distributed over several organization-specific storage groups, as shown here:

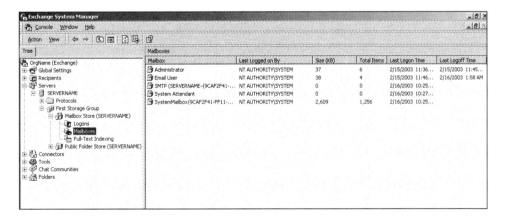

At the end of the following example we use the NativeObject ADSI representation of our user object to cast it into an IMailboxStore.

When you call `CreateMailbox()` on the CDOEXM object, you change the content of the hosting `DirectoryEntry`, which means that you must call `CommitChanges()` once again.

> *The user interface of Active Directory Users and Computers utility gives the impression that the user logon name, or its corresponding property, `userPrincipalName`, is mandatory. In Microsoft's course material, it is said that this value is one of the identifying keys of a `User` object in the Active Directory, but this is not really the case. You can verify this by using ADSI Edit; when you do, you will find `userPrincipalName` under the optional properties of any `User` object. The fact that `userPrincipalName` is optional can also be reflected in your code since it works flawlessly without the line that sets that property. Even though `userPrincipalName` is optional, you should make a habit of never leaving it blank because it is a cornerstone in Active Directory user management.*

```
using CDOEXM;

public void CreateMailbox(string fullName, string alias)
{
   DirectoryEntry container, user, rootDSE;
   IMailboxStore mailboxStore;

   string password = "newP@ssword";
   string domainName = "domain.com";
   string homeMDB = "CN=Mailbox Store (SERVERNAME),CN=First Storage Group," +
      "CN=InformationStore,CN=SERVERNAME,CN=Servers," +
      "CN=First Administrative Group,CN=Administrative Groups,CN=OrgName," +
      "CN=Microsoft Exchange,CN=Services,CN=Configuration," +
      "DC=domain,DC=com";
```

There are no big secrets about creating a mailbox-enabled account. Initially, you need to create a regular Windows 2000 account, as demonstrated in the following code.

```
   rootDSE = new DirectoryEntry("LDAP://RootDSE");
   container = new DirectoryEntry("LDAP://CN=Users," +
         rootDSE.Properties["defaultNamingContext"].Value);
   user = container.Children.Add("cn=" + fullName, "user");
   user.Properties["sAMAccountName"].Add(alias);
   user.Properties["userPrincipalName"].Add(alias + "@" + domainName);

   user.Properties["userAccountControl"].Value = 0x200;
```

The value `0x200` corresponds to the ADSI user flag ADS_UF_NORMAL_ACCOUNT, which means that this code represents a typical user account using default values.

Once you have created the regular Windows 2000 account, the fun begins. First you need to cast the `DirectoryEntry.NativeObject` to an `IMailboxStore` interface in order to call its `CreateMailbox()` method. `CreateMailbox()` creates a Mailbox in the specified storage and sets the homeMDB attribute of the account. Since `CreateMailbox()` modifies one of the attributes on the account object, you must call `CommitChanges()` to propagate the changes to Active Directory.

```
    user.CommitChanges();

    user.Invoke("SetPassword", new object[]{password});

    mailboxStore = (IMailboxStore)user.NativeObject;
    mailboxStore.CreateMailbox(homeMDB);

    user.CommitChanges();
}
```

Notice how there is no code for defining an e-mail address for the new recipient. However, you can use a feature called Recipient Policies that takes care of generating an e-mail address that complies with the corporate-wide standards. By default, this e-mail address is `alias@domain.com`. You can set this using the Exchange System Manager:

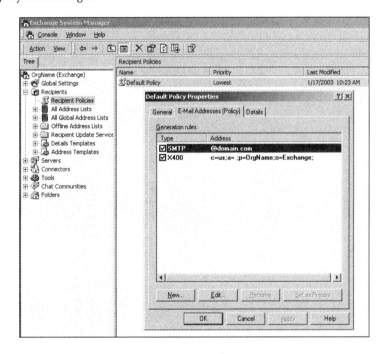

It is possible to generate multiple e-mail addresses for a user by following simple rules to define proxy addresses. For instance, `%d@domain.com` results in an e-mail address like `Email.User@domain.com` for an object with the display name `Email User`. If the new e-mail address conflicts with an existing e-mail address, an exception occurs and the operation halts.

The following table shows a few ways to define a proxy address template. For this example, we use an account with the first name `New`, a middle name `Email` and a last name `User`. Its display name is `New User` and its alias is `NewU`.

User Format String	Replacement String	Format String	Result
%g	First name	%g@domain.com	New@domain.com
%s	Last name	%s@domain.com	User@domain.com
%i	Middle name	%g.%i.%s@domain.com	New.Email.User@domain.com
%d	Display name	%d@domain.com	New.User@domain.com
%m	Mailbox	%m@domain.com	NewU@domain.com

You can easily change the Default Recipient Policy programmatically by modifying the following multivalued `gatewayProxy` property:

```
LDAP://servername.domain.com/CN=Default Policy,CN=Recipient
Policies,CN=OrgName,CN=Microsoft
Exchange,CN=Services,CN=Configuration,DC=domain,DC=com
```

It is still possible, however, to append additional e-mail addresses to a mailbox-enabled account by adding the following line:

```
user.Properties["proxyAddresses"].Add("SMTP:Specially.designed.addy@domain.com");
```

Any e-mail address related to the Recipient Policy is called a *proxy address*. A proxy address is also known as an *e-mail alias*, which is the more commonly used term on other platforms. If you open the property pages of a user, the proxy addresses are what you find on the **E-mail Addresses** tab along with the bold primary e-mail address. The primary e-mail address also appears on the **General** tab, and it is for this primary e-mail address that the other addresses serve as proxies. To modify an e-mail address, simple change the `mail` property, as shown in the following code line:

```
user.Properties ["mail"].Value = "Main.Addy@domain.com";
```

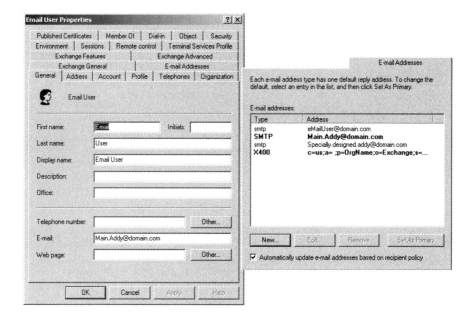

Deleting a Mailbox

Deleting an Exchange 2000 mailbox without removing its related Windows 2000 account is not as simple as it was with Exchange 5.5. Since the directories have been integrated into one, it is hard to take away one without the other. It is possible, but you nave to use a different class library. You will see how to do this with CDOEXM at the end of this chapter.

> *When you use* System.DirectoryServices, *you cannot delete a mailbox without deleting the related Windows 2000 account.*

For now, take a look at an example of how to remove an entire user account, including the mailbox. You have already encountered this type of code elsewhere in the book, since this is a standard way of deleting a known directory object.

```
public void DeleteMailbox(string ldapPath)
{
  DirectoryEntry trash = new DirectoryEntry(ldapPath);
  DirectoryEntry parentObject = trash.Parent;
  parentObject.Children.Remove(trash);
}
```

Alternatively, you can simply hide the Mailbox from the address lists. That way the Mailbox becomes invisible to the Exchange users and no additional messages appear. On the other hand, hiding the Mailbox does not get rid of the megabytes of messages that the Mailbox stores: it still functions normally, it just doesn't show up in any address lists, such as the one used in Outlook.

By setting the attribute msExchHideFromAddressLists to true, you hide the Mailbox from any address list. The Mailbox still function like any other, and the user will not notice any difference, except for the lack of incoming messages.

Typically, a hidden Mailbox functions as a send-only Mailbox.

```
public void HideMailbox(String ldapPath)
{
  DirectoryEntry user = new DirectoryEntry(ldapPath);

  user.Properties["msExchHideFromAddressLists"].Value = true;
  user.CommitChanges();
}
```

Connecting to Exchange Without DirectoryServices

Although this book should cover things from a System.DirectoryServices perspective, these classes are not always the easiest to implement, nor are they always the recommended solution for Exchange development. You can use one of a host of other programming interfaces; we will briefly cover some of the more common ones in the following pages.

Using CDO

CDO is short for *Collaboration Data Objects* and was first introduced as OLE Messaging. After that, there was a brief period when it was called Active Messaging, before it finally became CDO. CDO is the technology of choice for those who build applications with messaging capabilities. You can, for example, use CDO to create, send, and receive e-mails or simply to create new appointments in the corporate Exchange Calendar. It is also used to store and display items in the Exchange Public Folders, where items are available with company-wide access.

CDO has no managed code support, which means you have to use COM interop and reflection to access this application programming interface (API). Using CDO takes some extra work, but we assure you that if you are planning a messaging application, CDO is the class that you should use.

To illustrate just a portion of the functionality of this COM component, we have included a method that returns the subjects of all messages contained within an Inbox chosen from the Choose Profile dialog available from CDO.

By providing the System.Reflection with type Missing.Value, you can access the default value of an input parameter. When you use the mailbox with the Session.Logon() method's ProfileInfo parameter, it is defined by the profile you choose in the Choose Profile dialog. You can provide a profile string instead of Missing.Value, and by doing this, programmatically define to which Exchange Mailbox you should connect. Unfortunately, the reflected object only identifies itself as an object type, which forces you to create a number of intermediate objects if you are trying to access a member object of a collection. An example of this behavior appears in the following code, where we normally define messages as session.Inbox.Messages instead of taking the extra steps of creating the intermediate inbox object.

The following code iterates through the messages in the Inbox, storing the subjects in a string that is then returned.

```
public string GetSubjects()
{
  MAPI.Session session = new MAPI.Session();
  string retVal = "";

  object emptyVal = Missing.Value;

  session.Logon(emptyVal, emptyVal, true, true, 0, true, emptyVal);
```

CDO's `Logon()` method is a bit peculiar and has three distinct ways of operating. Its syntax is as follows:

```
session.Logon( [ProfileName] [, ProfilePassword] [, ShowDialog] [, NewSession]
[, ParentWindow] [, NoMail] [, ProfileInfo] )
```

CDO is a class library primarily intended for client-side use. For that reason, it also allows for a dialog box to appear under certain circumstances when logging on. This occurs when, as in the previous code section, you submit any `ProfileName` or `ProfileInfo` and, at the same time, set `ShowDialog` to `true`. A second option is to set `ShowDialog` to `false` and provide a `ProfileName` and `ProfilePassword`, which will log on to the session with the specified profile. Finally, you can provide a `ProfileInfo` string and set `ShowDialog` to `false`. That lets you create a profile on the fly and is the most commonly used routine for server-side programming.

> *If you specify a* `ProfileName`*, the profile must already exist on the computer from which you run the code. You can create CDO profiles either from within Outlook or from the Email Control Panel snap-in. Profiles are stored locally on each computer and you cannot use a profile created on one computer when you are running the code on another.*

Unfortunately, you need to cast each instance in the COM hierarchy to its real class type. This, in turn, means that you cannot traverse the object hierarchy as you would have done in regular COM programming. The following code section corresponds to two lines of VB6 code:

```
' VB6 code
objMessages = objSession.Inbox.Messages
objMessage = objMessages.GetFirst();
```

The two VB6 lines of code above correspond to the following lines in C#. Notice how we need to cast each value into a recognized type.

```
// C# code using COM interop
MAPI.Folder inbox = (MAPI.Folder)session.Inbox;
MAPI.Messages messages = (MAPI.Messages)inbox.Messages;
MAPI.Message message = (MAPI.Message)messages.GetFirst(emptyVal);
```

After setting references to the `Messages` collection and its first `Message` item, you can iterate through the collection and store the `Subject` of each `Message` in a string, which is returned once all `Message` items have been parsed.

```
while (message is MAPI.Message)
{
  retVal += message.Subject.ToString();
  message = (MAPI.Message)messages.GetNext();
  if (message is MAPI.Message)
    retVal += "\r\n";
}
return retVal;
}
```

Using CDOEX

CDOEX is short for CDO for Exchange 2000 Server. Unlike CDO, which is designed for client use, CDOEX is meant to be a platform for server-based programming. CDO 1.2.1 is normally an optional install with Outlook, whereas CDOEX installs with Exchange Server 2000. CDOEX is a superset of CDO for Windows 2000, and though it reroutes the Registry entries for CDO for Windows 2000, it is fully backward compatible. Unlike CDO, which is based upon Messaging API (MAPI) technology, CDOEX relies on Internet standards and the Object Linking and Embedding database (OLE DB) to access the Exchange Server.

In addition to the functionality inherited from CDO for Windows 2000, CDOEX also lets you access and create, modify, or delete items in the *Exchange Calendar* and *Contacts*. The Exchange Calendar features include distribution and handling of appointments and meeting requests. Contacts can be managed via CDOEX, whether they are stored in the user's own contact folder, an Exchange Public Folder, or even the Active Directory.

The following sample shows a very basic method in which CDOEX is used to create and send a message.

```
public void CDOEXSendEmail()
{
  CDO.Message message = new CDO.Message();

  message.From = "Administrator@domain.com";
  message.To = "EmailUser@domain.com";
  message.Subject = "Testing some CDOEX functionality";
  message.TextBody = ""up, it seems to be working"          + "
ok!\r\n\r\nCheers,\r\nMikael";
  message.Send();
}
```

Note that the ProgID for CDO is actually MAPI, whereas CDOEX uses the ProgID CDO. Thankfully Microsoft let the ProgID for CDOEXM be CDOEXM.

Using CDOEXM

CDOEXM is short for CDO for Exchange Management and, in terms of its function and use, can be thought of as a mix between CDO and `System.DirectoryServices`. Unlike CDO and CDOEX, CDOEXM is a COM API strictly for management purposes. It enables you to manage objects such as Exchange servers, public folders, and Exchange recipients.

`DeleteMailbox()` is the opposite of the CDOEXM `CreateMailbox()` method that was used earlier to finalize the creation of a mailbox-enabled account. It deletes the Mailbox from the storage group and dereferences it from the Active Directory account. The procedure for deleting a Mailbox is similar to the procedure for creating one. You need to create a reference to the Active Directory object from which the Mailbox will be deleted and cast its `NativeObject` into an `IMailboxStore`. As illustrated in the following code, `DeleteMailbox()` changes an attribute on the Active Directory object just as `CreateMailbox()` does, and therefore it requires a call to `CommitChanges()` to propagate the changes to Active Directory.

```
public void CDOEXMDeleteMailbox(string ldapPath)
{
  DirectoryEntry user;
  IMailboxStore mailboxStore;

  user = new DirectoryEntry(ldapPath);

  mailboxStore = (IMailboxStore)user.NativeObject;
  mailboxStore.DeleteMailbox();

  user.CommitChanges();
}
```

A deleted Mailbox is not destroyed immediately. It remains disconnected in the store, as a tombstone, for a period of time that is specified in seconds by the `msExchMailboxRetentionPeriod` property in the Mailbox Store.

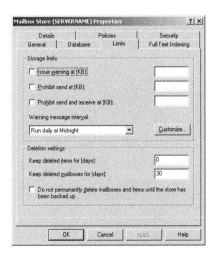

The rationale behind this is that if you accidentally delete or, for some other reason, regret deleting a Mailbox, you will be able to reconnect it to a Windows 2000 account. If you need to reconnect a Mailbox, simply create a new Windows 2000 account and connect it to that Mailbox. To do that, either use the CDOEXM `CreateMailbox()` method, as described earlier in this chapter, or use the Exchange System Manager. You can see this being done in the following screenshot:

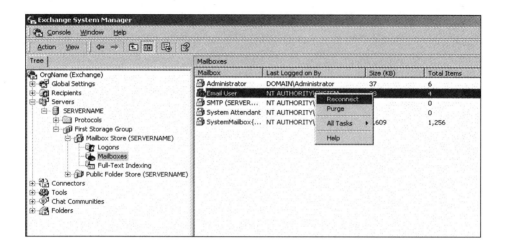

Summary

It is never easy to design efficient tools for querying catalogs and directories or databases in general. Microsoft has relieved us from the pain of resorting to parsing filtered container objects, and has instead released the `DirectorySearcher` object, which provides not only tools for filtering and searching, but also classes to hold the results of these actions. Since the structure and functionality of `System.DirectoryServices` follows well-documented Internet standards, it has become easier to design complex, yet highly efficient queries to the Active Directory.

Creating Exchange Mailboxes has never been easier, apart from the fact that you cannot do it using `System.DirectoryServices` alone. This represents a reasonable obstacle when you consider that CDOEXM, the additional class library required, is only installed with the Exchange Server. This means that you must run any code that creates Mailboxes on the same computer as Exchange Server.

In this chapter, you have discovered how to program for Exchange Server with System.DirectoryServices. In particular, you have learned

❑   What tools Microsoft provides to analyze and traverse the Exchange Server directory

❑   How to create specific address lists, based on custom filter criteria

❑   How to modify Exchange Server objects and attributes of the Active Directory schema

❑   How to add and remove references between Exchange Server objects and corresponding Active Directory objects

❑   What other class libraries are available for Exchange Server programming

When working with `System.DirectoryServices`, you cannot delete the Exchange 2000 Mailbox without deleting the entire Windows 2000 account. On the other hand, when using CDOEXM, deleting Mailboxes is very straightforward. This is a result of Windows 2000 and Exchange Server running a joint directory.

Microsoft provides a few class libraries specific to programming Exchange Server: CDO, CDOEX, and CDOEXM. If you are serious in your Exchange developing efforts, it is a good idea to look into these subjects. Unfortunately, as of this writing, they only exist as COM components, but there will almost certainly be .NET equivalents in the not-too-distant future.

Index

forums.apress.com

JOIN THE APRESS FORUMS AND BE PART OF OUR COMMUNITY. You'll find discussions that cover topics of interest to IT professionals, programmers, and enthusiasts just like you. If you post a query to one of our forums, you can expect that some of the best minds in the business—especially Apress authors, who all write with *The Expert's Voice*™—will chime in to help you. Why not aim to become one of our most valuable participants (MVPs) and win cool stuff? Here's a sampling of what you'll find:

DATABASES
Data drives everything.

Share information, exchange ideas, and discuss any database programming or administration issues.

PROGRAMMING/BUSINESS
Unfortunately, it is.

Talk about the Apress line of books that cover software methodology, best practices, and how programmers interact with the "suits."

INTERNET TECHNOLOGIES AND NETWORKING
Try living without plumbing (and eventually IPv6).

Talk about networking topics including protocols, design, administration, wireless, wired, storage, backup, certifications, trends, and new technologies.

WEB DEVELOPMENT/DESIGN
Ugly doesn't cut it anymore, and CGI is absurd.

Help is in sight for your site. Find design solutions for your projects and get ideas for building an interactive Web site.

JAVA
We've come a long way from the old Oak tree.

Hang out and discuss Java in whatever flavor you choose: J2SE, J2EE, J2ME, Jakarta, and so on.

SECURITY
Lots of bad guys out there—the good guys need help.

Discuss computer and network security issues here. Just don't let anyone else know the answers!

MAC OS X
All about the Zen of OS X.

OS X is both the present and the future for Mac apps. Make suggestions, offer up ideas, or boast about your new hardware.

TECHNOLOGY IN ACTION
Cool things. Fun things.

It's after hours. It's time to play. Whether you're into LEGO® MINDSTORMS™ or turning an old PC into a DVR, this is where technology turns into fun.

OPEN SOURCE
Source code is good; understanding (open) source is better.

Discuss open source technologies and related topics such as PHP, MySQL, Linux, Perl, Apache, Python, and more.

WINDOWS
No defenestration here.

Ask questions about all aspects of Windows programming, get help on Microsoft technologies covered in Apress books, or provide feedback on any Apress Windows book.

HOW TO PARTICIPATE:

Go to the Apress Forums site at **http://forums.apress.com/**.

Click the New User link.